```
MW00438203
```

(b i z - b u z)

BUSI *BUZZ*™

(b i z - b u z)

STANLEY,

I HOPE YOU, YOUR
STAFF, AND THE
FOLKS WAITING
PATIENTLY TO SEE
YOU AND/OR YOUR
STAFF ENJOY THIS
"BREAK IN THE ACTION."

ALL THE BEST,
Randy ☺

Stanley,

I hope you, your
staff, and the
folks waiting
patiently to see
you and/or your
staff enjoy this
"break in the action."

All the best,

:) Randy

**Business Buzzwords for Survivin'
and Thrivin' in the Big City**

Words with Wallop
Phrases that Pop
Spice Up Your Speech
Punch Your Statements
Ace the Meeting
Close the Deal

don't small talk...BIG TALK !

It's All In Here...

J. Randy Gordon

Booksurge, LLC
North Charleston, South Carolina
Royal Blue Gymbag Productions, LLC
Birmingham, Alabama

Interior Illustrations: Pete McDonnell
Logo Design: Menotti Creative Design /
     Pete Menotti
Cover Design: Jeffry Eaton
Proofreading: Linda Jay Geldens
Interior Design: Pete Masterson,
     Aeonix Publishing Group
Website Design: Emanuel Saba, Sabagraphix
Back Cover photograph: Robert Holmes
Legal-ese, Counsel, and Guidance:
     Robert G. "Bob" Pimm
Additional illustrations: © 1987–1995 by T/Maker Co.

Copyright © 2006 by J. Randy Gordon. All rights
reserved. This book may not be reproduced in whole
or in part in any form or by any means, electronic
or mechanical, including photocopying, recording,
or by any information storage and retrieval system
now known or hereinafter invented, without written
permission from the publisher.

LCCN: 2006900649
ISBN-10: 1-4196-2124-6
ISBN-13: 978-1-4196-2124-6

This book may be ordered by mail from Royal Blue
Gymbag Productions, LLC.
Please add $5.00 for postage and handling.

Royal Blue Gymbag Productions, LLC.
Attn: Jay Randy Gordon
1293 Greystone Crest
Birmingham, AL 35242

Printed in the United States of America

*T*his book is dedicated to the memory of
my friend Craig Tartasky
…he loved the sports business and he left for
heaven the very day of Opening Ceremonies
of the Athens Summer Olympic Games

To Mom and Dad, Nikki, and Beatty…
and to Michael and Barbara Safris,
thank you for the support and belief in me.

And to all people who are willing to listen,
and who have something to say…

ORG CHART

CEO
Chancellor Emeritus

Lady Shark
Co-V.P.

Alpha Dog
Executive V.P.

Acknowledgments

FOREWORD BY:
Leigh Steinberg
    CEO—Leigh Steinberg Enterprises

SECTION INTRODUCTIONS:
Jeffrey Fox, Vice President, National Marketing
    —Taco Bell Corp.

Karl Frey, Vice Pres., Mesirow Advanced
    Strategies, Mesirow Financial

Munir Haddad, Founder,
    MarketingJuice (formerly of MTV)

Geoffrey DeStefano, Founder and CEO – The
    Strategic Content Group, LLC

Peter Moore, Corporate VP, WW Retail Sales
    and Marketing —Xbox 360/Xbox
    (Microsoft, Corp.)

Dennis Gilbert, Chicago White Sox Executive/
    President of Gilbert-Krupin, Inc.

(the late) Craig Tartasky, Chairman and
    Executive Director, International SPORT
    SUMMIT

Scott M. Kaufman, CEO – Young & Successful
    Media Corp.

Tony Seiniger, The Critics' Collection
    (former President, Seiniger Advertising)

Jeff Powers, Marketing Superpower / Account
    Management, Viacom Outdoor (formerly
    of G-Shock)

> *"Live by your words…*
> *and mean what you say"*
> —*J. Randy Gordon*

Extra Special Thanks To:

COCA-COLA, SOBE ADRENALINE Rush, Sugar-Free Red Bull, and to Jones Soda's Whoopass for the help keeping me awake during the long nights of writing. Special thanks as well go to Tom Finnegan of Nimbus Design for his years of patience and suggestions, and thanks to past and present *ESPN SportsCenter* Late Night hosts (especially to Stuart Scott, Linda Cohn, Dan Patrick, Rich Eisen, Scott Van Pelt, and "the Swami" Chris Berman), in addition to David Letterman, Craig Kilborn, Jay Leno, Conan O'Brien, Adam Carolla, and Dr. Drew Pinsky — you all kept me typing during semi-comatose, night-owl hours and helped me finish this book.

Thank you to my friends… and to all of those folks over the last 15-plus years who helped contribute to this recurring dream of mine that started in Chapel Hill, North Carolina, and stayed with me through New York City, Atlanta, Birmingham, Alabama, and California, … that one day I would write a book.

I believe it was Moliere who said: "I live on good soup… not fine words." Well, Moliere, "no soup for you"… and this book is not for you anyway.… and to Buddy Hackett's Mom (who supposedly had two courses at each meal)… well, I feel the same about this book as she did her meals: "Take it or leave it."

Contents

Contents

Contents

Illustration Credits

Illustrations by Pete McDonnell are the opening "Org Chart" and on pages 6, 7, 19, 22, 33, 37, 44, 45, 47, 49, 54, 56, 62, 64, 65, 72, 74, 82, 83, 87, 91, 93, 97, 101, 107, 110, 117, 120, 123, 127, 130, 132, 135, 136, 139, 148, 149, 151, 153, 155, 160, 162, 163, 165, 166, 170, 176 (bottom), 177, 182, 183, 184 (bottom), 185, 187, 189, 190, 192, 193, 194, 198, 207, 217, 221, 226, 229, 233, 235, 238, 241, 249, 251, 252, 255, 259, 262, 268, 269, 270, 271, 272, 273, 283, 289 (bottom), 292, 293, 305, 313, 316, 318, 325, 328, 338, 339, 340, 342, 343, 344, 349, 351, 352, 354, 356, 359, 360, 362, 366, 370, 373, 375, 377, 385, 390, 393, 394, 400, 405, 414, 417, 421, 429, 435, 438, 445.

Other illustrations from ClickArt Cartoons Fun 5 Pak, T/Maker Company.

Foreword

by Leigh Steinberg
CEO—Leigh Steinberg Enterprises (Newport Beach, CA)

IN THE WORLD of sports representation, language can serve as either a barrier or a bridge. Our vernacular has become so diverse that the same player can be called "a good-looking prospect" and "an animal" without making any reference to external appearance. It's easy to get lost in the world of "sportspeak" or within the jargon of the modern business world. With so much *BusiBUZZ* in today's sports lingo, one needs a vivid imagination just to keep up.

A FEW YEARS ago, I signed a new client named Kwame Harris, a multi-talented offensive tackle from Stanford University. Kwame was the total package on the field, with an NFL body and tremendous coordination and athleticism. Off the field, Kwame was equally well-rounded. A devoted student, he mastered both the piano and violin and was involved positively in the Palo Alto community. When I met with NFL teams to discuss

Kwame, I mentioned all of his qualities, showcasing his skill and character. However, the question posed by many teams was:

"Does he possess 'The Nasty'?"

"The Nasty" does not refer to a maladjusted personality, but rather to a mean streak, or to the ability to motivate yourself to get tough against your opponent. Generally speaking, "The Nasty" would likely be a bad trait. In offensive linemen, "The Nasty" is an especially relevant attribute that can separate the superb from the mediocre. This is the significance of knowing the vocabulary in my world; without it, I'm flying blind.

Expressions like "The Nasty" are commonplace in the language of sport. To some, their only function may seem to be confusion, but these terms can actually enhance conversation. A quarterback can be a "franchise player" whom a team can be built around, or a "cerebral type," who thinks clearly on the field. A defensive lineman can be a "monster off the end who can flat-out fly," meaning he has a great speed burst and a keen ability to disrupt the passer. Some expressions are more useful in the negotiations themselves, as they refer to offers and not to players. When a team presents an offer not to my liking, I can simply respond with, "That's a non-starter" or "That's whack." Of course there is always the classic, "Are you confusing me with someone who cares?"

One particular expression has transcended the sports world. It spawned from Cameron Crowe's 1996 film *Jerry Maguire,* for which I served as technical consultant. Cuba Gooding, Jr.'s character, a wide receiver named Rod Tidwell, instructs his agent Jerry Maguire (played by Tom Cruise), to "Show him the money." Now, nearly a decade later, the masses use the expression in situations that have nothing to do with sports, proving that a simple phrase can evoke a variety of emotions, eventually fusing into a household saying.

Like all elements of language, sports phrases can have various implications. I had recently added a client named Ben Roethlisberger, a quarterback from Miami University (Ohio), whom some teams viewed as "raw," or lacking experience. Citing his three years as a college quarterback (as opposed to the norm of four) and the fact that he played in what was unfairly perceived to be a less-talented conference, a few General Managers saw his experience as a drawback. I viewed this "raw" quality as more of a positive, a chance for Ben to develop more as a player. I would compare him to quarterbacks like Chad Pennington and Michael Vick, the former coming from the same conference as Ben and the latter having played only two seasons of college football. Considering that Ben had three consecutive seasons with 3,000 yards passing, I would argue that he has had ample experience. Moreover, Ben has the potential to be a "franchise quarterback"—not just a player you can win with, but a player you win because of. With good looks and allure, a "franchise quarterback" has the ability to do for a franchise what very few athletes can do, resulting in benefits in ticket sales, concession sales, broadcasting rights, and a revitalized spirit within the franchise. Ben possesses all of these qualities, demonstrating how the notion of "raw" can easily be spun as a negative or as a tremendous positive, depending upon how you approach it.

When Randy Gordon told me about his idea for the book, I saw it as an intelligent idea that was both practical and relevant. Every profession

and field has its own lexicon and jargon that needs translation. Having worked for me in 1994 when I represented the collective interests of players on the U.S. World Cup team, Randy appreciates the value of understanding the everyday phrases of the sports and business world. *BusiBUZZ* provides a comprehensive listing of the modern vocabulary that is essential to today's working man and woman. It may help you gain a competitive edge, "The Nasty," if you will, in the business world.

Preface

My Universal And Intergalactic Disclaimer, Should I Unintentionally Plagiarize:

by J. Randy Gordon

A ND SO IT BEGAN… please note that any use of movie titles, song titles, book titles, printed phrases, movie quotes, lyrics, paraphrases, direct quotes taken out of context, dialogue from a play, recounting of ancient scripture, company slogans, ad phrases, copy, taglines, personal mantras, quotes directly attributable to one person in particular, team mottos, phrases cast in stone, derivations not listed, military creeds, previously made statements, published pieces, and any other "works-in-progress" is strictly unintentional and I remain profusely apologetic for any such infringements. Call me on it, or just call me.

Well, you know what they say, right? They say (whoever "they" are) that the root of all rhetoric is a play on words… that colloquialism is a secret language all its own. Well, for fifteen years, I have recorded phrases and words from "the public domain" that are "in play," the catchy sayings, the ten-dollar words, the dazzle dialogue, the ice-breakers, the conversation starters, the street slang, the office gossip, the water cooler talk, the ear candy, the nuggets, and the coined phrases, again, all from "the public domain," that keep us immersed in banter or thought. I have engaged in multiple conversations, eavesdropped, really listened in when people thought I was not paying attention, and have even jotted down sayings from people whom I admire, and notes from inadvertent daydreams, professors, guest speakers, keynotes, perfectly-coiffed TV luminaries, fast-talking radio

DJs, conference room meetings, boondoggles, business dinners, phone calls, and in-person one-on-ones… from the bullpens to the boardrooms, from the cube farms to the fishbowls, and from the bars to the ballgames, primarily relating to: **BUSINESS.** No doubt, this is *BusiBUZZ* for the "wannabes, up-and-comers, and players"… a book of lists… and, in short, stuff you can use.

Colleges and undergrad B-Schools teach theory… and case studies… and what is practiced. They do not necessarily know, show that they know, or demonstrate the "spoken language"… for it is conversational language that is too informal in diction or style to make for quality prose, text, or headlines. These institutions of "higher learning" (at least in the '80s and '90s, and hopefully they have upgraded their tools) did not even show you how to put together a marketing deck (I am not sure if they even knew to call it a "marketing deck," but that is a subject for another book). This book is not about professing "where it comes from" or telling you "who said it first"… or hypothesizing about "in what context it should be used." It does not provide you with structure or cadence guidelines. Those books are to be found in the reference sections of most major bookstores. This book will provide you with colloquialisms of content and style, the barbs of the recent boom times, the quick hits and stingers, the sharp-tongued showstoppers, the grandstanding gab, and the verbiage of the day… AND it will literally give you examples to help you "talk shop," so to speak.

This book is meant to be a quick read (a layup or slam dunk) particularly for those either interested in business, interested in getting ahead, or just getting that head start or leg up on the competition… or the "co-opetition." It can turn "just making conversation" into "just making money." While this book is a non-comprehensive compilation, it should be used as a springboard… to learning "the gift of the gab." Let's face it, how many times do you read a book, and even though there is solid, cohesive writing, you just come away with the main idea/storyline? So you read *Winning With Integrity* by Leigh Steinberg, or *The Marketing Game* by Eric Schulz, or *The End of Marketing As We Know It* by Sergio Zyman?… Good for you. All great reads… but what did you come away with? Did you save the books and make marks with a yellow highlighter to refer back to it at a later date? Maybe. In fact, that's great if you did. And maybe you do not even remember the gist… maybe you could not even give me a three-sentence summary or the Cliff Notes version… though you did focus and internalize it, right? …and yet, if and when you tell people you read it, you would or will look smart in the process of doing so. With *BusiBUZZ*, my hope is that you will read this compilation, you will internalize it, and come away with 25–50 new phrases that you will use in your everyday work and business dialogue. Make no mistake; this is the Official Book (or reference guide) for the rest of your working days and nights.

Make a quick list… tape it to the inside of your wallet… keep the book in the inside of your coat pocket… Whatever you have to do to start INTERNALIZING some of this book's content and actually USING the verbiage. After all, I am just trying to give the people some "love" and some good "nuggets"… a karma dividend from the universe, if you will… to throw a bunch of words and phrases against the wall and see what sticks… for you, I mean. Whether they are as "old

as the hills,"or "recently in vogue" vernacular (say, from the wireless space), the common thread is that it all applies to business (maybe a stretch at times, but, whether it is said by business people, or is about business, or is said in a business context, this book, I believe, is "all business").

In large companies, as in cottage industries, it is clear that good memoranda (memos or e-mails) contain certain key phrases or buzzwords to fit the culture. In some cases, what the emails actually say is not particularly important, but it is the reading between the lines that counts. Besides, if it were really important, someone would get you on their radar screen, discuss it with you in person, or leave you a voicemail. At The Coca-Cola Company, the key words are ubiquitous, relevant, cascade, utilize, activate, different, better, and special. Procter & Gamble marketeers like to "peel back the onion." And when Kraft Foods marcomm folks have a miscommunication of sorts, "they are getting a disconnect over here."

Slang is a barrier, and business communication and buzzwords can be so situational or topical, or relevant to only a few people, that the message can get convoluted or be difficult to comprehend. No doubt, slang creates the exclusivity and the camaraderie that keeps certain people "in the loop," in the same group or within an inner core, and, in turn, keeps certain people "out of the loop." Slang can be as subtle as a third-base coach tugging an earlobe, pointing to his nose, touching his belt buckle, and clapping his hands once... with the baserunner sliding his hand across his chest to acknowledge that the directive has been received... do you see what I am saying? ... Maybe you do and maybe you do not, but trust me, this collection of buzzwords and catch phrases will get you up to speed to where you need to be, get your competitors in the crosshairs, and hopefully put you "on the same page" with some of your higher-ups, colleagues, and compadres. Understanding buzzwords can bridge certain gaps... it completes a chain for those who get it and frustrates those who don't. The words themselves are not bridge-builders, but they do allow people to cross bridges... to actually "get it," to say things with a sincere ring of decisiveness, knowledge, and authority... and to understand, through all the muck, what is really being said. Face it, cool business people want to consort with smart business people.

For me, recording buzzwords and business jargon started as a tool to pay more attention, to listen more closely, to pick out key phrases... almost as a secondary game to simply listening to someone wax poetic or deliver a thought. I found that you must write it down when you hear it or it's gone... kind of like clay pigeons flying across a shooting range... you either pull the trigger or miss getting a shot off. Words can certainly be used to force the action, push the envelope, and give someone the "heads up" on where they stand. In business, there is a subtle but common language that is truly accessible and available to everybody who cares to inquire about what something meant or who cares to follow up and ask for clarification. There are memorable and catchy words that provide an instant reference point... typically, a meaningful phrase packed into a limited space or sentence. The sense or meaning that the word or phrase conveys can be the difference between an action-oriented "high five, a close-fisted tap, or a 'bro' hug" versus just the frozen pose of a handshake. Buzzwords and catch phrases are not just gobbledygook or overheated rhetoric. No, mi amigos... my peeps... my homies, this is a subtle yet available language.

THIS IS *CODE*. It's speaking in code to those in the know—and for those who do not know, they want to be dialed in, teed up, brought up to speed, on the same page, they want "in," in the house, to be hooked up, "indy," in thar, to be a part of the inner circle. Using buzzwords, catch phrases and short anecdotes is the social currency of our time—the time that has been—and the time yet to come. Buzzwords are a window into what is happening during the day—they are passwords into the elite boardrooms, the verbal indicators that show that you indeed belong in the meeting, that you are part of the core group, the think tank, the "A" team, the preferred stockholders' list, the V.I.P. guest, and that you are a keymaster to the executive washroom. These are certainly the "barbs" of Gen X, Gen Y, the PlayStation Generation, the Baby Boomers, the Echo Boomers, the Hardcores, the Influencers, The Leading or Bleeding Edgers, ... it ain't necessarily for the masses, the mainstream, the vanilla, the middle-of-the-roadsters, the yellow-liners, the sheep, the heartlanders, the old schoolers, the rank-and-file, and the "mom-and-pops." As someone once said, "At the end of the day, it is what it is."

> "A good woman is still a woman, but a good cigar... that's a smoke."
> —*Winston Churchill*

But who came up with "a cat has nine lives," or, better yet, the following "nine" expressions? Hint: it was probably not the most famous #9, Ted Williams (a.k.a. "Teddy Ballgame" and "The Splendid

Splinter"), and it was also not "The Clovers," who did in fact sing "Love Potion #9."

- The whole nine yards
- Dressed to the nines
- Niner
- A stitch in time saves nine

Who knows? Better yet, what do these words and phrases even mean? Here goes...

I may not smoke, but I do puff on an occasional cigar (so I believe I know what Winston Churchill meant)... and this phrase can certainly be used as an appropriate quote after a nice cigar following a round of golf or a fine business dinner. The "whole nine yards" is a military term signifying the length of a rack of ammo... which can also be a business battlecry in the heat of a negotiation or a rally to action (e.g., "Give 'em the whole nine yards."). "Dressed to the nines" is also a term of military origin that means donning your finest garb or clothing. Niner, which can be short for "forty-niner" as in participants in the 1849 gold rush or members / fans of the San Francisco NFL football team, is also an aviator number term / call sign frequently heard in airport control towers that can also be used by bean counters (a.k.a., accountants). Finally, a "stitch in time saves nine" is a stopgap, a band-aid, or something preventative against future problems, and this can be used by CFOs or finance people during budget time to make cuts, report earnings, and to verify a number. ($900 = niner-zero-zero). BUT, let's be clear, this book will not help you out in this regard... this is not a dictionary. It is a reference guide... a grouping, but it does not remotely qualify or try to show that a certain phrase was said circa-whenever or when exactly you should use it—that part is still up to you, the reader (or the talker). "Google™ it."

As we have now crossed the threshold of the new millennium, and entered the new frontier of business post-9/11, what is in store for us? What are the emergent technologies? What will be the watershed events? What will, in fact, be the new trends that we track? In the relatively recent age of whistleblowing on companies like Enron, the downfalls and phoenix of iconic people like Martha Stewart, and the semi-recent collapses of corporate behemoths like Global Crossings and Worldcom, will we now realize the errors of our self-centric ways, roll-up our proverbial sleeves, and simply go back to the "basics of business?" NO WAY, JOSE. With shady bookkeeping techniques and questionable discretion and disclosure policies by once-reputable beancounter firms, coupled with seemingly baseless speculation and stock pumping that ran rampant in the business community in the late 1990s and early years of the first decade of 2000, will we now eliminate spinmasters, optimistic earnings reports, glib spokespeople, and forecasting embellishments, and go back to the common standards and practices of the dry but truthful sort? STARTS WITH "ENN" AND RHYMES WITH "OH" (or at least Sarbanes-Oxley will be one cleanup mechanism). Will business around the office, beat-down and berating e-mails, and smack talk on IM (Instant Messaging) move by the wayside to make room for the drab-and-drone of the "straight-and-narrow" day-to-day dealings as we go beyond 2006? NEGATIVE, NYET, and I THINK NOT.

At the end of the day... the bottom line... is that people need to keep talking to one another...

to LISTEN AND LEARN from one another... but most importantly to KEEP COMMUNICATING (be it verbally or non-verbally). What I have ultimately detected and transcribed... amounts to an abridged compilation of words, catch phrases, barbs, mantras, sayings, anecdotes, jargon, slang, nuances, entendres, innuendos, euphemisms, big-people speak, words from the business ballfield, some words from the street, and both catchy and slick uses of the language... that can describe anything from technology... to the intersection of technology and daily life... to, well, anything —in business, that is. The rest, as it always is, is up to you... TIMING is where luck and preparation meet opportunity, and it can be practiced —the skilled ear and eye prompts the prepped brain and mouth to quickly scan what you have in your oratory and communication artillery (even your silence and body language) to denote what is best to say (or not say) during a given situation and at the appropriate time. We live in a bullet-point society where abbreviations and acronyms abound. In an elevator pitch situation, a sitdown, or a real-time bull session, you had better know how to talk, what to say, and the hot-button words and phrases to use... or to at least sound like you know what you're talking about. STUDY, EXPERIENCE, PREPARE, LISTEN, and BE READY... and remember, TIMING and luck are everything.

So, in the future, be hip to the vernacular... be in the know next time... and all the time... add some timing, some non-verbal body language... and you can take over the discussion and grand-stand your way to the next promotion or simply nail the interview. I hope you take something away from it to enhance your knowledge, your entertainment value, and your own speech enhancement. Now, get out there… break through the clutter… consolidate and dominate… ace the meeting… close the deal… kick ass… and take names. Say what you mean… and mean what you say. After all,"You da man."

> "Believe everything you see, half of what you hear, and some of what you read." —*J. Randy Gordon*

QUESTIONS: *www.BusiBUZZ.com* or
E-MAIL: *info411@BusiBUZZ.com*
SUBMISSIONS FOR NEXT BOOK:
Nuggets@BusiBUZZ.com or *bizbuz@BusiBUZZ.com*

And be sure to look for forthcoming editions, including:
BusiBUZZ (the deuce): Re-Hash
and
BusiBUZZ (three-ball): The Third Time's The Charm

> —written in San Francisco,
> California

The View From 50,000 Feet

$$\$$

by Jeffrey Fox
Vice President—National Marketing—Taco Bell
   Corp. (Irvine, CA)

Sᴵᴛ ɪɴ ᴏɴ ᴀɴʏ ᴍᴇᴇᴛɪɴɢ—and I sit in on a lot—
and you'll start to go lifeless with the acronyms,
colloquialisms, and *BusiBUZZ* that takes place.
Expressions fly left and right. Some you get right
away. Others you're not so sure you're tracking
with. And, when the rest of the room seems to be
nodding along, you're sure to feel like an outsider
looking in, a foreigner in your own country.

So, if you haven't sat through the mind-numb-
ing amount of conference calls, deck presentations,
status updates, alignment meetings, hallway conversations, bathroom chatter, and hundreds of
thousands of voicemails and e-mails that I have—
and that goes along with learning to communicate in the business world of the 21ˢᵗ century—or

you haven't read this book, then sit down, shut up, and fasten your seat belt because you're in for the ride of your life.

Being a consumer marketer, I try to understand, and, more importantly, appreciate the power of the English language. The subtleties are strong. The American consumer rates small improvements in products and knows and recognizes the difference between "best, preeminent, paramount, finest, and greatest." So if you think you can sit in a business meeting and succeed without understanding the basic difference between the thousands of *BusiBUZZ* words and phrases that Randy points out, you can pack up your briefcase, because you're buzzard meat.

When I was asked to write an introduction to this book, "The view from 50,000 feet," if you will, I thought I'd recount my days of working with and at some of the best and largest companies in their respected fields. What words may I have adopted over time or maybe even coined? What *BusiBUZZ* words were in my mental lexicon from too many years of meetings and presentations? Wow, I thought I'd have to get out a pad of paper and really think back and prepare for the task.

But all I really had to do was unknowingly sit through one—yes, one—product positioning meeting and the *BusiBUZZ* words were flying. Literally "flying." In my first meeting of the day we were "flying at 30,000 feet, flying in tighter and tighter circles, flying blind, flying by the seat of our pants, flying without a parachute, flying into a wall, and flying for flying's sake." And that didn't even include the fact that we were "looking for air cover, had a touch-and-go landing, and were in need of air traffic control." All that in only one meeting.

One meeting made me take notice of how often *BusiBUZZ* is used. But, what's scary is that Randy has been collecting these *BusiBUZZ* words for years and years. Trust me, I've seen him. When he worked for me, it was an everyday occurrence to see him in any meeting with his trusty stack of yellow stickies. Honestly, it was a bit disarming and, at the time—I must admit—a bit weird. There was Randy, throughout a meeting, writing down what you said. Not the important stuff, mind you, but the *BusiBUZZ* words. He collected hundreds and then thousands of those sticky notes and was, unbeknownst to me at the time, on his way and onto something.

Truly, J. Randy was, and is, spot on. *BusiBUZZ* is its own language, its own culture. But, rest assured, you don't learn *BusiBUZZ*. It takes control of you like an unsuspecting virus. It molds you into a working collection of hidden, almost sacrosanct secret talk that is as different at each major corporation in Americas as are the vernaculars of the Deep South, New England, and Southern California.

Listen in and you'll know. Soon, if not already, you will *BusiBUZZ*. Not because you want to, or even because you have to. Simply, it creeps into your subconscious and takes hold and you don't even know you're using it. You just are. You learned it via immersion and you come out the other side with the words sitting on your frontal lobe, ready for the using. They seep into your conversation. They become the best way you know how to say something; and, more importantly, the best way others know exactly what you mean.

BusiBUZZ is kind of like reaching into French, Spanish, or Yiddish for a better word than the English language has. Not because you or I can't speak fluent English—come on, I was born speaking English—just because some words or phrases are better, more exact, in another language. They bring clarity, more precise emotions, or better understanding. That's what *BusiBUZZ* will do for you. It will provide you with a way of saying things that others will nod and smile along with. It will let people know that you know that they know that you know. All in the matter of a few words... a few *BusiBUZZ* words.

Hot Words
From 2000 – 2006

The Prompt

WHY ARE THESE the particular words and expressions that break through? Who knows? Do they actually help us to sound "cool" if we use them? Can they stand the test of time? Hit me back.

Blackberry me
Hit me on my Blackberry
Crackberry
Tag me on my Treo
Treo tag
Skype number
Skype me
Epic battery life
Hotspots
Going Nano

Digerati
If the skrilla is killa
Traction
Wireless
Robocalls
Ping
Ping me back
Ping you back
Ping ya later
Voice-activated dialing
Voice-activated anything
Wiretaps
Pocket-sized IM devices
Spam-proof
Nastygrams
Immune to viruses
Expanded cell phone keyboards
Call me on a landline
Litmus test
Red flag it
Sidebar
Scalable
Activate
Utilize
Cascade
Social catalyst
Amber alert
Opt-out
We are inside the cone of silence
Vaulted conversation
Cyberterrorism
H264 (the name of the video code that will make all video playable on multiple platforms)
He's high-dij ("dij" is short for digits, meaning a high-salaried individual)
Think of your own shelf life (how many years do you have left to be viable at what you do?)

Sarbanes-Oxley Act (new legislation that regulates the reporting of financial position of a company)

SOX-compliant (also SARBOX-compliant)

Webisodes (typically 3-minutes long (or so) news clips on the Internet)

Webisodics (typically 3-minutes long (or so) news clips on the Internet)

BREW - Binary Runtime Environment for Wireless (programming platform developed by Qualcomm for use with their chipset used by many carriers)

GSM (protocol for phones currently used in Europe and by T-Mobile and Cingular)

CDMA (protocol for phones currently used by Sprint / Nextel and on some BREW phones)

J2ME - Java 2 Mobile Edition (Programming platform (version of Java) from SUN used by GSM and CDMA carriers)

3G (third generation of wireless; faster wireless data)

MVNO (virtual mobile network using other company lines)

Carriage (TV cable carrier lingo and cell phone lingo)

P2P (peer-to-peer; find and share digital data)

Blogs (Web logs / diaries based on Web pages, not for chats)

VOIP (Voice Internet Protocol)

GPS (Global Position Satellite)

GPS-enabled

AOP (annual operating plan)

201(k)—(a hurting 401(k))

Nanotechnology (machines of submicroscopic size)

Intelligent buffers (digital recorders with instant replay and rewind if music and TV)

Bluetooth (wireless technology that eliminates the use of cables between electronic devices)

i-mode (Japanese service offering wireless web browsing and e-mail on mobile phones)

Sceddy (schedule)

IM (instant messaging)

IM sessions (instant messaging sessions)

B2D (Back To Disney)

Chad (from voting cards)

Wi-fi (wireless fidelity)

Waptop (wireless laptop)

VDSL (very-high-bit-rate DSL; 25 to 50+ Mbps transmission over very short distances)

Deleters (someone who starts deleting to expand a computer's memory)

Uncle Joe (a Web site that consistently loads slowly)

Farquad and hadback (an underhanded payoff)

PDAs

PC maintenance

Spyware

Java-based

Patch me in

Plugging into life

Platform

Privacy filters (prevent wandering eyes from watching your laptop screen)

Living in the digital world

Virtual mobile network

On Demand

Streaming

Downloadable shows

Complexity of content

Video iPods

Podcasts

Porting code

Porting the product

Technical workaround

COPPA (Child Online Privacy Protection Act)

COPPA-compliant

There is a democratization of media happening right before our eyes

Democratization of entertainment delivery

Hol-la atcha boy (please respond back to me, it would be great—or an individual's approval)

Hol-la (I approve)

Auto reply day (the day before a major holiday when everyone sets their e-mail on auto-reply)

A hard stop (I need to have a "hard stop" at 3pm in order to go to another meeting)

Can you unpack it for me (break it down for me and explain it)

Air cover (when a senior manager agrees to take the flak for an unpopular decision)

Alpha pup (market research fun referring to the "coolest kid in the neighborhood")

Bleeding edge (beyond the cutting edge; the creators may not even know where it's heading)

Business ecosystems (when companies in the same market work cooperatively and competitively)

Cookie jar accounting (accounting practice where a company uses reserves from past good years)

Defenestrate (throw someone or something out the window)

Dial it back (tone it down)

800-pound gorilla (a company that dominates an industry short of having a compete monopoly)

Future-proof (create a product that will not be obsolete by the next wave of technological advances)

Ideation (brainstorm session)

Market cannibalization (when a company's new product negatively affects sales of its existing base)

Netiquette (the etiquette on the Internet)

Netizen (citizen of the Internet; someone who uses network resources)

It's all Optics (it's all how things appear)

Pain points (consultants used to describe places where an organization is hurting due to poor structure)

Pockets of resistance (a person or group that attempts to stall, block, or kill a project)

Reaching critical mass (having enough customers or market share to become profitable)

Repurposing (take content from one medium and repackaging it to be used in another meeting)

Reverbiagize (to re-word a proposal in hopes of getting it accepted this time around)

Tszuj (pronounced "zhooh!"); to tweak, finance, or improve)

Value migration (used in industries where there is little market growth)

White space opportunity (new high-potential growth possibilities)

Etcetayada (combination between etc etc etc and yada yada yada)

Red state / blue state (from TV election night, the map that shows the country's deep political division)

Insurgents (media-certified word for the other side in Iraq; loyalists; terrorists)

Christmahanukwaanza—(Christmas / Hanukkah / Kwaanza time period)

Wimax

Wide-Area Wireless

2.5G

Avatars

Bluetooth phones
Skype name
Fanisodes
AIM name (AOL Instant Messager name)
Packets
Acronym Soup
HTTP (Hyper Text Transfer Protocol)
LAN (Local Area Network)
WLAN (Wireless LAN)
PAN (Personal Area Network)
WAP (Wireless Application Protocol)
SMS (Small Messaging Service)
RFID (Radio Frequency ID)
QOS issue (Quality Of Service Issue)
DSSS (Direct Sequence Spread Spectrum)
RSS (Really Simple Syndication)
CDMA protocol (Code Divided Multiple
    Access)
CDMA carriers
GSM (Global System for Mobile)
GSM carriers
GPRS (General Packet Radio System)
WPA (Wi-fi Protected Access)
Podcasts
VPN (Virtual Private Network)
IEEE ("I-triple E"; Institute of Electrical and Elec-
    tronics Engineers)
802.11A (IEEE protocol)
802.11B (IEEE protocol)
802.11G (IEEE protocol)
Open Source
Mash-ups
Social networks
Non-Open Source
SSID
Walled gardens (location-based, high-speed ports
    for broadband delivery in airports)
Crossfire

Last Mile problem
Back-of-the-envelope calculation
Flash banners not compatible with tech specs
Chips and salsa (hardware and software)
Multi-modal issues
Shoot me an e-mail, I am on Blackberry all week-
    end
Five-channel sound
Surveillance and wiretaps
Multi-line rollover capability
Cellular telephone device
Search engine marketing
Contextual targeting
Text advertising
Graphical advertising
Online localization
Digital wallets
Frameworks
Middleware
Security encryption
Bench strength
Drop an F-bomb
On the downlow
Non-endemic
Your in-between-gigs insanity
Put a deck together
In-between opportunities
Numbers in the ionosphere
What is the kill code?
Moneygood
First prover
It's a real tension convention
Low carb financial situation
Low carb
Anticybersquatting consumer
Antispamming law
Autonomy privacy
Border and transportation security

Cyberpiracy
Cyberterrorism
Directorate
Digital Millennium Copyright Act
Digital signature
Hot potato rule
Wardrobe malfunction
Girlie men
Duuude
Machinima
Websplosion
WIKIs
Matrix organization
Weapons of mass destruction (WMD's)
Homicidal violence
Blueprint for success
Botox parties
Odor print
Severance package
Compensation package
Golden parachute
Regime change
Gen Y-ers
Toxic investments
What's up?
Wassup?
Quit e-mauling me
E-mauling
Your yellular problem
Yellular
Helicopter up
Rollin' up
Favored nations status
Orange alert
Homeland security
Embedded
Firewalls
It's back to wait-and-see

Back to the old B2C
Grass2Mass
Content plays
Pure content plays
Material breach
Mandatory overtime
Bandwidth
Cross-collateralize
Electricity brokers
Rolling blackouts
Energy alerts
Handhelds
Re-connect
Manage up
Pressure-test it
This is off-strategy
E-tailers (same as click-and-mortar retailers)
Vulture capitalists
Parody jargon
Convergence
Tech-savvy
Unsecured revs
What's the delta?
Telephone tennis
Take it offline
Upload
Deep-dive on that issue
Workshopping it
Digital signatures
Digital watermarks
Security encryption
Complaint threshold
Opt-in
Double opt-in
Backbone
Platform
Titanium laptops
G4 editors

Deliberate indifference
Declassify the information
Style points
Dot-bombs
Parachute packages
Soft landings
Grounded birds
Sabbaticals
He's backfill for that position
People plan with backfill
Let's do a deep dive
Globallistic
Go ballistic
Gun maker immunity
Mergers and acquisitions are back in fashion
Our company jets have the West Nile virus
Get in on the ground floor
Inscrutable fault
Internally-displaced person
Mutual fund wrap account
Online Sexual Addiction
Docu-Dramas
Outer Space Treaty
Repressed Memory Syndrome
Stealth juror
Strategic National Stockpile
Terrorism insurance
Zero-tolerance policy
In-game advertising
Best practices
Best of breed
One-to-few marketing
Stay financially solvent
Ground sensors
Cell phone intercepts
It's all siloed
Business phoenix
Turnaround situation

Data marts
Skin in the game
Eat what you kill
Getting in deep
Live 2day, die 2moro
Stage 5 hurricane
Category 5 hurricane
Three days' rest
Illiquid
Chain death letter
Blocked ID
Heavy lifting
Drill down
Do a deep dive
Marketecht
Marketechture
Comforts of modern society
Elaborate communication intercept systems
I'm in NYC, call me when U get back to LA
Hired guns
Radioactive dirty bombs
Blu-Ray
EVDO
Bluetooth phones
Dynamic advertising
Hockey-stick projections
TAM projections (Total Available Market projections)
Closed-box thought processes
Downstream revenue opportunity
Best of Breed
The run rate
Proof points
Cash Grab
A little slow on the uptake
Take a bio break

High-Frequency Usage Words / Phrases Since The Mid-1990s

(Keep It Simple, Stupid)

The Prompt

SURE, SOME OF these "are overcooked" and some may match or be similar to "Words / Phrases That Were Popular To Say In The 1990s (And 1980s)," but face it, many have been "run into the ground" and "beaten to death." But, do these phrases make you want to "vomit dayglow"?

Keep it simple, stupid (KISS)
World-class
Follow up
Follow through
Out-of-pocket
Paper trail

Working stiffs
Push the envelope
Venture capitalists
Mindshare
Paradigm shift
Touchy-feely
Pass the buck
We need a "walk before we run" project
We may have to step on a few toes
Run with it
Consolidate and dominate
Nature of the animal
Stick to what got you here
Go with what brung ya
Stick with what you know
Play telephone tag
Telephone tag
Angel investors
Too much hand-holding
The tech wreck
Shareware
Do-able
Broad strokes
Litmus test
Synergy
Added-value
Nip it in the bud
Politically correct
Seal the deal
Brouhaha (pronounced "brew-ha-ha"; a really
    bad situation)
Out-of-the-box thinking
Think outside of the box
Run it up the flagpole and see if anyone salutes
Run it up the flagpole
Ancillary revenue streams
Ancillary

Run the numbers
End-to-end solutions
Value-added
Da bomb
Step up
Backward compatibility
Barriers to entry
Water under the bridge
Revenue streams
Critical path
Authentic
Full-service
Done deal
You the man
You da man
In the grand scheme of things
Radar screen
A drop in the bucket
Small potatoes
Activate
Interactive
Paradigm shift
What's the business model?
Boondoggle
Turnkey
Dog and pony show
Jump through hoops
Rainmakers
Learning curve
Move the needle
Best efforts
Cut the crap
Sense of purpose
Incentivize
Fire off an email
Shoot off an email
Touch base

Mission-critical

Go after the low hanging fruit

Do lunch

We get it

He gets it

Don't go there

Fish where the fish are

Brilliant

Bricks and clicks

Brick and mortar

Click and mortar

E-commerce

Broadband

Too many cooks in the kitchen

Spread thin

It goes down well

Catch some flak

Feast or famine

Millennium

Open-door policy

Short list

Hidden agenda

Bury the hatchet

It pops

Break through the clutter

Been there, done that

Tight

Craft a proposal

Hone your craft

Other fish to fry

Go after the low-hanging fruit

Low-hanging fruit

Monetize (pronounced "mah-nah-tize")

The Department of Redundancy Department (usually Human Resources Department)

Push the envelope

Get on the stick

Rolling in dough
It's a lost cause
Jump on 'em early
Word of mouth
The 80-20 rule
User session lengths
Uniques
How many hits?
Impressions
Ducks in a row
Come full circle
Parallel path
Expedite the process
Time is money
Piece of cake
It's cake
A leg up on the competition
Green light
Irons in the fire
Burning the midnight oil
Hands-on experience
Word-of-mouth
Concerted marketing efforts
Spending on the cheap
Street date
Real-time
Wink-wink, nod-nod
Reverse engineering
You are wise beyond your years
Time to clean house
It's a go
Give him some kudos
Props
Get on the same page
Manage expectations
Take it offline
Call me on a landline

Rode hard and put away wet
Drink the kool-aid
Flabbergasted
Millennium bug
Y2K
Kick the tires
Well-oiled words
Pipe dream
Slick spin

MID-1990's (AND BEYOND)

Nukes
Mucky-mucks
Let me give you the download
Re-focus
Re-envision
Re-connect
Re-establish
Blamestorming
Mouse potato
Paralysis by analysis
Paradigm shift
What's the model?
At the end of the day
I'll deny ever saying this
Hurry up and wait

The man behind the curtain
Build up your chits
Angel investors
Angels
VC people
Flake cadet
Space cadet
Project creep
Be careful what you wish for
On the down low
On the QT
All over the board
Scalable
Bailiwicks
Barriers
Safeguards
Barricades
Parameters
Constraints
Segues (pronounced "segways")
It's their bailiwick (area of expertise)
WAP (wireless application protocol)
Recos (recommendations)
CYA (cover your ass)
Uber (as in "uber cool" or way cool)
CC'd (pronounced "see-seed" / carbon copied)

Words / Phrases That Were Popular To Say In The 1990s (and 1980s)

The Prompt

POPULAR WORDS AND phrases that you heard all the time? Oldies and newbies? Tag, you're it.

Chiefs
Mules
Indians
Soldiers
Smoke and mirrors
We have other fish to fry
Temporary fix
Raising the bar
Raising the standard
Don't get defined
The tick list
Honey-do list
Respond vigorously
The "To-Don't" list
In no uncertain terms
It dominates the water cooler talk
Second-guessed but not abandoned
Outside chance at best

Blunt force trauma

Pure business experience

Entrepreneurial bent

Welshing on their markers

Supercharges

A call seeking comment

Hardball tactics

Booking ad revenue

Brand groups

Knock them off your perch

Push the envelope

Don't upset the apple cart

If it ain't broke, don't fix it

Out-of-the-box

Stick-to-it-tive-ness

Big Blue (nickname for IBM)

The Evil Empire (nickname for Microsoft)

The tech wreck (downward spiral in stock prices for tech companies—late 1990s)

The Asian flu (downward spiral in stock prices for Asia-based companies—late 1990s)

When things are critical, choose union not division

Until there's a dead body in the street, no one will think to put up a traffic light

At this point, the project doesn't even have a blinker on (not sure where it's going; not sure direction)

Immersed

Immersive

Interactive

The new millennium

Millennium

Reverse engineering

Core competencies

Word-of-mouth

Buzz

Boondoggle
Cohesive team
Watershed event
Paradigm shift
A look-and-feel
Feel of venue
Hot
White hot
En fuego
The ball is in their court
Water under the bridge
Internet gold rush
Internet
The Net
The Web
Shareware
Groupthink
Net-net
Stay on track
Go the extra mile
The unexpected "aha" point
The Dotcom phenomenon
Dotcoms
Dotbombs
Cyberworld
Cyberspace
Cybersquatters
Double standard
Computer games
Videogames
You don't get it
He gets it
Don't go there
Let's not go there
Who's your daddy?
That's what I'm talking 'bout
Yeah, baby

Visceral
Grass roots
Groundswell
Analog
Digital
Integrated
Synergy
Streamlining
Foster relationships
Re-engineering
Downsizing
Rightsizing
Decommissioned
De-installed
Employee package
Compensation package
No downside guarantees
Evaporating on the upside
Do the math
Run the numbers
It all adds up
Logo guidelines
Style guides
Body of work
Double standard
Been there, done that
Been there, done that, bought the t-shirt
It's simply the best part of my day
Highbrow
Fish where the fish are
Window of opportunity
Circadian cycle
Circadian rhythms
Dynamism
It ain't brain surgery
It pops
It breaks through the clutter

Cut through the clutter
They were drinking the kool-aid
Talk smack
Flip 'em off
The gold standard
Heady stuff
It's a go
The clock is ticking
Buzzword bingo
Run the table
From cubicles to conference rooms
Drones
Peons (pronounced "pee-ons")
Incentive
Proactive
Impactfulness
Step up to it
Information superhighway
Paradigm
Stakeholder
A greater say
Optimizing
Below the radar
What's the deliverable?
Voice of the customer
Sugar-coated bad news
Core competencies
Shortcomings
A shot in the arm (a boost)
M&A (mergers and acquisitions)
Foster relationships
Under the radar
Upset the apple cart
Campy
Kitschy
Please treat me like a grownup

Reap what you sow
More than you can shake a stick at
Let's not reinvent the wheel
Nature of the beast
Make a silk purse out of a sow's ear
Comeback story
Jump on 'em early
Objectivity out and reality in
Cut the crap
Sense of purpose
A path that is fraught with danger
Keep things moving forward
It's all about going forward
Take it in stride
Topped out
Bested
Another day, another dollar
Best practices
Results-driven
24/7
Paradigm shift
Touch base
Strategic fit

Summary / Status / Bottom Line / Final Synopsis

The Prompt

JUST GIVE IT to me straight—what's the bottom line?—the final number…

What's the topline?
The net-net
Net-net
At the end of the day
What's the deal?

What's the dilly?
What the deezy?
What's the status?
Where are we on that?
Where are we on this?
The quick and dirty
When the dust settles
The topline
The bottom line
The straight skinny
The skinny
Give me a big fat recap
Update
Debrief
Download
Let the chips fall where they may
Once the chips fall
Thumbnail sketch
The downlow
What's the crux?
The crux
The deal
What's the gist? (pronounced "jist")
The gist
Zero sum game
Has the jury reached a verdict?
Where do we stand?
The situation update is as follows
Let's know our own status
For all intents and purposes (the right way to
    say it)
For all intensive purposes (the wrong way to
    say it)
The cut to the chase
Cut to the chase
Please cut to the chase from this long diatribe
It's done

Done deal
It doth not protest too much
Etched in stone
Cast in concrete
Out of ammo
The company is flush with cash
It's a house of cards
House of cards
It's a dog with fleas
Lead status report
The take-away is this
Dependency reports
Having said that
That said
The logic behind the end result
The bake sheet
In the grand scheme of things
A whole new ballgame
The way the ball bounces
When the smoke clears
It serves all the masters
Put on your business goggles

Acronyms / Abbreviations / The Numerology Alphabet (86-it / 24-7-365)

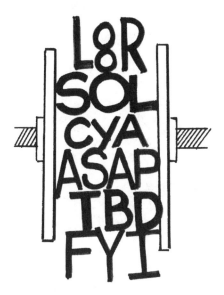

The Prompt

Aₕ, ᴛʜᴏꜱᴇ ᴛʜʀᴇᴇ- or four-letter sequential expressions that can make all the difference. We live in a bulletpoint society that loves to abbreviate, to shorten, "to make easier." And the language of tomorrow is all numbers: 4U (for you) and 2BAD (too bad). Seeya later is now L8R. C?

CYA (cover your ass)
FYI (for your information)
SOL (sh** out of luck)
PDQ (pretty damn quick)

ASAP (as soon as possible)
DK (didn't know)
NA (not available)
N/A (not applicable)
T&E (travel and expense)
T&E (training and experience)
OOO (out of office)
OOTO (out of the office)
OOP (out of pocket)
SOS (help)
ABC (always be closing)
SOP (standard operating procedure)
MO (modus operandi)
NLT (no later than)
COB (close of business)
EOB (end of business)
EOD (end of day)
CPC (cost per click)
CPA (cost per acquisition)
CPA (certified public accountant)
SRO (standing room only)
SO (standing ovation)
M&A (mergers and acquisitions)
The CIO (Chief Idea Officer)
The CMO (Chief Motivation Officer
CXO (chief level; commanding officer)
LOL (laugh out loud)
SOS (someone special)
CC'd (carbon copied)
WAP (wireless application protocol)
Y2K (year 2000)
EOM (end of message in an E-mail)
EBIT (earnings before interest and taxes)
EBITDA (earnings before interest, taxes, depre-
    ciation, and amortization)
A&Os (achievements and objectives)
ZOPA ("Zone" of Possible Agreement)—range of
    terms or amounts open to negotiation

WYSIWYG (what you see is what you get)
BOHICA (bend over, here it comes again)
WTF (what the fu**?)
STFU (shut the fu** up)
KISS (keep it simple, stupid)
HMFIC (head motherfu**er in charge)
PK (player killer)
CS (Counter-Strike, the videogame)
TOOC (totally out of control)
BSD (big swinging dick)
SWAG method (scientific wild-ass guess method)
SWAG (stuff we always get)
GLOM (give the loser our merchandise)
BYO (bring your own)
WI-FI (wireless fidelity)
SMP (strategic marketing plan)
OYL (out of your League)
BBFN (bye bye for now)
P2P (path to profitability)
P2P (peer-to-peer)
B2B (business-to-business)
B2C (business-to-consumer)
B2C (business-to customer)
B2D (back to Disney)
VCs (venture capitalists)
VCs (vulture capitalists)
AI (artificial intelligence)
VAD (voice-activated dialing)
STO (standard training operations)
QT (on the "QT"—quiet; hush-hush)
C-YA (see ya)
LYLAS (love you like a sister)
UMPH (that extra "UMPH")
ULL (you'll; you will)
GIGO (Garbage in, Garbage out)
MSOs (Multi-System Operators)
O&Os (Owned and Operated)

CPM (cost per thousand—advertising measurement)

CPM (complaints per million—direct marketing E-mails)

CPM (cost per message—direct marketing E-mails)

UR (you are)

TVTO (TV timeout)

OOFAU (out of funds as usual)

DOE (depending on experience)

PC (politically correct)

SNAFU (situation normal all fu**ed up)

FUBAR (fu**ed up beyond all recognition)

MOTs (members of the tribe; Jews)

NR (not required)

TLAs (three-letter acronyms)

G$ (G-Money)

GL (good luck)

GG (good game)

CSDs (carbonated soft drinks)

QSRs (quick service restaurants)

QOS (quality of service)

NORDO (no radio contact)

ROI (return on investment)

ROL (return on life—a concept)

PPB (principal place of business)

DCs (distribution centers)

QSBs (qualitative systems for business)

HTTP (hyper text transfer protocol)

DART (most popular ad server)

GPs (General Partners)

LPs (Limited Partners)

VLTs (video lottery terminals)

T&M (time and material)

USA (you're still away)

FISO (fu** I'm still out)

SYT (still your turn)

NSF (not so fast)
COB (close of business)
COPPA (Child Online Privacy Protection Act)
IRC (Internet relay chat)
LMAO (laugh my ass off)
FWIW (for what it's worth)
VNR (video news release)
DC it (discontinue it)
BFD (big fu**ing deal)
BS (bullsh**)
DOA (dead on arrival)
KOD (kiss of death)

Acronyms—Inspired by the Internet and Web Chats

AFAIK (as far as I know)
AFK (away from keyboard)
BRB (be right back)
BTW (by the way)
MVDO
VLOG
MMO (massively multiplayer online)
GIF (graphic interchange format; can be displayed on web browsers; pronounced "giff")
PDF (portable document format)
FTP (file transfer protocol)
JPEG (joint photographic experts group; pronounced "jay-peg"; graphic format newer than GIF)
HTTP (hypertext transfer protocol; the format of te World Wide Web)
ISDN (integrated digital services network; high-speed dial-up connections to the Internet)
DSL (digital subscriber line; copper loop transmission technology through a dedicated phone line)

IDSL (ISDN DSL)

IMHO (in my humble opinion; in my honest opinion)

IP (Internet protocol)

ISP (Internet service provider)

IRC (Internet relay chat)

IM (instant messaging)

OSP (online service provider)

MIB (management information base)

MODEM (MOdulator DEModulator; device to connect your computer to a phone line for Net talk)

MORF (male or female)

MSO (multiple system operator; cable industry term; a company operating more than one system)

NAP (network access provider; typically DSL-related)

NOC (network operations center; centralized point of network management within large-scale network)

PPP (point-to-point protocol)

RTF (rich text format)

SDSL (symmetric digital subscriber line)

SOHO (small office / home office)

TCP/IP (transmission control protocol / Internet protocol; suite of protocols that defines the Internet)

TTFN (ta ta for now)

UI (user interface)

URL (uniform resource locator; used with the Web as an address, e.g., http://www.*BusiBUZZ*.com)

VDSL (very-high-bit-rate DSL; 25 to 50+ Mbps transmission over very short distances)

WAN (wide area network; a computer or communication network that covers a geographical area)

LAN (local area network)

HTML (hypertext markup language; coding language to create documents on the WWW)

WWW (World Wide Web)

UFI (user friendly interface)

GUI (pronounced: "gooey"; graphical user interface)

FAQs (frequently asked questions)

VLAN (virtual LAN; a network of computers that act like they are connected to the same wire)

VPN (virtual private network)

ADSL (advanced digital subscriber line—high-speed transmission technology)

FFS (for fu**'s sake)—(British)

WTF (what the fu**?)

DBA (database administrator)

RHIP (rank has its privileges)

SNC (snooze and cruise)

VOD (video on demand)

MM (double M; $1 million; one million dollars)

M ("emm"; $1,000 or 1 million; one thousand or one million)

K ("kay"; $1,000; one thousand dollars)

G ("jee"; $1,000; one thousand dollars)

G-NOTE ("jee note"; one thousand dollars)

HI-FI ("high fidelity"; $500; five hundred dollars)

DEUCE ("doose"; $200; two hundred dollars)

C-NOTE ("see note"; $100; one hundred dollars)

HUN-D ("hun-dee"; $100; one hundred dollars)

FI-T ("fitty"; $50; fifty dollars)

10-spot ($10; ten dollars)

5-spot ($5; five dollars)

The Numerology Alphabet (86-it / 24-7-365)

86-it (cancel it or cut off)
80-20 rule (like the iceberg principle - 20% of
    something may yield 80% of revenue)
404 File Not Found (computer error message)
L8R (later)
411 (info)
911 (emergency)
8 (ate)
2 (to)
2 L8 (too late)
1 (won)
4 (for)
U (you)
4U (for you)
U1 (you won)
2moro (tomorrow)
2day (today)
GR8 (great)

tlk2ul8r (talk to you later)

Go 4 2 (go for two)

Live 2day, Die 2moro

That's it 4 now

Go 4 it

Take 1-4 the team

2-2-much (too too much)

2 minute drill

Everyone knows that 20! / 10! 10! = 184,756

10-7 (leaving the site)

10-4 (okay; understood)

4-score

2-bits

10-spot

Deuce

Trey

High fiver

Fiver

Why was 6 afraid of 7?… because 7-8-9

We cannot be throwing 55-footers (coming up short)

Marketing Insights / Generic Statements / Big-time Advertising

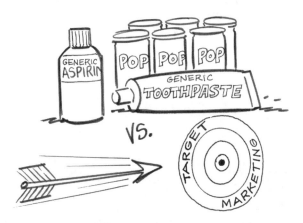

The Prompt

WHEN THERE IS nothing else to be said, yet you are looking for solid closure in the conversation, well, all I can say is try some of these "zingers" and "mainstays." Many of these terms are taken out of context, and while some of these phrases or statements will not universally apply to any given situation, they can stand on their own or be smart-sounding fillers. Listen up.

The sizzle can sell the steak
First you need the steak and then the sizzle
What wins on Sunday sells on Monday
Get some bang for your buck
You need to push the envelope
You don't wake a snake to kill it
I do not have my PC hat on right now

The socioeconomic status is broad-based

In parallel with the demographic skew

Ethnicity usage profiles

Consumptive enhancement

Purchase probability

Purchase intent

Social catalyst

Pushbutton issues

Pushbutton

Turnkey events

Turnkey

Icon marketing

Cross-collateralize

A whole new ballgame

Think broad strokes

Vanilla statements

The 3 c's (customer, company, competition)

It is that cool demographic that I want to deal with

No matter how big your budget... it is still too small

You do not get what you deserve... you get what you negotiate

The angle of the dangle equals the heat of the meat

Change is inevitable, except from a vending machine

A day without sunshine is like, well, night

When the chips are down, the buffalo is empty

Those who live by the sword get shot by those who don't

I wonder how much deeper the ocean would be without sponges

We do not want any value-added that will impact the promotional budget

It's so easy to work your craft when you're surrounded by such a fine ensemble cast

Nothing is foolproof to a sufficiently talented fool

Flashlight: a case for holding dead batteries

Paper trail

Turnabout is fair play

The way the game is played

That sentence packs a wallop

The newspaper game is a game of inches

A game of inches

The business environment

It's right in front of your eyes… in living color

Cherry-pick the markets

Go after the low-hanging fruit

Consolidate and dominate

Ascertain the marketing mix

Plan the work, work the plan

Move the needle

Cash is king

Did it spike?

Did it do a 5? (rating)

Did it at least do a 1? (rating)

What won the night?

Air check

Blanket clearance

End-to-end coverage

The spot market

Remnant space

4-wire

Flyaway

Preso (presentation)

Doing reach / frequency scenarios in your sleep

Let's go over the preso tomorrow (preso = presentation)

Depression is only anger without enthusiasm

The only easy day was yesterday

If you're dissin' the sisters, then you ain't fightin'

the power

We must have the openness to accept good ideas and the strength to reject bad ones

A fine is a tax for doing wrong… a tax is a fine for doing well

Light travels faster than sound, which is why some appear bright until you hear them speak

Hard to understand how cemetaries raise burial costs and blame the high cost of living

The things that come to those who wait may be things left by those who got there first

Marketing efforts

New smash hit

New hit show

Romance the rest of our coverage

I'd rather do no advertising than bad advertising

More mass market and mainstream

Television is a close-up medium… not many long-shots

TV has critical mass issues

Grass2Mass

Antithetical message

Didn't raise me to a level

PSA-type feel

Build up equity with sequential spots

The hook

Hit the button

Impact measurement

Based on a truism

The great American public

Implied profanity

Counter to the brand values

Familiarity factor

Body of memory

Buckets

Up the growth curve

Coalescing the management team
The stars we look to
The altar you worship at
Preaching to the converted
Compensation plans
Tasking them with the following
Take them to task
Eliminate issues of silos
Supply holistic communications
Crushing margin blows
The next generation of talent
Churn
That kind of turnover and churn
A big issue is P and L division within companies
Through proactive management or by default
Reputation could be your brand
Synchronization… each message links to another message on the purchase continuum
There are a dearth of new business opportunities
A stirring at the farm
Indication of activity
C-level versus V-level
It bodes well for the business
A shot across the bow
Manage the marketing mix
Compel consumers
They consume the messages they want to
Aligned behind strategy and key messaging points
Branded content
Find the Alpha (the beginning)
Find the A
Contextual link
Be there when they are ready to buy
Compel or make available

Move to the narrowcasting model

The era of narrowcasting communication

Choose on a granular basis

If you want to find it, google it

Take issue with that spot

Buy over a whole range of media

Demonize

Look at the diagnostics of it

Slapstick humor in advertising

Physical comedy

Won the round on all cards

Advertising is a privilege

Advertising is a conversation with customers

The musings of our industry

The next Renaissance of advertising

What won the night?

Are you dealing with C-level or V-level? (as in VP-level)

Fundamental shift from broadcasting to narrowcasting

It's all about ratings and viewable hours of programming

A high degree of clutter in the marketplace and a lack of relevant messages

There was a stirring at the station, for the word had gone out (Australian)

Darwin's Principle of Adaptation—if adapted, then there is mass potential for growth

Back to the taproot

The taproot of the brand

Intersperse and interact

Filling out RFPs and waiting in the queue

Front and center on the agenda

Agency-client model

Enhance collaboration across P and L's

No cataclysmic changes

The rush to press release marketing

Online… it's just part of the marketing mix

Use the mix if it is relevant

A holistic approach across all touchpoints

Media fragmentation

Media proliferation

Losing the aggregated knowledge

Create a meaningful message in the right platform

It's about the marketing mix

The world is revolving around search engines

Search engines are the ultimate target marketing

The message you are trying to extol

AIDA (awareness interest desire action)

The fastest growing area of media is paperclick

Media and tracking methodologies

Classic test and role scenarios in direct marketing

Do the background tracking

What was the business pull-through?

Had to mine and get a hold of it

The mail that makes the kitchen cut

I feel that there is a disconnect

Sales, move product, or branding

Lead clients and lead disciplines

Come at it from a holistic perspective

Analyzing ROI and lead generation

Preparatory process

Sync up

Contextual advertising to convert sales

There is always a brand component

Every product has a brand

Multi-layered process

Online is an integral part of bonding with the customer

Semblance of continuity

Casting a wide net (targeting broad)

Resonates with the target

Word-of-mouth

Creative hot shop

Creative boutique

Big box media house

Agency conglomerates

Big behemoths

Mid-level shops

Mid-levels

Standalone agencies

Standalones

Deep in the trenches of catch-up

Give us a flavor or a taste of what you think it may be

We're playing catch-up

The work ethic, integrity, and competencies observed leads me to the following opinion

They know how to best lineup the goals and objectives of numerous partners and stakeholders

Capable of building and executing solid business plans

There has been a shift in business focus

Effective and efficient (should apply to all recommendations)

I have some bandwidth (available time on my hands and can take on another project)

Consumers are shifting how, when, and where they see and consume media

SF was the mecca of creativity from the dotcom-craziness to postage-stamp-size ads

Brand message period… use all of your vehicles to bond with customers

Branding is all-encompassing… it's all about the action and the experience

Experiential marketing

Bringing the brand to life and giving it some character

One-to-one consumer marketing

Cherry pick the markets

Low-hanging fruit

Surround strategy

Dynamic in-game advertising

The Money Section /
It's All About The
Benjamins

$$

by Karl Frey
Vice President –Mesirow Advanced Strategies–
Mesirow Financial (Chicago, IL)

MAKE NO MISTAKE about it, the business world
is a beehive of *BusiBUZZ*. From the board
room to the trading floor, a plethora of expressions,
metaphors, anecdotes, and analogies, saturate the

honeycomb of daily dialect, enriching it if not redefining what otherwise might be considered ordinary language. Naturally, individual areas of specialization will develop their own unique, proprietary jargon, with certain verbiage the equivalent of a secret handshake. Moreover, a fair degree of commonality exists across these speech sweeteners, and not just transcending the various financial arenas, but spanning other professions as well. For instance, "low-hanging fruit" conveys an attractive opportunity with little-to-no-risk and/or effort to the investment portfolio manager, just as it does to the insurance salesperson. The bottom line—*BusiBUZZ* is all around us, and the greater our command of it, the better our ability to effectively communicate with others as well as to impart individualism into what we say.

I have been involved in the financial markets for the better part of ten years, and unequivocally, this space is a proliferation of *BusiBUZZ*. During most of this time, I was a corporate debt originator (first with regional money center bank First Chicago, and then with Dutch banking giant ABN AMRO), which required that I spend much of my time in a trading room environment, involving markets such as bonds, swaps, and foreign exchange. It is a difficult atmosphere to appreciate unless you have been there, but expressions like the following epitomize the general mentality:

"eat what you kill" (compensation largely based on the profits that you generate)

"skin in the game" (one's own money at risk)

One of my early experiences involved a seasoned bond trader whom I worked with to collect various bond security information (e.g., pricing, position, levels, volumes). Like most traders, a short attention span and high-strung demeanor were "par for the course" or standard, so it was critical that any dialogue be clear and concise. Also, I regularly had to contend with the distractions of constant trader babbling as well as the nearby squawk box and its regular barrage of bond quotes. During one particular encounter, after patiently waiting for my chance to intervene, I unfortunately learned that the trader had recently "hit a rough patch" involving the security of my interest, causing him to unleash a litany of fury. The gist of the tirade was something along the lines of "taking a bath because his shorts were being squeezed, forcing him to take an inverted position." Now, at the time, I had no clue as to what that all meant, but I was fairly confident it was not good. Loosely translated, the trader was losing money on a short-sell trade, forcing him to pay an above-market price to close out of the position. Needless to say, I remained pretty ineffective with this guy, not only in terms of gathering market intelligence but also in developing a rapport, until I learned to speak his language.

For the past year and a half or so, I have been involved in the area of investment management, and specifically, hedge funds. This new endeavor shares some of the same *BusiBUZZ* picked up during my capital market days, but as well has introduced a whole new set of idiosyncratic references. For instance, when prioritizing prospects, we commonly list our top picks as "trophy mandates," "elephant trades," or the "800-pound gorillas." Also, when sizing up opportunities, we will "take a pulse," "test the waters," or "do a thumb-suck." I find that this type of language that not only facilitates communication and understand-

ing, but also projects style and personality into one's speech.

So, in the business world, like so many other professions, effective communication is "mission-critical," including one's grasp of this mostly unofficial terminology. Embrace it and leverage it, both in terms of navigating the daily routine as well as demonstrating that you are "in the know." And, perhaps, someday you will be creating your own buzz in the beehive of your profession.

Money

The Prompt

WE ARE A little tight on fundage and could use some more cash-ola. Do you have enough bank to make this happen? Because, if you do, can you throw us a little more scratch? Just show me some of that long green... and we will keep this thing going.

Cash
Cash-ola
Cash-eesh
Coin
Clams
Cake
Gelt
Serious coin
Cha-ching
Change
Serious change
Currency
Kaish
Lettuce
Cabbage
Green
Long green
Bread
Dough
Dough-ray-me
Moola
Bills
Bling bling
Skrilla
Scratch

Funds
Fundage
Dinero
Dalloo
Bills
Bank
Bomb
Bundle
Boatload of cash
Boatload
Buck (could be $1; could be $100; could be $1 million)
Beaucoup bucks ("boo-koo bucks")
Bucks
Buckage
Bananas
Jack
Jang
Jing
Jingle
Honey
Greenbacks
Shekels
Doubloons
Swag
Take
Skins
Scoobies
Scoots
Wad
Big wad of cash
Texas bankroll
Bits
Two bits
Pence
Pounds
Poundage

Digits
Dij (digits)
Chump change
Wampum
Loot
Smackers
Semolians
Buttaz
Flash
Ettygrat (Jamaican)
Donny (Bahamian)
Lana (Mexican)
Ends (Mexican)
Jale (pronounced "Hah-lay"—Mexican)
Escarole (Italian)
Duckets
Dead presidents
Bazillion
Sugar
Stipend
Kickback
Honorarium
Lump sum
Appearance fee
Participation fee
Ante
Donation to the cause
Are you loaded?
Loaded
The fu**-you fund
Mad money
Deep pockets
Flush with cash
Fu** you money
Flash cash
The double comma club (millionaires)
Grand ($1,000)

Grover Cleveland ($1,000)
G-note ($1,000)
Singleton ($1)
Deuce ($2)
Finsky ($5)
Honest Abes ($5)
Abes ($5)
Ten-spot ($10)
Jeffersons ($10)
Sawbuck ($10)
Double sawbuck ($20)
Jacksons ($20)
Fitty ($50)
Hamiltons ($50)
Benjamins ($100)
Franklins ($100)
C-note ($100)
Hundo ($100)
Hundy ($100)
Dime (gambling = $1,000)
Nickel (gambling = $500)
Dollar (gambling = $100)
Half dollar (gambling = $50)
50-small (gambling = $50)

Funding-related / Consulting Terminology /

Accounting / Banking / Saving Money

The Prompt

WELL, WE GET slapped a lot, but we don't ask for cheap money

You can find money with words and you can hide money in numbers

Now that you've taken me on a "numbers run," let's just bankroll the deal

The project has not reached all the limbs on the decision-making tree

Sacred cow
Try to catch a falling knife
Catch the falling knife

Exit strategies
Investment motivations
Lead investor
Angel investors
Angels
Angel deals
Corporate angels
Clinch the deal
Deals are rolling in
The due-diligence process
Attrition rate
Sector specialization
What does your gut tell you?
Guts
Protect the financial downside
It's looking up
Financial windfall
Valuation methods
Bang for your buck
Consolidate and dominate
Put it in an index fund with gains
Paycap gains
The attrition rate of investment opportunities
Bootstrapping (financing small firm through
    creative acquisition without borrowing bank
    money)
VC (venture capital)
EBITDA (earnings before interest, taxes, depre-
    ciation, and amortization)
EBIT (earnings before interest and taxes)
Deal flow (number of potential investment opps
    to which an investor is exposed)
Potential exit routes (liquidity; exit an investment
    and still realize returns)
Screening the deal (scanning investment to find
    one or more that match the investment cri-
    teria)

Equity gap (a stage of business financing usually involving less than $500,000—outside funds difficult)

Do your due diligence (rigorous investigation and evaluation of opp before committing dollars)

IPO (initial public offering; going public; sale or distribution of firm's stock to public for the first time)

LBO (Leveraged buyout—investment strategy involving acquisition w/ high degree of debt+no equity)

Holding period (length of time an investment remains in an investor's portfolio)

Lemon (an investment that has a poor or negative rate of return)

Lemons ripen before plums (an old VC investment adage)

Plum (an investment with a very healthy rate of return)—Plums ripen later than lemons

Break-even point

Business devils

Venture capitalists
Vulture capitalists
Dead cat bounced
The promise of enormous financial returns
Competitive venture
Strong growth potential
Sluggish gowth
A growth in sales
Modest returns
Glamour stocks
Wonder stocks
Penny stocks
Cats and dogs
Wildcat stocks
Sweat equity (give to founders in recognition of their effort to start to build a venture)
Snowballing (using one contact to find others through personal referral)
Seed stage (idea still has to be developed and proven)
Takedown schedule (plan stated in a fund prospectus specifying transfer of funds)
Vesting schedules (timetables for stock grants and options that can be earned over time)
Equity gap (a stage void of finance)
The 3 F's (founder, family, and friends)
Drive-by VCs (venture capitalist firms who don't have time to help individual startups)
Declining profits (the reason consultants are in business)
The business angel market and its untapped potential
P2P (path to profitability)
We conservatively project... blah blah blah
BATNA (best alternative to a negotiated agreement)
Flotation (when a firm's shares start trading on a formal stock exchange)

Plankton (a startup that gets eaten by bigger fish)

Living dead (a company too sick to grow but too healthy to die)

Living dead (VC investments not generating healthy returns but managing to survive)

Gatekeepers (persons or organizations that advise limited partners as to where to invest)

Ratchets (one party can increase share of equity stake in venture depending upon equity's performance)

Buyback provision (firm purchases a leaving employee's stock at a preset price)

Captive funds (a VC firm owned by a larger financial institution)

Piggyback rights

Your interests are at stake

One-trick pony

Low-hanging fruit

Don't skimp

GPs (General Partners)

LPs (Limited Partners)

Reality check

Reverse engineer the numbers

We have a 6-month lead time

We have a 6-month window

Dumb as a box of rocks

Ride the ups and survive the downs

The entrepreneur seeks capital

Commit your capital

Bush league

I-banking associate

Investment deals

Limited funding options

Inherent challenges

Second round

Mezzanine round

Searching for market inefficiencies

Arbitrage opportunities
Harness the power
Get in on the deal
Invite them in on the deal
Start-ups
Value-add
Deep pockets
Daddy Warbucks
Dangerous scum
Investor consortiums
Duck soup
The verbal
The verbal okay
I can go with a verbal
A verbal contract isn't worth the paper it's written on
Apples versus oranges
Net worth
The company is flush with cash
Do not let them talk you into doing a 100% complete job
It is difficult to see the picture when you are inside the frame
Nothing ever gets built on time or within budget
We bring the page… they bring the package
There's dew on the melon
The client is holding us hostage
Interagency foreplay
Institutional wheels
Bankroll the project
Find the backers
That'll take kidneys
That'll cost you a couple of lungs
The spigot gets turned off
Consulting fees
Hostage fees

Streamline
Disintermediation
The unexpected "aha" point
Actionable advice
Numbers-oriented
What's the delta?
I need qualitative info
Optimize
Cost-effective
Utilize
Rock solid
Critical path
Risk management
Deer in the headlights

Parallel path
We're talking pennies
Bells and whistles
Set the stock afloat
Flotation
Hot issue
Blowout

Cooling-off period
Free riders
Stags
Wall Streeters
Lions
Dinosaurs
Barefoot pilgrims
No matter how big your budget… it is still too
     small
Retrofit the idea to the strategy
Back into the numbers
Back into it
Pinch pennies and spend dollars
Cottage industries
Niche marketing
Boutiques
Fired on the spot
Know when you're on stage
Husbanding your money
The burn rate
The project's burn rate
Flaunt it
Mad money
Flash cash
Texas bankroll
Big money guys
Takeover artists
Build your business
Too much coin
Cost-prohibitive
Too rich for my blood
Very hit and miss
Head count
Workflow issues
Twiddling your thumbs
The jackpot would be…
Best-case scenario

Worst-case scenario
Drill down on it
On the same wavelength
The market bottomed out
The market is troughing
The stock price is cresting
Cresting
Troughing
Focus on long-term initiatives
Streamline operations to cut costs
It is a pretty rich price structure
The dollar figures are laced with cream
Remain comfortable with analysts' profit expectations
Do not simply establish short-term guidance
Down to brass tacks
A come-to-Jesus meeting
Dog and pony show
Bulletproof
Take a breeze through it
Back integration issues
Rollout tools
Path to profitability
Incentivize
Finger on the pulse
Kick it around
Kick around some numbers
Toss around some numbers
Best ever
Throw it around
Cutthroat
Up for grabs
That's a gray area
Strange bedfellows
A walk before we run
Modest gains
Short rally

The Santa Claus Rally
Bull Market
Eroding cachet
The market rallied
Rev share
Barefoot pilgrims
Glamour stocks
Wonder stocks
Penny stocks
Cats and dogs
Wildcat stocks
Blue chips
Pale blue chips
High-fliers
Fancies
Traps
The restructuring playbook
Stem a stubborn sales decline
Corporate turnaround whiz
Go after the low-hanging fruit
String of financial embarrassments
We are looking for first prover, not first mover
Dance around but don't sleep together
At the end of the day, the net-net is "it is what it is"
Workouts ("Wall Street" slang for company restructurings)
Think of us as a gas station, we are here to fill you up this time
If you need a refill, we are here for you, but I'm asking that you not come back for a while for a refill
Are we moneygood? (we will get our initial investment back at a minimum, we will get paid first)
Moneygood

Stockbrokers and The Street (Wall Street Terminology)

The Street

The gold-paved street

The golden canyon

The canyon of heroes

The street of sorrows

The Alley (British; UK)

Exchange Alley (British; UK)

Amex (American Stock Exchange)

The Little Board (Amex)

The Irish-American Exchange

P-Coast (Pacific Stock Exchange)

PSE (Pacific Stock Exchange)

The KNIFE (New York Futures Exchange)

The OTC (Over-The-Counter)

The Third Market (OTC)

The old guard (Wall Street)

The MERC (Chicago and New York Mercantile
  Exchange)

Wall Street of the West (Los Angeles, Pacific Stock Exchange)

Bellwethers (stocks that lead the way up in rallies and down in declines)

Red herring (preliminary draft of a company prospectus)

Sweethearts (congenial buyers who outbid raiders)

Pure plays (going long on companies with only one pursuit)

Take a flutter (armed with advice to play the market in a speculative play)

VD (Volume Discounts—trades more than 1,000 shares)

Window dressing (buying showier stocks before the performance is judged)

Greenmail (repurchasing stock by a company from an unwanted suitor at a high price)

Greenmailer (company threatens to continue to raid unless quickly bought out at a premium)

Whitemail (elaborately concealed large corporate bribes)

Pac man strategy (eat your opponent before he eats you)

A biteback (delay tactic as opposed to a serious bid)

Bodyrain (leftover people from a takeover, merger, or failure)

Milking the street (manipulators making money by depressing a price through rumor)

Stoking the boiler (when the boiler room caller calls a prospect)

Goose job (forcing up the price by buying outstanding shares at increasing prices)

Dynamiters (high-pressure salesman; highest on boiler room hierarchy)

Trading on margin (trading with little money)

Short-squeeze play (forced to buy at artificially high prices)

Big swinging dicks (big-time brokers or traders)

Take a flier (take a chance)

Lollipops (sweet to everyone but a raider)

Elephants (institutional investors)

Squawk box (interoffice two-way cable radio)

Cleaning up (making $$$)

Standing on velvet (making $$$)

Arbs (Arbitrageurs)

Risk arbitragers

Goldbugs (Speculators in the gold market)

Razz (high-pressure sales pitch)

Goosing the market

The mark (the victim)

Alley waddlers (dishonest bankers)

Plunger (risk-taker)

Scalping the market

Punter (small-scale speculator)

Piker (punter)

Tailgating (what tailgaters do)

Bulls (believe prices of market will rise)

Bears (believe prices of market will fall)

Hot stuff (promotional literature)

Paper (promotional literature)

Shadow market (options market)

Melon (dividend)

Plum (dividend)

Sweeteners (extra incentives)

Kickers (sweeteners)

Munis (municipal bonds)

Discos (bonds selling at a discount)

Whisky diskies (discos)

Zeros (zero coupon bonds)

Zippers (zeros)

Ballooning a stock (create artificial upward trend)

Golden handshake (lucrative severance package)

Blowout (offering of an issue that sells fast)

Gunning a stock (create artificial downward trend)

Tailors (ride the coattails of market leaders)

Floor animals (those with an instinct of trading successfully)

Position traders (buy stocks and hold them)

The fix is in (pre-arrangement for a situation, mainly through bribery)

Scalpers (trade small quantities of stocks and quickly see price moves)

Boutique indexes (sum up the performance of specialty stocks like utility stocks)

Cut the melon (when a company delivers an unexpectedly high dividend)

Silver bullets (government bonds and securities that contribute(d) to the war effort)

War babies (stocks or bonds whose worth increases during the war)

Flipping (buy it on first issue and sell it at first rise in price at the end of the day)

Green shoe option (underwriters issuing an additional 10% of stock under certain conditions)

Strong hands (investors who hold securities for long periods of time)

Weak hands (investors who hold securities that they would sell for slight profit)

Golden parachute (exec salary benefits for a year or more after corporate takeover)

The great crash (1929)

The great Bull Market (1920s)

Coolidge Boom

Hoover Bull Market

Eisenhower Boom

Sputnik Market (1957)

Kennedy Bull Market (1962-1963)

Johnson Bull Market (1964)

October Massacres (1978 and 1979)

The Asian Flu (1999-2000)

The Tech Wreck (2001-2002)

Dotbombs (2000-2003)

Black Monday (10/19/87)

Black Tuesday (10/29/29)

Black Wednesday (7/26/1893)

Black Thursday (5/9/1901)

Wild Friday (1/23/87)

Yaks (salespeople)

Needlemen (salespeople)

Fronter (inexperienced seller)

Coxey (front call man)

Salting them down (buy the stock and put it away)

The floor (of the New York Stock Exchange)

Getting down to brass tacks (finish the business at hand)

Getting into a scrape (disagreeable predicament)

Triple witching hour (3 P.M. to 4 P.M.—last hour of the day of the Quarter)

Pulling in their horns (Wall Streeters pulling in their stocks due to a nervous market)

Hit the bid (market order to sell at a bid price)

Blow out the position (sell stock immediately)

Played him for a point (broker made a trade just for the sake of commission)

Running for the hills (prices begin dropping in droves and investors hurry to sell)

Escape the flood before everyone liquidates

Bailing out (selling quickly without regard to price)

Unloading stock (selling large amounts of stock)

Hammering the stock (lowering the price by dumping large amounts)

Blown out (lose everything that is invested)

Going through the financial wringer

Holding the bag (investor owning stocks that are no longer desirable)

Pony up

Spill the beans

Penny stocks

Pass the buck

The quick and dirty

Down and dirty

On the curb

Curb stocks

Tech stocks

The gutter market

Young turks

Off the board

Blue Mondays

Blue Monday Syndrome

Good stocks recover, but cats and dogs die

Go long

Play the market

Dumb money

Get in on the ground floor

Ride stock up

Chasing the market

Block trades

Hot stuff propaganda

Tip

Tipster

Tipster sheets

Pointer

Blue chips

Blue chip raiders

Hostile takeovers

Unfriendly takeovers

Black knights
White knights
Teddy bear pats
Blood is in the water
Wall Street piranhas
Hired guns
Killer bees
Sandbagging
Tapped out (complete loss)
Taking a bath (large losses)
Hedging (balancing out positions)
Lobby rats (what brokers call idle tape watchers)
Walk-ins (unsophisticated new customers who
    try their hand at the market)
Stockwatchers
Tickerhounds
Tape worms
Tickerosis
Bullpens
Bucket shops
Dialing for dollars
Back-office crunch
Inside information
Inside dope
Big operators
Filthy rich
Flush with cash
War chest
Jackscrew it
Hammer it
Straddle it
Dump stocks on it
Bloodthirsty market
New issue fever
Merger mania
Bulletproof the targets
Key raiders

Making a killing
Pyramiding
Trading on a shoestring
Bottom feeders
Bottom fishers
Going short
Short selling
Short positions
Caught short
Tryin' to be bigger than the market
Check the arbs
Boiler rooms
Boiler room call boys
Switching and twisting
Smiling and dialing
Big operators
Smart operators
Hip shooters
High steppers
Bird-dogging information
Turn the screws to 'em
Poison pills
Poisoned tips
Bullish
Bull runs
Bull traps
Bearish
Bear drives
Long position
Short position
Short the stock
Sucker rally
The smart money
Smart money men
Wise money boys
Wall Street talent
Gnomes of Wall Street

Chartists
Titans of finance
Technicians
Play the market
Long and wrong
Rocket scientisis
The jewel in the crown
The lynchpin of the deal
A diamond in the rough
In play
Issue overhang
Watered-down stocks
Bells and whistles
Naked option writers
Several options
Strips
Straps
Saddles
Spreads
Spread eagles
Straddle the market
Hedge strategy
Notes
Last-ditch effort
Gunslingers
Wolves
Little guys
Little people
Stock market lambs
Lambs
Lilies
Suckers
Sucker list
Sucker play
Lobby lizards
Big wigs
The big store

Big board
Big con game
Bootstrap bust-ups
Caught in a corner
Cut and dried
Dead ducks
From soup to nuts
From womb to tomb
From cradle to grave
One-stop shop
Boutique firm
Cottage industries
Out of the money
First rule of thumb
Trainwreck
Lock, stock, and barrel
Locked into a stock
Dumping stock
Spilling stock
Pounding
Banging the market

Banging
Bangers
Rechannel the tension
Cornered the market
Big loser
Cleaned out
Tap city
Taking a cleaning
Wiped out
Take some gas
Go to the wall
Be burned
Going South
Holding the baby
Churn 'em and burn 'em
Churn, burn, and bury

Real Estate Terminology

Bubble (when the market is inflated)
Beat down (hold it down as in the price)
Cash eater (high burn rate usually on land)
Cash burn (same as "cash eater")
Radio silence (same as "going dark")
Hard corner (a true corner with a light signal)
Main & Main (the best location in the market)
Squeeze down (same as a "beat down")
That dog won't hunt (the deal makes no economic sense)
Too much hair (the deal is too complex with too many problems)
Lotta hair (same as too much hair)
Trophy property ("A"-class)
Pig (bad real estate with no long-term appeal)
Vanilla shell (Building or space with no frills)

Vanilla box (same as "vanilla shell")

Fish or cut bait (make a required decision or move on)

Back of the envelope calculation (a pro-forma that is a quickie)

Beauty contest (when numerous buyers are competing to purchase a property)

Wise guy (New York-type; talks fast; no substance)

Big hat, no cattle (for a promoter who oversells what his true abilities are)

Bottom fisher (a buyer who only purchases when prices or properties are distressed)

Grave dancing (people who chase owners or lenders who are in deep trouble on a deal)

Brain damage (when a deal or person is causing undue stress)

Cherry pick (when looking at a portfolio of properties and only bidding on a portion of the properties)

Dead cat bounced (when the cycle hits bottom, goes slightly up, and then goes even lower back down)

It doesn't pencil (economics of the deal does not make sense)

Double dip (economy dipped a second time before improving)

Eat what you kill (you find it, we pay for it; the way brokers live)

Get on the board (the desire to monetize a development and put some money in the bank)

Get the clock ticking (commit a buyer to start the due diligence period during escrow)

Going hard (when you purchase money deposits and they became non-refundable; soft luck, hard commitment)

Going vertical (when construction commences from the foundation upward)

Gone dark (other party won't return calls or correspondence)

Greenmail (someone who has what you need and demands more money than it is worth)

Ground floor elevator (getting into a deal at the right time and letting the market upswing be profitable)

Holding us hostage (same as greenmail except may not consume money)

Lowball offer (an unrealistic offer to test where the seller's bottom line is)

The mom & pops are killing us (non-credit tenants who aren't paying rent)

NIMBY (not in my backyard)—(when a community activist lobbies against a development)

Pigs get fat, hogs get slaughtered (okay to be a pig and make good profit; hogs get greedy for too long)

Pushing a rope (don't try now because there is nothing to be gained)

Pushing a string (a futile effort; trying to "push a string" uphill)

Re-trade (when you renegotiate a purchase price lower than the contracted amount)

Red herring (a preliminary prospectus; draft document only)

See through building (a property that has no tenants)

Shill (a seller uses you to get the sale bid higher even though he has no intention of selling to you)

Shopworn (deal has been around a long time with no takers)

You snooze, you lose (when you wait too long to make a deal and someone else picks it up)

Cram down (when a financial party takes all of the upside away from the operating partner)

Making Money / Revenue Generation / Affordable / Rewards

The Prompt

THE COMPANY IS sitting pretty... they are flush with cash

A million bucks for them is only a drop in the bucket... they make major moolah

You should try to make your second million first because it is easier than the first

You can start your economic engines because we need to bring in some more dough

Clocking dollars
Bringing in bills
The guy is minting coin
Minting coin
Time is money... and we have time

The market's exploding
Start your economic engines
Coins were coming in
The green is rolling in
The cash is tumbling in
We are swimming in the green
Living the P-Diddy life
Taking in buckets of dough
Making money hand over fist
Raking it in
It's like we're printing money
Pots of gold all along the rainbow's curve
That's just a drop in the bucket
That's chump change
That's just flash cash
That's just some mad money
It doesn't even dent our bank account
Sweet cashflow
Cost-effective
In the black
In the pink
Sitting pretty
The company is flush with cash
The reward is a carrot and not a whip
Bull market money
Filthy rich
Flush with cash
If the skrilla is killa
Modest gains but advances nonetheless
A heaping war chest
War chest
Bankroll me
Pocket some cash
Get all you can
They make more money than most third-world
    nations

Losing Money /
Not Making Much Money /
Cost-prohibitive

The Prompt

MAN, I'M JUST trying to get by and pay the Williams, but my bank account is ka-put

We have been bleeding red ink for the last two fiscals

We are having as much success as we would if we were trying to sell ice to the Eskimos

It's like trying to rearrange the deck chairs on the Titanic… it's useless… this is a no-win

Strapped for cash
Hemorrhaging cash
We are pretty price-
    sensitive on this
Light in the wallet
Circular discussion
We blew the budget
The market's tanking
Out of funds
Way overbudget
Going down like a
    power window
Square peg in a round hole
The twelfth of never
Doom and gloom
Bleeding red ink
In the red
Redline it
Flatline
Treading water

Too rich for our blood
Tightwad
Penny pincher
Cheapskate
Belt tightener
For scraps and fragments
That'll cost kidneys
Time is money
This is a time suck
This is a cash suck
The never-ending well of draining our cash dry
It is a crazy job, but that is why I make the middle money
One of these days is none of these days
If the cost is too high, we will have to eat it
Money pit
Merry-go-round of losses
Significant world of hurt
Burning money
A high burn rate
It's not a never-ending pot of money
When you're out, you're out
It is a pretty rich price structure
Too much coin
No bank left
Blew the lot
Blew the nest egg
Cost-prohibitive
Too rich for my blood
That'll cost you a couple of lungs
Pour through a wealth of
Simply running through the cash
Investment trappings
Bear market
Frightfully expensive
The dollar figures are laced with too much cream

It's like walking in loose granular
Champagne taste but a beer budget
OOFAU (out of funds as usual)
OOF (out of funds)
To the Budweisers of the world, $30,000 is lunch…
    but not to me
Like carrying coals to Newcastle… it's done

It's All Good

$$$

by Munir Haddad
Founder, MarketingJuice (formerly of MTV)
Sausalito, California

"It's All Good Until It Is What It Is"

IN 1997, I MOVED from Chicago to San Francisco to work in electronic entertainment. Not dot-coms, but video games or "vids." Northern California was experiencing its all-too-famous boom-and-bust cycle, and I was in the thick of things. It was "all good."

Occasionally, I would have to suffer through

a bit of "portfolio inferiority complex" as I discussed my traditional compensation package with the "millionaires on paper." They would regale me with stories about how they were "leveraging their portfolio assets" to do all sorts of things that I could only dream about. For one person, it was a trip around the world, for another, it was a second vacation home, and still another was planning the purchase of his first Ferrari when his options matured. Games, after all, were just games, and if I wanted in on the action, I was counseled by these "young guns" to go the Internet route. "It's all good," I would respond, "but ya see, I'm a bit 'risk-averse'."

All their dreaming led me to believe that these "netrepreneurs" weren't really working. Instead, they were just "resting and vesting." Don't make waves, and stay employed until those paper millions became real. It was all good—at least it appeared to be for them. Who knew that most of their high-flying start-ups would become "dot-bombs"?

The longer I stayed in the Bay Area, I began to see "It's all good" as more of a philosophy than a phrase. And the folks in "NorCal" would use it as a defense. Times were often so stressful that you'd get a bit "agro," but if you held to the philosophy, you could just walk it off. Even a bum deal, a dot-bomb, or your "cube farm" were all "money." Someone rear-ends you on "the 101," they get out of their car and are apologetic, saying, "Oh man, I'm so sorry." You may want to kill them for a second, but then you'd automatically respond, "It's all good."

This philosophy becomes "crystal" when contrasted with the East Coast. I eventually moved back to New York City, where I grew up, and my

West Coast friends would call and ask me what I found to be the differences in attitudes between the cities. Besides the fact that New Yorkers laugh when Bay Area residents refer to San Francisco as "The City," the difference is attitude. In New York, if someone looks at you funny on the street, let alone rear-ends your car and is stupid enough to stop for a second and apologize, the reaction, if it isn't a tirade of epithets and gesticulations, is, "It is what it is" (which is the modern day "sh** happens").

In New York City, you "sh**-can a bad idea before it comes back to bite you in the ass." And in negotiations, the concept of a "win-win" is often replaced with, "Screw them before they screw us." It's aggressive. That fatalistic, aggressive response defines the difference in attitude that is borne out in every facet of New York, including the native choice for "*BusiBUZZ*." There's a lot more "dropping of F-bombs" (using the "f-word" and "Fu**-'em") in New York City. It certainly "ain't fu**ing all good," and it rarely ever is, because "It is what it is." Fatalistic versus optimistic. You were bound to fu** up, and I was bound to be in your way when you did. "It is what it is."

"Pay attention, motherfu**er, or you might get "run over by a Mack truck." "When in Rome, do as the Romans do." Take in and use the *BusiBUZZ* and the attitude of the folks around you. Or just "stick to your guns" and "fu**-'em if they can't take a joke." But whatever you do, pay attention to the *BusiBUZZ* people are throwing around you. It might just give you the edge. Beyond being "gravy," it might get you "added value" from your program, a "lucky strike extra" in a deal, or let you walk away "laughing all the way to the bank."

Positive Vibes / Very Good Things / Optimism / Happy / Hot

The Prompt

IT'S ON THE straight and narrow... it's on the level... it's on the up and up

I do not own a farm, but if I did, I would bet it—it's a sweetheart deal

It is definitely on point—well on track to make it

Yes in a big way

Sweetheart deals
Coins were coming in
Like a kid in a candy store
It'll take wing
I've got pull

Peachy
The table is set
The idea has teeth
Do-able
Greenlight
Frolicking in the madness
Tickled pink
Hunky-dory
Happy camper
Happy camper syndrome
Feels like an oasis

Looks like an oasis
Put a plus in front of it all
Smiles all around
Drinks all around
Drinks for all my friends
That's a feather in your cap
A strut in your step
A spring in your step
Collective, public, spirited interest
Double-digit growth
Really yahooey

It moved the needle
Fear is the other guy's problem
You've got muscle in the marketplace
Double down
I agree with you 1,000%
Ducks in a row
Ducks on a pond
We're talking pennies
The wind in your sails
Feelin' pretty brilliant right about now
Reap the benefits until the cows come home
The stars are in the right alignment
The stars are in synch in the right quadrant
Dancing on the edge of the volcano, but every-
   thing is cool
He's the picture of health
Whatever you say, Irie man
Put a plus in front of that deal
A-team
On the same page
Get on the same page
Full steam ahead
In concert
Short list
Make the pie bigger
Dominate and satiate
I cannot disagree with you
Make hay while the sun shines
It's better than the alternative
A real up-and-comer
A star on the rise
Self-starter
I think it will fly
Utilize it to the hilt
Make the most of it
Always the optimist
Happiness is positive cash flow

A diamond in the rough
Oldie but goody
Make some waves
There's credence in the comment
Optimism cookies
High on chuckleseeds
Knock on wood
A sanguine shower (upbeat)
Cash flow keeps the dream alive
No problems
No worries
It's Irie
As simple as agreement, deal, contract
You catch more flies with honey than vinegar
In this case, you can fall on your sword and be
    happy about it
Trippin' the light fantastic
Gain steam
It's a lock
We are making some headway
Big points
Bet that

Positive Outcome / Positive Situation / Good News

The Prompt

It's spot on—and sitting pretty
I'm like a kid in a candy store
We're hitting on all cylinders
You can take it to the bank

A banner day
Icing on the cake
It's all good
It's all to the good
That's good stuff
Good stuff
Run the table
The table was set
It's as sure as the world

Guaranteed done deal
Done deal
Good deal
It's spot on
Spot on
Boondoggle
Check plus
Frosting on the cake
The exclamation point
The cherry on top
In the black
In the pink
Yes in a big way
Feather in your cap
Sweetheart deal
Exclamation point
Reward with a carrot rather than a whip
The whole shootin' match
Thanks for the tip
They saved my bacon
You were yelling… I was yelling… but we got it done
You were dealing like a kid in a candy store
Don't forget about the vig after a deal like that goes through
Hot stone massages and bath butlers
Reap the benefits until the cows come home
Off the hook
All the rage
Out of the woods
Supercharged
Layup booty call
Off the chain
Off the hook
Holla
In the hizzy
It went off without a hitch

Knee deep in hooters and gin joints
Dip your beak
Shooters shoot
Jackpot
Paydirt
Shoot the moon
Cha-ching
That's butter on some tasty toast
A shot in the arm
A boost
A bump up
The sweet spot
Up to snuff
Passed the sniff test
Nothing's better than that
You can't beat that
You can't top that
That hits the spot
Turn a negative into a positive
A business phoenix
We pulled some strings to get you here
An incredible run
It was a great run
By hook or by crook
It was a back-end solution
It solved all of our problems
Amped up
Jacked up
Keyed up
He's lit
We're in the friend zone
Pie-in-the-sky

Cool

The Prompt

THE BOMB
Sweet
It's the sh**
He's a cool customer… Cool as a cucumber

Boss
Hot
Sweetness
Sweet dock
Pimp
Butternut
Cool beans
Cool out
Cool cat
Easy street
Cherry
Peachy
Peachy-keen
Solid
Kosher
Bet
Be chill
It's tracking
It's spiking
It's within arms' reach

Do-able
Everybody just take a sec and be cool
Everybody be cool
Is everything to your liking?
Me likee
It's all good
I ain't mad at ya
In thar
All that
All that and a bag of chips
Bag of chips
Wicked
Fresh
Fresh and fly
Cutting-edge
Bleeding-edge
Leading-edge
Smooth operation
As cool as the other side of the pillow
Guay (pronounced "gway"; Spanish for cool)
Can everybody just be simpatico?
Simpatico (Spanish for nice)

Easy / Relaxing / Calming / Predictable

The Prompt

COOL, CALM, AND collected
    Piece of cake
A walk in the park
    If you want to make it easier, then ask us
Randy Gordon's last-name type questions

A layup
A slam dunk
Ducks on a pond
Duck soup
How easy is that?
No worries
Painstakingly easy
I want everything to be modular
Clean and green
Comfort factor
A lock
That's a two-putt green

A two-foot putt
A gimme
Inside the leather
Money in the bank
In the history book
It's academic
No-brainer
Cut-and-dried
A cut-and-dried issue
Easy street
Easy money
Easy easy
It's an easy game
Gravy
Keep your powder dry
Take a chill pill
Take a pill
Take a powder
It serves all the masters
It doth not protest too much
The no-stress part of the day

Path of least resistance
Cool your jets
Be chill
Everybody chill out
Everybody be cool

No need to create a lot of white paper over it
In these enlightened times when hubby is at work
    and you are sitting on your butt
A non-confrontational idea
Drowning a kitten would be easier
A case of beer and a bag of prawns
A glass of rum in a quiet, warm place
Don't get caught looking at strikes
Child's play
Catch air
Calm waters
Clear as a bell
A tap-in
A cakewalk
Mr. Smooth
Mr. Consistency
According to plan
Right on time
Still waters run deep
Milk and cookies
Funnelcakes and kettlecorn
Chill the fu** down
Chill the fu** out
Simmer down now
Drop a Valium
Take an Ambien

Booze / Beer / Bartalk

The Prompt

Here are some of the terms that put smiles on our faces… and numb our throats… call it what it is or order what you want… the drinks are on the house.

Booze / Alcohol

Booze
Hooch
Liquor
Highballs
Libations
Liquid libation
Firewater
Pisswater
Sauce
Spirits
Nog
Healing juice
Lunatic juice

Nightcap
Evil potion
Frolic
Frivolity
Tie one on
Paint the town red
Chat her up
Pour me some smooth
Pour me some solid
Smooth sippin'
Another drinky
Drinky
Drinky-poo
Spice it up
Spice things up
Let's shoot up with…
Inject some…
Light on the…
Heavy on the…
Shots
Double shots
Shots all around
Shots fired
Jigger (shot)
Double (double shot)
Speed well (speed rack)
Splash (a tiny amount of)
Tall (a tall Collins glass)
With some onions
With some olives
With some salad
Truth serum
On the rocks
Over ice
Over
With a water back (shot glass or cocktail glass of
    water to the side)

Rocks (a shot of booze in a glass filled with ice)

Speed rack (the rack attached to the ice well; behind and under the top bar)

One count (approximately one quarter of a shot)

Pony shot (one ounce of booze)

Shot (one-and-a-half ounces of booze; usually a three-count pour)

Neat (this is how you order when you want booze straight from the bottle to your glass with no ice)

Nice and neat

Up (chilled over ice; stirred or shaken, then strained into a glass)

Straight up (same as "up")

Bruised (light crystals of ice within the drink, once shaken or stirred)

The gun (a hose with a multi-buttoned nozzle for dispensing mixers)

Slammed (when the customer's demand for drinks equals the bar staff's ability to supply them)

Virgin (a drink without booze)

Wilted drinks (once a drink passes its peak in terms of flavor; "up" drinks become warm and wilted)

86ed (could apply to a bar patron no longer welcome on the premises or a cancelled drink or food order)

Amateur hour drinks (seldom-ordered drinks that are usually fruity or sweet)

Fru fru drinks (usually fruity or too sweet)

Beer

Cold ones

Cool ones

Nice, tall cool one

Coldies
Frosty ones
Frosties
Brewskies
Brewsky
Brew
Tall boys
Pops
Road pops
Brew pops
Beer pops
Grain
Ale
Grog
Suds
Hops
Beeya
Golden goodness
Gold
Some o' them thar gold
Dead soldier (empty beer bottle, glass, or can)

Toasts

Up the rebels
Bottoms up
Tally ho
Another glass of courage
In your eye
Here's mud in your eye
Here's looking at you sideways (a toast with a
    friend)
Here's lookin' at ya
Here's to you
Here's to nightcaps
I love all o' yez
Pass the lips, over the gums, look out, stomach,
    here it comes

Down the hatch (a toast with a friend)
To your health, happiness, and success
Here's to a short life and a merry one
L'Chayim
Banzai
Skol
Prosit (pronounced "prohst")
Sante (pronounced "Son-tay")
Ost
Chin chin
Cheers
Arriba, abajo, al centro, padentro

Bartalk

Let's go paint the town... a night on the town
Chit-chat in the taproom
How about a nightcap?
Let's stay a half a glass longer
Let's stay for another round
One more round
Call it a night
Hold down the fort
Should we call it a night?
Let's tie one on
Let's get stinking drunk
Let's get stinking
Let's get snot-yanking drunk
Let's get drunk off our asses
Let's get slobberknockered
Let's get sh**faced
Let's get sh**housed
Let's get housed
Let's get sloshed
Let's get nogged (Christmas time drunk)
Let's do something stupid
Let's water the horses
Everybody's soused (drunk; Irish)

Everybody's scuddered (drunk; Irish)
Everybody's palatic (drunk; Irish)
Plastered (drunk)
Wicked hammered (drunk)
Hammered (drunk)
Drunk in the gutter
Drunk and laid out in the gutter
Three sheets to the wind
Liquored up to the eyeballs
Liquored up to the gills
Good and liquored
See ya at the pub
See ya at the beer parlour
Slop the hogs
Cheers (thanks; Here's to…; Please; Goodbye; Whatever)
And your own… (said to a bartender or barmaid when giving them a tip—typically 10 pence - 1 pound)
Bottoms up (drink up; said to someone or to people in a group)
Tally Ho (drink up; goodbye; or "off we go" at the beginning of a fox hunt)
Beers in (get beers from the bar)
Down and in
Kill off a few soldiers

Another dead soldier

Rally the troops

Circle the wagons

On the house

Roundup

Another round

Another round for the boys

Another round for my people

Top me off

Top it off

Top off

Give me a topper

Topper

What's your poison?

Put it on my tab

Tab out

Check, please

Close out

Go for the finish

Thank you, sir, may I have another

Living large

Last call for alcohol

Last call

One for the road, then one for the sky

One for the road

Touch base

Let's reconvene

Let's go live "la vida loca"

Blowing smoke

86 it (out of stock; Navy code for out-of-inventory)

Pull up to the trough like gutter pigs

Gutter pigs

No-tell motel time

Well (the entry, hand-level booze; the more inexpensive stuff you get if you do not order by brand)

House brands (same as "well")

Call (these are the moderately priced name brands; a step above "well")

Back-bar (the large fixture against the wall behind the bar for "call" and top shelf booze display)

Top shelf (the best booze in the place; typically situated on the top shelf for premium positioning)

Bump (an extra charge for certain drinks such as "up" drinks)

Upcharge (same as a "bump")

Dash (this is the smallest amount in a drink recipe; usually just one squirt of something like bitters)

Float (booze added last and allowed to float on top of the drink; usually a one count or ¼ of a shot)

Tavern

Bar

Taproom

Tap house

Pub

Joint

Ale house

Saloon

Beer hall

Brew house

Beer garden

Beer parlour

Gin joint

Bar dust

Bar mud

Bar bilge

Rotgut

Road house

Waterin' hole

Honky-tonk
Wine bar
Martini bar
Prohibition bar
Bartender
Barmaid
Barkeeper
Barkeep
Beer boy
Beer jockey
Suds jockey
Hot toddy
Toddy
Nipper
Ice well (this is the sink-like bin behind the bar that the ice is kept in)
X-out (bartender or individual waiter settles up for the night)
Z-out (all bartenders or the whole bar settles up and clears out tabs for the night)
Highball (mixed drinks most often ordered usually consisting of one shot of booze over ice with mixer)
I need a good belt of something
Slingin' back drinks
A George (big tipper)
A Stiff (bad tipper or a non-tipper)
Double-fisted (carrying two drinks)
Tip
A dash
A little somethin' for the effort
A pat on the back
An attaboy
Double up
All dolled up
All done up
All gussied up

Dressed to the hilt
Dressed to the nines
Be chill
Chillin'
Chill like big daddies
Hittin' the sauce
Lie in a gutter and drink
Pull up to the oasis

Excuse my French
Toss some back
Knock 'em back
Hoist 'em up
Hoist a few
Drink till your nose turns red
Slide one down
Slide one over
Slide me one
Sop up the booze
Soak up the booze
Bladdered (drunk)
Arseholed (drunk)
Wankered (drunk)
Pissed (drunk)
Rollin' blank tape (drunk)
Stinkin' drunk
Blotto (drunk; intoxicated)
Floating on ice (drunk)

Pissed as a parrot (drunk)
Drunk as a skunk (drunk)
Full as a state school (drunk)
Getting snookered (being taken advantage of;
    getting drunk)
Three deep at the bar
Swamped
In the weeds (4 to 5 people deep at the bar)
86 the order (cancel the order)
How am I feeling?… poor… no, pour
J'moke (idiot)
Schlub
Primo
Vomit
Upchuck
Regurgitate
Repeat dinner in reverse
Yack
Yackfest
Praying to the porcelain God
Grab porcelain
Hollerin' down the hole
Yellin' at the tidy-bowl man
Yellin' at the toilet water
Metho (a derelict)
Technicolor yawn (to vomit)
Chunder (to vomit)
Kark (to vomit)
Lunatic soup (alcohol)
Tinny (can of beer)
Tube (can of beer)
Plonk (cheap wine)
Fourpenny dark (cheap, red, fortified wine)
Snake's piss (bad alcohol)
Dead marine (empty beer bottle)
Rort (an enjoyable party with dancing and vio-
    lence)
Stubby (a small Australian beer bottle)

Two-pot screamer (a cheap drunk; someone who
    can get intoxicated very quickly)
On the turps (in the process of getting drunk)
Top night (getting drunk amongst friends)
Split-second of humor injected into a stressful
    day
Burn time
Down time
Got any smokes?
Got any timber?
His head's throbbing like a sick robin's ass
A good belt of the sauce
What's the skinny?
What are you, some drama club sissy?
Shaken not stirred
She's good enough
Grab some coldies
Pound some brews
Rotgut
Of all the gin joints in all the world
Hold down the fort
A mouth like Cocky's cage (hangover)
In the weeds (swamped with orders / customer
    requests)
With destruction and desolation, there is new life
    here at the bar
Japanese "nomunicating" (drinking and talking)
2-Buck Chuck (derogatory term for Charles Shaw
    wine)
Get lit
That's the booze talking
On the house
When can we cocktail?
When can we coffee?

Make It Happen / Need It Quickly / Speedy

The Prompt

WE NEED IT PDQ (pretty damn quick), so just do it post-haste

We needed it yesterday or ASAP (as soon as possible)

Lickety-split
Double time
On the double
We are at the eleventh hour and need to move on it
We have to make a move
Time to sh** or get off the pot
You need to be Johnny-on-the-spot
You need to pay it off and fast
Pull out all the stops
Post-haste
ASAP or sooner
Exhaust administrative remedies
We don't have any long lead times
Expedite the process
Do whatever comes to mind
Be jacked, ready, and double tough
Move the needle
Fast track it
Spike the sales
Show a spike

Go into overdrive
Hyperdrive
Just the soup of the day and a glass of water
Don't take time to smell the roses
Don't be a tourist
Just get it done and done fast
Warp speed
Light speed
When does it need to go live?
When does it street?

It drives the boat
Exhaust the quick alternatives
No stone unturned
Come hell or high water
No holds barred
Anything goes
Cowboy up
Man up
Have some gumption
Get ready to move fast
On the way to go
We did the math
It's a sprint to the finish
We gotta push it
I am not the Dallas Cowboys… I need more than
      two minutes to get the job done

Simple / Keep It Simple / Simplify / Structured / Predictable

The Prompt

L ET'S USE THE KISS method (keep it simple, stupid)

Look, it ain't brain surgery—in fact, it's a slam dunk... or at least an easy lay-up

(Keep It Simple, Stupid)

Let me give you a thumbnail sketch (quick review)

A back-of-the-envelope calculation

This is not brain surgery

Painstakingly easy

Not a problem

Keep your powder dry

I want everything to be modular

Piece of cake

Comfort factor

About as basic as it gets

A lock

A two-foot putt

That's a two-putt green

A gimme

Inside the leather

Fish in a barrel

A layup

A slam dunk

Money in the bank

In the history book

It's academic

Cut-and-dried

A cut-and-dried issue

In laymen's terms

Let me cut to the chase

Let me give you a quick and dirty... and break it
down for you

No need to create a lot of white paper over it

Ducks on a pond

Easy money

Easy easy

Gravy

Hindsight is twenty-twenty (20-20)

It serves all the masters

It doth not protest too much

The no-stress part of the day

A non-confrontational idea

Consolidate and dominate

Cool your jets

Cakewalk

A walk in the park

Go with the hot hand

Legitimate

It's legit (pronounced "la-jit")

Keep it legit

Keep it fair

Maintain integrity, and it will fall into place

Monday-morning-quarterbacking can make anyone look like a genius

Just have a Bushmills and Percoset and call me
in the morning

I am simply looking for a two- or three-letter
answer (Y-E-S or N-O)

Running Smoothly /
Compliments /
Going Fine

The Prompt

It's RUNNING LIKE a well-oiled machine

It's your world… the rest of us are just paying the bills

If it ain't broke, don't fix it

We're all systems go

All systems five-by-five

A-Okay

Okey-dokey

Like clockwork

Three greens

We are go for launch

We haven't had problem one

On time

On sceddy (schedule)

I passed the "give me the once-over" test

Damn, we're good
Damn, I'm good
Smooth sailing
Smooth riding
Peachy
Peachy-keen
Don't sweat it
No worries
No prob
No problemo
Let it keep on rolling
Let's keep it rolling
Let it ride
Keep riding that horse
Let 'er rip
Full steam ahead
Full speed ahead
If it ain't broke, don't fix it
It'll fly
Whatever walks the dog
Whatever floats your boat
Out of the line of fire
We're in a safe zone
Safe zone
Ahead of the curve
Knock off around five
Seren-fu**ing-dipity
Keep on truckin'
R&R (rest and relaxation)

Understanding /
Learning / Clarity

The Prompt

I think we have come to an understanding
We had a Come-To-Jesus meeting… and everybody is now on the same page
I'm picking up what you're putting down
Ya see what I'm saying?

Crystal-clear
Crystal
Clear
10-4
Check
Checkmate
Roger wilco, over
    and out
Roger wilco
Copy
Copy that
Kinko
Damn straight
Damn skippy
Sit down session
Clarification session
I am now getting some clarity… it's less of a fuzzy
    picture
Blow the trumpet with some clarion sound
I'm telling you how it works… do I have to draw
    you a picture?
We've been through the wars
We know what's what
Blinding insight

A light bulb went on
Learning through subtle indoctrination
The unexpected "aha" point
Bingo
Let me learn you something
Informed, reasonable decisions
Deep-dive session
Discovery mode
Due diligence
Give me the once-over
Fair assumption to make or conclusion to draw
There you go
I hear ya
It's as sure as the world
Note to self
Factor it into the equation
Found religion after that outcome
Up to standard
We're exceeding expectations
We're beating Wall Street expectations
It's a sustained drive

It Ain't All Good;
In Fact, It's All Bad

Negative Vibes / No, In General / It Does Not Feel Right

The Prompt

WE GET CROSS-EYED with them every day
We have two feet in one shoe
I see the screw-up fairy has visited us again
We're in a tailspin… it's a downward spiral

Significant disparities
Go ahead, I always welcome being interrupted
Sluggish growth
Slumping sales
Evaporating profits
Declining revenues
Growth in losses
Minimal expansion

It mars the attitude
It muzzles the dog
We are on a much tighter leash
It spoils the day
Ruins my day
Yikes
Moan-day
It's a slippery slope
Tighten up your bank account
Better put your best foot forward, given the situation
The tail is wagging the dog
Just blowing smoke
I am out of my gourd
I don't know what the problem is, but I bet it's hard to pronounce
I'm out of my mind, but feel free to leave me a message
Like rearranging the deck chairs on the Titanic
Like catching up to an avalanche to give it some direction
Like brown shoes with a tuxedo
The beginning of the end
We're rudderless
We're flying blind
Lamentably, I suspect something is amiss
Serves a grisly purpose
Real quandary
Between a rock and a hard place
It's a double-edged sword
Therein lies the problem
Two sides to every coin
A bag of snakes
Gum on a shoe
Hit it, Alice
We need to eat our Wheaties
Behind the eight ball

Not my strong suit
Not gonna happen
It's just not my for-tay
Buzzkill
Sucks balls
Sucks dog
Blows dog
Fractured
The canoe talk
Bonehead ideas
Sh** rolls downhill
Asleep at the wheel
A bunch of hooey
Sound asleep
Not tight enough
Too restrictive
Cutty (hidden)
Pinner (weak)
It's pinna (weak)

Not that it will help, but…
Feels like a lot of hocus-pocus
On the precipice
On the verge
Hold your mud
Trainwreck
Bad voodoo
Into thin air
Get a cap to the dome
Lamentably, I suspect an orthographical lapse
Lamentably, I suspect something is amiss
Serves a grisly purpose
Work blue
Thin ice
Save your own hide
Just trying to survive in this shark tank
It's a grenade with the pin pulled
I don't give a flying fu**

Forget about it (pronounced as one word)
We're in a significant world of hurt
Slim pickings
It really frosts me
I'm hot under the collar
I'm hot and bothered
I'm hot
It really chaps my ass
C'mon guy
What's the freakin' point?
Take to high ground
Brace for impact
Run for daylight
Bands of rain
Stage 5 hurricane
Case of the chills
Creepy
Better fend for yourself

Fend it off
Anybody's guess
We are deeply divided on this issue
Deeply divided
Hung jury
Divided jury
These are just dumb-offs
We're in with the dirty water boys
It's so not gonna happen
It gives people the jumps
It spells the end
Fright factor
Just worry about the shark that's closest to your
    body

We cannot keep throwing 55-footers (coming up short)

On a safari, it's not the lions and the tigers that get ya, it's the mosquitos and the gnats

Well, what do you think you could support with the minimum spec?

Rowing the canoe in a different direction than the rest of us

I am doing a slow burn (talking myself out of it)

Negative Outcome / Negative Situation / Bad Deals

The Prompt

WE SHOT AN airball
We didn't hit a home run
Snafu (situation normal all fu**ed up)
Behind the eight ball from the start

Bad news doesn't get good with age
They will have a field day with this
Our back was against the wall the entire time
Back against the wall
It was a firestorm from the get-go
That's just lip service at this point
Lip service
Behind the times
Cut your losses
Nip it in the bud
Bite off more than you can chew

Open up a can of worms
A can of worms
Out on the limb
Ride a good horse to death
Do not poison my water hole
That's just gasoline on the fire
You just shot yourself in the foot
Faux pas (blunder)
A turkey shoot
Crisis management
It was a real dog fight
Crash and burn
Bend over
The chips are down
Tit in the wringer
Dick in a vice
Drop the ball
Between a rock and a hard place
Going down the toilet
I do not mind the umbrella up my butt, but don't
    try to open it
Buttslammed
We got jobbed
We were on thin ice to begin with
We got our bell rung
Pigeonholed
Fly in the ointment
Wrench in the works
Pain in the cucaracha
Pain in the ass
Sitting duck
House of cards
The beginning of the end
Rudderless
Are our oars in the water?
A bag of snakes
Well, if the shoe fits

The shoe is on the other foot now
Getting grilled
Called on the carpet
Upset the apple cart
Duck and cover
Bad theater
It's a pipe dream
You just hit a nodal line
It is a placebo, not a panacea
Gum on a shoe
The devil finds work for idle hands
It was like throwing darts in the dark
Spitting in the ocean
Better call security
Defcon one
White knuckler
Goatrope
Clusterfu**
Fubar (fu**ed up beyond all recognition)
I'm really easy to get along with once people learn
    to worship me
Houston, we have a big fu**in' problem
Crybaby soup
Do you want some cheese with that wine?
Good old fashioned butt-whippin'
Good old fashioned butt-kickin'
It is so not happening
Do not let things flame out
Flame out
Suction, quickly
Slow down the bleeding
Pull out the tourniquet
A grenade with the pin pulled
Significant world of hurt
Coming up empty
All it needs is a rhinestone collar
Poison pen letters

Poison pills
We're disappointed but not deceived
Hemorrhaging cash
Not a good thing
Bummer
Fess up
Come clean
Disaster city
Disaster
So you got the heave-ho
The economy tanked
That's a tough pill to swallow
The shots weren't falling
Call the nurse… I have just slit my wrists
It is a dog with fleas
Whatever it is, it spells D-O-G
Bring out the flea powder and pooper scooper
There was a substandard level of preparedness
Karmageddon
It could be worse, you could be signing off for
    delivery guys and replacing toner
We've got to build a better mousetrap next time

Questionable / Blunders / Mistakes

The Prompt

HE'S A FEW sandwiches short of a picnic
This was a really big faux pas (pronounced "fo-paah")—it's a colossal fu** up

With that latest decision, I think you are higher than domed-roof scaffolding

Dead brain mode
He is no rocket scientist
It conjures up some rather pointed questions
That's just plain wrong
That would be incorrect
Not gonna happen
Ain't gonna happen
What's up with that?
This would of course not be a good idea
Monumental piss-off
He (she) makes the question mark appear
In a pickle
It's a fumble
Fumble
Incorrect
Who is steering the ship?
Officially overwhelmed
Don't get caught sitting on your hands
Coughed it up
It's just blowing smoke
Needle in a haystack
Slinging a dead cat
It certainly ain't out-of-the-box
The tail wagging the dog

Colossal fu** up

Charlie foxtrot (colossal fu** up)

That's a Charlie Foxtrot

That's nasty

Get a whiff of this one

Whack job

It's like pissing into the wind… you just made a big mistake

I could see that one coming

It's like trying to catch up to an avalanche to give it direction

No one gets too old to learn a new way of being stupid

The light at the end of the tunnel might be a freight train coming your way

The elevator does not make it all the way to the observation deck

You haven't heard the half of it

Unethical Behavior / Dishonesty / Deception / Interference / Secretive Action

The Prompt

Smoke and mirrors and hidden agendas
Keep it on the down low
You're teetering on the ethics tightrope
He's pulling a fast one on you

On the QT
On the hush-hush
On the silent tip
Pulling a number on you
Doing a number on you
Getting ripped off
Rip you off
Monkey business
They're lying like rugs
Backdoor cuts
Backdoor antics
Backroom dealings
Backroom deals
Mask it
Under the radar
Underground system
Hidden matrix
Let's just say there was money passed
Palms were greased
Tills were filled
Money slipped under the table
Let's just say money changed hands

Not on the up and up
You're not being straight with me
Last chance to fess up
Can't trust 'em
Crooked (pronounced "cruh-ked")
Gotta build a better mouse trap
Game of cat and mouse
Bait and switch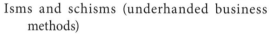
Smash and grab
Smokescreen
Backwater people
Set 'em up
Shifty little bastards
Shifty
Dance around it
Isms and schisms (underhanded business methods)
You're walking that line of being less than honest
It's indicative of him being a slimeball
Come clean
Drop dime (expose someone; tell on them)
The fix is in
It's fixed
It's fixed like the fight game
It's all downhill from here
It's very slippery slope from here
Slippery slope
Run some interference
Buy more time
Buy some time
Getting off scot-free
Closed-door policy
Turn up the heat
Hold their feet to the fire
Feet to the fire
Make 'em sweat it out

Sweat it out
They crossed over to the dark side
Went over to the dark side
The Hoboken Hustle
The Potomac Two-Step
Tomfoolery
Hijinx
Is that your best lift?
Is that your best pull?
Trading on somebody else's name
The devil finds work for idle hands
Struggling to find ways to pass the time
You're up to no good
It'll get you in the end
It'll come back to haunt you
What goes around comes around
Black market
Gray market
Don't try to snow me
Don't try to bullsh** a bullshi**er
Don't piss in my ear and tell me it's raining
They went back door on us
They pulled an end around
Don't ever go behind my back again
Wire taps
Head games
Mind games
Vulcan mind fu**
Mind fu** with 'em
Playing games

Take a bite of the apple
Drink the kool-aid
Go down the rabbit hole
That first hit of crack
There's no turning back
Red pill, blue pill
Crossed the line
Nobody needs to know the better
Nobody needs to be the wiser
What they don't know won't hurt 'em
I can't guarantee that nobody gets hurt
What are our projections for loss of casualties?
Hidden agendas
Shyster
Gray area
Offends all sensibilities
Cock-block
Crossed the line

Bombs/ Bad Situations/ Compromise/ Bad News/ Messed Up

The Prompt

IT'S A REAL CAN of worms—a total goat rope
Significant world of hurt—It's tanking
Crash and burn

Boom!
Sayonara
Titanic
Disaster city
Moan-day
Well, Hell's bells
Hell's bells
That's bunk
We're in a tight spot
Code blue
That's a fine kettle of fish
Out on a limb
Ride a good horse to death
Shoot yourself in the foot
A turkey shoot
Fight the fires
Identify the hot spots
Crisis management
Dog fight
Tit in the wringer
Dick in a vice
Merry-go-round of losses
Bend over
The chips are down
Bite off more than you can chew
Snafu (situation normal all fu**ed up)

Fubar (fu**ed up beyond all recognition)

Call the nurse… I have just slit my wrists

Tough row to hoe (the right way to say it)

Tough road to hoe (the wrong way to say it)

Bad news does not get good with age

Why don't you just throw some gasoline on the fire?

Drop down the fire retardant and mop up the hot spots

The rock and the hard place just became one and the same

I do not mind the umbrella up my butt, but don't try to open it

Drop the ball

Back against the wall

Go down the toilet

Pigeon-holed

It didn't move the needle

It didn't really scare the horses

It did not make anyone sit up and take notice

They're dead wrong

It's worse than charging a castle naked

Take them down

It's not even funny

Hard-hitting stuff

That dog won't hunt

Not even small potatoes but zero potatoes

Black ice

Black copters

Screwed the pooch on that one

Screw the pooch

Wither and die

Like being stoned to death with popcorn

House of cards

Off to the big house

Like brown shoes with a tuxedo

All it needs is a rhinestone collar

It is a dog with fleas

Whatever it is, it spells D-O-G
Bring out the flea powder and pooper scooper
That one came out of left field
A recipe for substance abuse
Do not let things flame out
Flame out
Slow down the bleeding
Pull out the tourniquet
A grenade with the pin pulled
Fly in the ointment
Wrench in the works
You just hit a nodal line
They cut the spigot
Behind the eightball
It is a placebo, not a panacea
Gum on a shoe
Idleness is the holiday of fools
Throwing darts
Flag it
Wild, horse-faced guffaw failure
A guffaw failure
The flop house
In a pickle
Spitting in the ocean
Defcon one
It's a pain in the cucaracha
It's a pain in the ass
Sitting duck
House of cards
Are our oars in the water?
A bag of snakes
Bloodbath
If the shoe fits
The shoe is on the other foot now
Wrench in the works
The devil finds work for idle hands

Nothing / Nothing New / Empty / Bankrupt

The Prompt

WHAT DID WE find? … Nothing, Nada, Goose egg, Donut hole

We came up with Bubkes, Zip, Zero, Zilch

No dice… it ain't happening

It's small potatoes… there's nothing here… I don't know what to tell ya

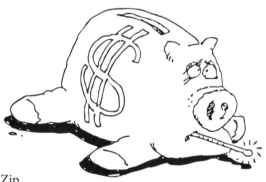

Zip
Zero
Zilch
Bunk
Goose egg
Donut hole
A drop in the bucket
Small potatoes
No there there
Nothing new under the sun
Same ol' same ol'
Miniscule
Stopped at the goal line
Dee-nied

Didn't get it
You cannot teach an old dog new tricks
Doesn't bring anything to the party
Doesn't bring anything to the table
Doesn't bring anything to the mix
Dead air
Dead weight
Beating a dead horse
Boiler plate
Cookie cutter
Vanilla statements
Vanilla documents
Diddly squat
Nada
Zippidee-doo-dah
Brick wall
Stonewalled
Halted in our tracks
Sent home packing
Aspiring to so very little
Throwing in the towel
Raising the white flag
No gas left in the tank
Look behind the shine and you will find it does
    not always gleam

Keep It Quiet / Be Quiet / Shut Up / End It / Eliminate

The Prompt

YOU CAN STICK a fork in it… it's done
Knock it off… Call it quits… Pull the plug…

Cone of silence
Siloed (pronounced "si-low-d")
Vaulted
Under lock and key
Zip it
Callate (pronounced "ca-ya-tay")
Shut it down
Shut it
Close the books
Call the time of death
Enough
Basta
Quitsville
DC it (discontinue it)
Hit the brakes
Go dark

Control-Alt-Delete
Up in smoke
Game over
Final gun
Cool your jets
Power down
Button your lip
Button it
Bottle it up
Give it the heave-ho
Steer clear
That's a wrap
Holster the weapon... that being your mouth
Cut the overheated political rhetoric
Do not burn out the synapses, because I am already
    there
Put the kibosh on it
Sh**-can it
Trash it
Junk it
Chuck it

Uphill Battles and
Tick-tock Situations

$$$

by Geoffrey DeStefano
Founder and CEO, The Strategic Content Group, LLC
(former TV Executive and Advertising Agency
CEO) (Los Angeles, California)

RANDY GORDON HAS been both my client and a consultant for me. He is a bright and energetic executive that has his fingers on the pulse of what is happening in the business community. He also has a keen ear for how people are communicating and what they are saying.

When he asked me to write an introduction for the "Uphill Battles and Tick-Tock Situations" section of his book, I was more than happy to

do so because I have spent most of my career in what seems to be uphill battles and tick-tock situations.

Having spent my first ten years in advertising on a range of multinational clients at the Leo Burnett Company, it seemed as though we were:

1) always up against an impossible deadline; and
2) inundated with inspirational sayings from Leo Burnett himself.

Whether it was the company motto to "Reach for the stars," or his speech from the tumultuous 1960s about "Integrity in times of change," (that is even more relevant today than it was then) the culture kept troops motivated and charging hard.

I spent a great deal of this time working on a global basis, and I can tell you that living and working in Tokyo and Hong Kong, and managing seventeen separate businesses across fourteen countries, we always "had our backs against the wall." It was tough business opening up offices in countries ranging in economic development from Japan to Vietnam. We encountered many situations when we had to say "it's gut-check time." Then again, you also knew when the Japanese started to wince and rub the backs of their necks that their was no fu**ing way that your project was going to get done. You have to look within and see what you have left in the tank. But you suck it up and do whatever it takes to get the job done and done well.

The interesting part of that experience is that it prepared me well for "swimming with the sharks of Hollywood" when I moved into the entertainment business. Spending the next six years developing and producing primetime television shows, I worked on shows like: *"Mad About You," "Party of Five," "Dawson's Creek,"* and *"Friends."* This exposes you to a truly rare breed of people that thrive on "green lights," "holding deals," and "if-come" money. As we all know, when it rains, it pours" especially in California. You always have to be of the mindset that "It ain't over 'til it's over," and live by the creed, "No defeat; no surrender." Working in Hollywood also gives you a true understanding that America loves a winner, but America also loves rooting for the underdog, and when you are really up against it, you claim underdog status, put on your rally caps, and get down to the business at hand. Working in the entertainment business where seemingly everybody is looking for fame, fortune, and the next hit, which especially means money, puts all the players in a similar situation of having the odds against you and having the pressure to deliver, no matter what, and at all costs.

I ran a creative company called Kastner & Partners that was ensconced in developing ideas to build brands and engage consumers on multiple levels across every communication channel imaginable. Whether it was commercials, branded content, grass-roots events, or core opinion leader programs, for us, it was about trying to engage our audience in interesting and innovative ways that further purchase intent of the product and yet still build the brand. We were the group that had helped launch Red Bull energy drink, worldwide, perhaps the most successful product launch in the last fifty years, created a whole new category of beverages, and changed the way products are marketed forever. In this day and age of TiVo and DVRs, the merging of entertainment and advertising, the ever-increasing speed with which audiences are adopting new technology, and the plethora of messages that consumers are hit with on a daily basis, we in the creative businesses are truly "under the gun" with "our backs against the wall" and fighting our way into a whole new era of communications.

Throughout my life, I have found that some words can intoxicate listeners and that some phrases are hit-and-miss, but the audible flavor of words is what inspires people to action. Just ask anyone who has attended a session by motivational orators like Tony Robbins, played for influential coaches like Lou Holtz, or heard inspirational leaders such as Dr. Martin Luther King. Truly hearing what is said rather than reading it, I believe, is what really galvanizes and inspires a connection between speaker and listener even more than a connection between writer and reader. You should also know that the days of jabber are unfortunately not "dead and gone," not by any stretch of the imagination. On the contrary, there are new chapters yet to be written (or spoken), and in this dawn of the new age of digital, broadband, and Wi-Fi, you can bet that the new "buzz" is just beginning to make it into general circulation.

The reason that there is a market for this book is that "Everyone wants to keep up with the Joneses," and the Joneses tend to communicate on a daily basis via Blackberry, phone, overnight delivery, IM, e-mail, snail mail, or good, old-fashioned, in-person one-on-ones. You should want to know a little bit about what they say in both the new and old business worlds. It just may help you with the day-to-day "uphill battles" and "tick-tock, time-is-running-out situations."

Running Out Of Time / Gloomy / Out Of Ideas / Stalled / Desperation

The Prompt

WE SEEM TO be chasing our tails… and not catching them

It is D-Day around here—total doom and gloom

We're almost out of ammo

Doom and gloom
What's the deal?
Does anyone have a scent?
The eleventh hour
Dark skies overhead
Dark hours ahead
Dark clouds looming
It's looking ominous
Stormfront coming
Almost out of ammunition
Welcome to Moan-day
Sink or swim time
Time to fish or cut bait
Two minute warning
Tick tock, tick tock
It's a tick-tock situation
The clock is ticking
No more change
Out of change
They're looking kind of lean
We are at the bone
There is no fat
Try not to finish "ass-out"

Nowhere street
Hang around 'til the very end
It's almost time for Control-Alt-Delete
Does anybody even have the foggiest idea of what's
    going on?
I seem to be working in a world that is largely
    unquantifiable but yet wants the numbers
Even if progress is not made, time seems to still
    continue to march forward
The last grains of sand are dropping through the
    hourglass
The car seems to be stalled on nowhere street
En route but not enough gas to reach the final
    destination

Milk the clock
Salt away some time
Salt away the game
Kill some time
Some time to kill
Running out of hours to fill
Past the point of no return
Past the point of no rejection
We've made our bed
We've dug our own grave
There's no going back
Bring in the closer
Down to our last firefighter
Play our last hand

Game over
Down to our last play
A 1-2-3 inning and we're done
Last gasp
Desperation heave
Hail mary time
Say your prayers
The twelfth of never
Bleeding red ink
In the red
Red-line it
Flatline
Time is money
Paper chase

Walking in loose granular
We keep hangin' around, but we're running out
    of time
I hope you brought your prayer book
Like trying to fit a square peg into a round hole
One of these days is none of these days
Like trying to rearrange the deck chairs on the
    Titanic
Like trying to catch up to an avalanche to give it
    some direction
Circular discussion
Circular dialogue
Circular conversation
Champagne taste but a beer budget
What goes around comes around
Turnabout is fair play
I would like to see a full court press on this
Turn up the heat
Running on fumes
I would do it if it were realistic
Everyone is firmly denying the existence of any
    agreement
It's gonna sink under its own weight

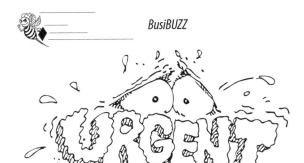

The only easy day was yesterday

My life for freedom

What is the more serious time frame on this?

Cherry-pick the critical item list

Decide what's important because that's all we'll
have time for

Fat chance

Almost out of ammo

Outside chance to still make it happen

Outside chance

Last-ditch effort

Chasing sunsets

Circuitous route to eventually get to the reality

Holding Pattern / Moving Slowly / Not Much Progress

Silver Bullets

THE CAR SEEMS to be stalled on nowhere
  street
It's like trying to walk in loose granular
It's a monumental piss off when he's ramrodding
the cattle drive and the bulls are not moving
Circular dialogue

Hovering
Project creep
Flat-footed
Saddled
Spilt milk
Paper chase
Chase your tail
Move into the left lane
It is on the back burner
Dead in the water
Dead air
Oozing like molasses
A cryogenic freeze of molasses
Moving at glacial speed
Airport speed not airspeed
Circling the airport
Too pooped to pop
Parking lot that idea
Tickler file
Put it on hold
Shelve it for now
On the shelf
The bulls are just out there on the trail

Do not get caught sitting on your hands

Real blunt edge-type movement

That patchy coastal fog time of the day

Long run for a short slide

Like trying to find the tallest midget

The project's in cryogenic freeze

In the deep freeze

Bottlenecks

Chokehold

An "If Come" deal (TV business—paid only if it's made)

A "Hold" deal

This is going slower than molasses uphill on a cold day in Maine

Problem Areas /
Not Happening /
Not Working Out

The Prompt

NO DICE
The rock and the hard place just became one
and the same
It's a sticky situation
Fly in the ointment

Chasing sunsets
Chasing shadows
Identify the hot spots
Water off a duck's back
A long run for a short slide
The tail wagging the dog
Duck soup
Goal line stand
Didn't get it
Pissing into the wind

Watering flowers into the wind
Needle in a haystack
Do not feed oats to a dead horse
Who is steering the ship?
Sitting on your hands
As they say in golf, it's right in the Sahara
Barriers to entry
Undesirable situation
Undesirables looming
It's hovering
It's idling
If all you have is a hammer, then every problem
is a nail
You're yelling… I'm yelling… we will get it done
Like carrying coals to Newcastle (just not fea-
sible)
Like selling ice to the eskimos
Kaput
Cart before the horse
Paint yourself into a corner
Two feet in one shoe
The beginning of the end
A real tension convention
All it needs is a rhinestone collar
It is a dog with fleas
Whatever it is, it spells D-O-G
Bring out the flea powder and pooper scooper
It will sink under its own weight
We're shooting blanks
We're rolling blank tape
A tailspin
Rudderless
It's all Greek to me
Up to my ears in alligators
A bag of snakes
Major problemos

Heavy lifting
Significant world of hurt
Back against the wall
Sh** runs downhill
We have a situation
Like nails on a blackboard
Ride a good horse to death
Behind the eightball
Fight the fires
Crisis management
Dog fight
Crash and burn
Bend over
The chips are down
Between a rock and a hard place
Wrench in the works
Pain in the cucaracha
Pain in the ass
We're sitting ducks
Tough row to hoe (the right way to say it)
Tough road to hoe (the wrong way to say it)
When the going gets tough, everybody leaves
Are our oars in the water?
Bug up your ass
It is a placebo, not a panacea
Throwing darts
Spitting in the ocean
Flag it
Call the nurse... I have just slit my wrists
You just hit a nodal line
A grenade with the pin pulled
Like brown shoes with a tuxedo
More nervous than a long-tailed cat in a room
   full of rocking chairs
We need to drop down the fire retardant and mop
   up the hot spots

Difficult + Risky Situation /
Uphill Battle /
Face Adversity

The Prompt

Y OU'RE BETWEEN A rock and a hard place
Set up a triage and tend to the wounded
It's a grenade with the pin pulled
A bag of snakes

Dog fight
Last-ditch effort
Out on a limb
This will be bloody
Use good discretion
You won't get off scot-free on this one
Get your head back in the game
Get back in the game before it's over
This may not last another two seconds
Make the most of it
Crisis management
Back against the wall
Pound the pavement
A long road to hoe
Risk management
Fly in the ointment
Wrench in the works
Pain in the cucaracha

Sitting duck
Swimming upstream
Are our oars in the water?
Behind the eightball
It is a placebo, not a panacea
It's like throwing darts in the dark
The chips are down
Let's take the hill
Have Plan B at the ready
Tighten up your bank account
Defcon one
Do not let things flame out
Flame out
Gusher
You just hit a nodal line
A real hair-raiser
An insurmountable amount of sh**
Nose to the grindstone
Can you make any headway?
That dog won't hunt
Like charging a machine gun nest
Take a stab at it
Give it the old college try
You'll get schooled quickly
Bit me in the ass
This could take some hazard pay
Sale-able but fail-able
Up sh**'s creek without a paddle
Good fortune is the result of hard work
Nervous nellies
It will be a cold day in hell before that happens
We may have to look into other arrangements
Desperate times call for desperate measures
You may not want to invest your skills points in
        that project
Have a look-see because it doesn't look good
No one said it would be easy

Solve The Problem / Remedy A Difficult Situation

Silver Bullets

THERE ARE NO problems, just situations that
need more attention
There's more than one way to skin a cat
Can we course-correct this in time?
Drop down some fire retardant and mop up the
hot spots

The only easy day was yesterday
Do you have a fix or recourse?
We can course-correct with time to spare
Set up a triage and tend to the wounded
Let's start by untying the Gordian knot
We can make our way through the labyrinth
We can make it through the wars
This is not a tough maze
Out on a limb
Don't throw gasoline on the fire

Don't shoot yourself in the foot

Let's fight the fires

Cool your jets

Set the priorities

Identify the hot spots

Crisis management

The squeaky wheel gets the grease

It is a panacea... a cure-all... not a placebo

Find the right solution

Flag it

Do not let things flare up

The flame is out

Pull out the tourniquet

Slow down the bleeding

Defcon one

No doubt, we have the power to unlock some of the conundrums of the universe

The quicker you fall behind, the more time you have to make it up

Let's start with the shark that's closest to your body

The rock and the hard place just became one and the same

I do not mind the umbrella up my butt, but don't try to open it

It's a grenade with the pin pulled... figure out what to do next

Like brown shoes with a tuxedo... pick a different combo

You're in a significant world of hurt... and you need to get out

Be thick-skinned and forge ahead at 100 miles per hour

You can slice it and dice it so many different ways

Going Global /
International /
"From Across The Pond"

$$$

by Peter Moore
Corporate Vice President of
  Worldwide Retail Sales and Marketing
  Home Entertainment Division
  Microsoft Corporation (Xbox 360 and Xbox)
  (Redmond, WA)

> *"I'm off down the apples and pears to*
> *get on the dog and bone to ring the*
> *trouble and strife"*

THE ALMOST UNINTELLIGIBLE sentence above
is rhyming slang, a "language" formed as
a cultural code understood only by those born
within the sound of Bow Bells in London, oth-
erwise known as "cockneys." It has developed

and evolved over centuries, utilizing the popular parlance of the times, creating a communication tool only really fully understood by "insiders," simultaneously providing a tangible badge of belonging to this geographically-linked tribe of practitioners. (By the way, the sentence simply states that I am going downstairs to call my wife on the phone.)

Likewise, we can view the language of modern business as a tribal code, understood by those on the inside, strange and almost impenetrable to outsiders. Driven by the need for speed in our Web-based dealings with each other, it almost seems like we have lost the ability to form full words or complete sentences anymore. On my first day at Microsoft, among the materials provided was a URL (an acronym for a Web site) explaining the meanings behind all of the acronyms that I was about to be exposed to during the myriad meetings to come. We "Softies" (as Microsoft employees are known) seem to have created our own abbreviated form of the English language, where no word or expression is not subject to retrofit in the interests of expediency, and I have no doubt it is the same in other large corporations that have developed their own unique verbal identifiers within their ecosystem. It's almost as if we pay by the letter in e-mail nowadays... so keep it snappy (and incomprehensible).

As a Brit who has lived in the U.S. for over 20 years, my language and vocabulary is a hybrid that resides somewhere in the mid-Atlantic, a sad state of affairs that was further compounded by working for Reebok, a U.S. company with deep British roots, for over seven years. As a result, I know enough of both cultures to realize what makes sense to them and what doesn't. For example, if you are applying all resources to be successful in a particular business situation, there is no use telling the Brit we are going for the whole enchilada, nine yards, shebang, or swinging for the fences. All the marbles, maybe, kit and caboodle, likely, but you are more likely to be understood if you simply explain we are going to give it "the full monty." That'll get his attention. The blurring of geographical business lines is also impacting our in-office vocabulary. As the head of the U.S. arm of Sega, the colleagues that "as *gaijin*, we will have to do some serious *nemawashi* if we want to get *the ringi* signed at the next *tenken*." (Translation: as foreigners, we need to do some lobbying to get the authorization signed at the next business meeting in Japan). It made perfect sense to both of us, but it would have been complete gibberish to anyone eavesdropping.

So the next time the meeting gets a little boring, play "*BusiBUZZ* Bingo," a little game concocted to help you get through the monotony until somebody calls time for lunch. Rules are simple—give out a blank template to your cohorts, and they fill out the "biz-cliches" that they feel are likely to be espoused during the meeting. First to complete a line, be it horizontal, vertical, or diagonal, WINS !

B U S I *B U Z Z*

B	**I**	**N**	**G**	**O**
Take this offline	Readers' Digest version	At the end of the day	Is it a show-stopper?	What's the worst case scenario?
Syner-gistic	Is he adding value?	Always on	The bot-tom line is…	It's a win-win for all parties
Core compe-tencies?	It's spot on	Is this mission-critical?	We need some air cover on this	Ducks in a row?
We need to think outside the box	Neces-sary band-width?	The net net	Pro-active	Bench-mark
Add what-ever	Add what-ever	Add what-ever	Add what-ever	Add what-ever

British (UK) Buzzwords and Catch Phrases

The Prompt

Bollocks
It's spot on
It's rocking
Brilliant

Spot on (exact, perfect, absolutely correct)
Wicked (awesome, quite young and trendy)
Off to the gallows
It's rocking (very good, excellent)
Buzzing (great news, very good news)
Sorted (all correct and ready to go)
Footy (soccer; football)
Telly (television)
"P" (pronounced "pee"; short for pence; also, going
     for a piss)
A "note" (any paper money)

Quid (a pound)

Fiver (five pounds)

Lady Godiva (Londoner or Cockney rhyming slang for a "fiver")

Tenner (ten pounds)

Bollocks (testicles; rude slang for "oh sh**")

Windbag (person who talks too much)

Battered (hit hard, as in "our stock is getting battered")

Solid (you can count on it; difficult or tough)

Dodgy (uncertain, deserving suspicion)

Pester (persistently hassle, can be used as a noun or verb)

Valid (true)

Barney (trouble)

A Barney (a fight or disruption)

Mug (someone who is being taken advantage of)

Wally (dumbass)

Spa moron (dumb person)

Chap (male)

Bloke (male)

Mate (pal, friend)

Chum (pal, friend)

Fella (a man, or a friendly term: "Alright, fella")

Wanker (someone who masturbates a lot; rude insult; a jerk; an ass)

Tosser (less obscene than "wanker"; also a jerk; an ass)

Tool (a jerk; a dick)

Knobhead (a dickhead)

Mind your P's and Q's (mind your manners; mind your pints and quarts)

Leave it out (come on, what the hell; should not have happened)

Out with it

Crack pot

Gonzo

Grab your knickers (get ready)

Going to a do (going to a big event)

Shenanigans (crazy happenings, hijinx, off-topic antics)

You've lost your marbles (crazy; gone mad)

See ya at the pub

See ya at the beer parlour

Bird (female)

My bird (my girlfriend)

Your one (that woman)

Tottie (good-looking woman)

Fit bird (good-looking woman)

Minging (unpleasant, ugly)

Minger (ugly woman; pronounced "ming-uh")

Slag (a woman of loose morals)

Tart (a woman of loose morals)

Geezer (old man; silly old geezer's lost his marbles)

Nick (steal)

Skint (to have no money)

Trump (to pass wind, fart)

Cheers (Thanks; Here's to…; Please; Goodbye; Whatever)

Beers in (get beers from the bar)

Getting snookered (being taken advantage of; getting drunk)

Bladdered (drunk)

Arseholed (drunk)

Wankered (drunk)

Hammered (drunk)

Pissed (drunk)

Floating on ice (drunk)

Pissed as a parrot (drunk)

Lightweight (someone who cannot handle their drink / responsibility)

And your own... (said to a bartender or barmaid when giving them a tip—typically 10 pence - 1 pound)

Bottoms up (drink up; said to someone in a group including yourself and them)

Tally Ho (drink up; goodbye; or "off we go" at the beginning of a fox hunt)

Good show (a job well done)

Right-Oh (usually used when you agree to do something)

Righty-Oh (same as above)

That's a fine kettle of fish (perplexing confusion; predicament)

Put the kibosh on it (put an end to pointless or endless discussion)

Hurly burly (state of chaotic confusion; also "hurleigh burleigh")

Good bloke (good man)

You couldn't swing a cat in here (small space; from 19th Century British Navy—a nasty 9-tailed whip)

Like carrying coals to Newcastle (like trying to sell ice to the Eskimos; just not feasible; act of folly)

Wet blanket (a killjoy)

Make a quid (make some money)

Me daisies (boots)

Daisy roots (boots)

Fu**ed in the head (crazy)

Dull as dishwater

Poofter (homosexual)

Bob's yer uncle (everything is okay; there ya go)

Hit the nail on the head

A bit strong (hurtful remark or action)

Happy as Larry (very happy; happy as a clam)

Come up smelling of roses (a piece of luck)

Cranky (bad-tempered or crazy)

Don't get sarky with me (sarcastic)

Two bricks short of a load (stupid)

Show willing (ready to help or work hard)

Dead set unlucky

Dead cert (guaranteed to do well; a winner)

Copper (policemen; constable on patrol)

Ding dong (impromptu bout of fisticuffs; a fight)

Get into a ding-dong

A punch up (a fight)

Get into a punch up

I'm dirty on him (annoyed by him)

Down the drain (things turned out for the worse)

A fair go (a fair chance)

Give it a go (take a shot; have a try)

Yank (American)

Frog (French person)

Sheep shagger (Welsh person)

Joies (people from Johannesburg, South Africa)

Mick (Irish person)

Paddy (Irish person)

Geordie (someone from Newcastle)

Manc (someone from Manchester)

Scouser (someone from Liverpool)

Brummie (someone from Birmingham)

Northerner (someone from North of Birmingham)

Maccam (someone from Sunderland)

Cockney (someone from inner city London; lower class London, England accent; Bow Bells East Ender)

Londoner (someone from London)

Farmer Giles (someone from rural Southwest England; rhyming slang for "Piles" or hemorrhoids)

Midlander (someone from the midland area of England)

Southerner (someone from "down South" or South of Birmingham)

Scally (snobbish term directed at someone from a lower-class, crime-ridden area)

Wide Boy (someone who is working-class but has stature due to violent/criminal activity)

Ikey mo (a British or Australian derogatory term for a Jew or a "money lender")

Knuckle down (a good worker)

To knuckle down (work hard)

Pass muster (be acceptable)

Grub Street hacks (bad writers)

Better than a poke in the eye with a blunt stick (better than expected in a roundabout way)

Where there's money, there's bound to be a fiddle

Lakker (nice)

JOL (party)

Shame (expression of sympathy)

My china (my friend)

Let me tune you (let me tell you something)

Veld (field)

Baf (fart)

Irish Buzzwords
and Catch Phrases

Shagged and nackered (tired)
Going to a do (a big event)
This place is like mad woman's shite (messy)
Would you ever fu** off (piss off; up yours)
I'm shagged
I'm knackered (tired)
I'm wrecked tired (exhausted)
I'm wrecked (really tired)
You're wrecking my head (you're annoying me)
Going to a do (a big event)
Everybody's soused (drunk)
Everybody's scuttered (drunk)
I'm sozzled (drunk)
I'm langers (drunk)
I'm out of my tree (drunk or high)
I'm lamped (drunk)
I'm gee-eyed (drunk)
I'm shit-faced (very drunk)
I'm bollocksed (really drunk)
Everybody's soused (drunk)

Everybody's scuddered (drunk)
Everybody's palatic (drunk)
Pissed as a coot (very drunk)
Everybody's palatic (drunk)
I'm bolloxed (really drunk)
Kick in the goolies (low blow)
You piss-ant (insult)
You knob (insult)
You dipsh** (insult)
You muppet (insult)
You geebag (insult)
You dickwad (insult)
You clown (insult, usually lighthearted)
You sack (insult, as in "sack of sh**")
You shite-hawk (insult)
You don't know Jack Sh** (you're ignorant about
    a particular topic)
What a gonad (idiot)
Póg mo thóin ("Kiss my ass" in Irish)
My arse (expression of disbelief)
I'm bursting (I need to urinate)
My back teeth are floating (I really need to uri-
    nate)
I need to drop a bomb (defecate)
I've got the scutters (diarrhea)
I've got the scuts (diarrhea)
I've got the runs (diarrhea)
I've got Delhi-belly (diarrhea)
You dirtbird (you are a pervert, lighthearted)
Gobsheen or gobshite (idiot)
Like flies on shite (attracted to something)
On the ging (trying to attract a woman)
She's a lash (she is beautiful or sexy)
She's a ride (she is beautiful or sexy)
She's a fine thing (she is beautiful or sexy)
I'd like to ride her (have sex)
Get your hole (have sex)

Throw your leg over (have sex)
Blue balls (haven't had sex for a long time)
She's a dog (she is ugly)
She's a howler (she is ugly)
She is minging (she is ugly)
She has a face like a slapped arse (she's ugly)
Deadly (really good)
Mad craic (good fun)
The life of Reilly (great time)
Flek (poor person)
Scobie (poor person)
Knacker (poor person or itinerant)
A real windup (person who talks too much; major
    windbag)
Stitched 'em up (set 'em up for a fall; sold 'em
    down the river)
Guestimation

Australian Buzzwords and Catch Phrases

The Prompt

Who do you barrack for? (root for in sports)

Good on ya, mate (nice going; well done)

Bloke (guy)

Bonzer (good)

Good bloke (good man)

G'day (pronounced "G'die")

In the arvo (in the afternoon)

The arvo (afternoon)

Shonky (suspect)

Dodgy (suspect)

Back at Bourke (long way away)

Fu**ed in the head (crazy)

Aussie battler (little hard worker)

Beaut (pronounced "Byute"; very good or excellent)

Bewdie (pronounced "Byu-dee")

Possum (term of endearment; "you little possum you")

Humdinger (something very good or excellent)

It's not half bad (excellent taste or quality)

Rapt (happy)

Fair dinkum (really true)

Bloody oath (exactly)

Tucker (food; meal)

Tucker ration

Bloody (very)

Bludger (lazy person)

Stickybeak (nosey person)

Yobbo (uncouth person)

Cranky (bad mood)

Airy fairy (unsubstantial)

BYO (Bring your own)

Crook (sick)

Chuck a sickie (have a sick day off work even if you are not sick)

Be sent to the sin bin (a sportsman ejected and sent to the locker room)

Counter lunch (lunch in a pub)

Smoko (morning or afternoon tea break)

Give him a fair go (give him a chance)

No worries (no problem)

Tall poppy (successful person; someone who aspires to educational excellence)

Tickets on himself (stuck-up and arrogant person)

Pommie fag (a discriminatory term to be said towards a British person)

Pommie bastard (could be sarcasm for a good person; could be bad name for British person)

Ocker (unsophisticated Australian)

You reckon? (you think?)

You're not wrong (you're right)

Strike me pink (fancy that happening)

Starve the lizards (expression of amazement)
Bob's yer uncle (everything is okay; there ya go)
Everything is Jake (okay)
Oz (Australian)
Pommi (Australian for Englishman)
Pom
Chook (chicken)
Sanger (sandwich)
It's spot on
Hit the nail on the head
Yacker (work)
Hooroo (goodbye)
You little ripper (expression of joy)
Whacko (expression of joy)
Alf (fool)
Bazz (fool)
Dill (fool)
Droob (fool)
Dunderhead (fool)
Drongo (stupid person; idiot)
Billy (a friend)
Abo (an insulting term; short for Aborigine)
A bit strong (hurtful remark or action)
Apesh** (completely mad or crazy)
Sheila (woman)
Good sort (good-looking woman or Sheila)
Happy as Larry (very happy; happy as a clam)
You float my boat (approval; acceptance)
Giddy up (really good)
Dinki di (telling the truth about something; the
    real McCoy)
Technicolor yawn (to vomit)
Chunder (to vomit)
Kark (to vomit)
Driving the porcelain bus (to vomit)
Talking to the big white telephone (to vomit)
Having a bark at the grass (to vomit)
Crook in the guts (sick)

A case of the collywobbles (sick)

I've got the wog, and I've got see a quack (got the flu and going to see a doctor)

Balmain bug (related to the lobster and crayfish; a tasty crustacean with an unpleasant name)

Barbie (a barbequed meal cooked on a hot plate over hot coals)

Barrack (to cheer one's team from the sidelines)

Bloody pansies

A real drop kick (wimp; nerd; or someone on drugs)

Bloody bastards

Come across (have sex)

Shagged (exhausted from hard work)

Even Blind Freddy could tell you that would happen

Come up smelling of roses (a piece of luck)

A good cove (good bloke or good man)

Bloodhouse (a terrible hotel)

Blow-in (an unwanted guest)

Crack hardy (being courageous or toughing it out)

Swagman (bum; wanderer)

Swag (a bedroll containing one's personal possessions)

Matilda (having one's personal possessions rolled up in a blanket)

Humping the bluey (bumming around)

Throw your swag into the bushes (waste your money)

You've done the rent (wasted your money)

Drum (the truth)

The good oil (the truth)

A bloody furphy (a lie)

Over the odds (a lie)

Battler (someone who has had a hard life but continues to battle, no matter what)

Phoney as a two-bob watch (tricky and untrusting person)

Bull artist (short for bullsh** artist or con-man)

Illywhacker (a smartass trickster; someone not to be trusted)

Bloody bulldust (a lie or worthless piece of information)

Duckshove (to pass the buck; give someone else the responsibility)

Duds (clothing for men)

Not worth a brass razoo (worthless item)

As useless as tits on a bull

As useless as an ashtray on a motor bike

As useless as a dead dingo's donger

Arse into gear (necessity of at least appearing to do work while the boss is around)

Everything will be Jake (okay)

Billy-Oh (had a great time at a party—"I played it up like Billy-Oh")

Big smoke (a country expression for a big city... similar in the U.S. to a "honky tonk")

Better than a poke in the eye with a burnt stick (better than expected in a roundabout way)

You're as game as Ned Kelly (unprepared but ready, willing, and able anyway; stupid but raring to go)

Hang yourself from the handy beam of a nearby shanty (give up after wasting your money)

Pie eater (person of no consequence; a dickhead)

Ratbag (dickhead)

Rabbit (weak person)

Weak as cold piss on a plate (weak person)

Dead-set bastard

Do it like a rat up a rope (do something quickly or half-fast)

Up a gumtree (on the wrong track)

Living off the smell of an oil rag (hard worker)

Get it on tick (get it on credit)

Not worth a bumper or a crumpet (worthless)

Bung on a blue (cry)

Turn on the waterworks (cry)

Cadge (beg, borrow, or steal in a friendly way)

Camp as a row of tents (flamingly gay or homosexual)

Shirt lifter (homosexual)

How's the cheese and kisses? (how's the Mrs.;
one's wife)

Stop chaicking me (stop being sarcastic with
me)

Copper (policemen; constable on patrol)

Demons (policemen)

Ding dong (impromptu bout of fisticuffs; a
fight)

Get into a ding-dong

Get into a punch-up (a fight)

A punch-up

A stoush (a fight)

Prone to punch-ups at the drop of a hat

Stir the possum (to create an uproar)

A dingo's breakfast (nothing at all)

A piss and a good look around (did not find anything)

To dip one's lid (take off your hat to salute)

Punch the bundy (check into work on time; punch
the clock on time; willing to do hard work)

White ant (to destroy another's character through
gossip or truthful but damaging stories)

The ringer (whatever gets it done the fastest)

Bushweek (everything is a bloody mess or similar
to Murphy's Law... what can go wrong will
go wrong)

What do you do for a crust? (how do you make a
living? or make money?)

I didn't come down in the last shower (I wasn't
born yesterday, you know)

Like sh** off a shiny shuffle (fast)

Chock-o-block (full)

Braise the balls off a brass monkey (really cold)

I'll dip out on this one (renege; refuse to participate)

I'm dirty on him (annoyed by him)

He gives me a dose (annoyed by him)

Don't do the dirty on me (don't let me down)

Timid fish (someone who does not like to work)

All the bloody dogs are barking (everybody knows)

Done like a dinner (to have been badly beaten in a fight or a business deal)

Down the drain (things turned out for the worse)

Drag the chain (loafing on the job; not drinking fast enough)

A fair crack of the whip (a fair chance)

A fair go (a fair chance)

A fair suck of the sauce bottle (a fair chance)

Give it a go (take a shot; have a try)

Go for the doctor (pulling away to win a race)

Go under his neck (take unfair advantage)

Face like a stopped clock (ugly person)

Full bore (to go all out)

Hit the kapok (go to bed)

Snatch a stretch of shut-eye (go to bed; take a nap)

Knocker (bringer of bad luck)

Put the kibosh on (stop it from happening)

Get the readies (get the money; particularly for the next round of drinks)

Kick the bucket (to die)

King hit (to knock someone down unfairly with one hit; to knock someone senseless)

Kinged (to get hit badly)

Knuckle sandwich (a punch in a fight)

Put the hard word on her (talk her up; chat her up; try to get laid)

Knock back (to get rejected)

Knuckle down (a good worker)

Feather duster (a "has-been"; soon-to-be-obsolete person, like a politician)

First cab off the rank (the person who is next in line or at the head of the queue)

The middle of the bloody day and not a bone in the truck (nothing is getting done)

Do your block (a warning to a friend or enemy to not lose his temper and start throwing punches)

Lie doggo (keep quiet about matters and remain inconspicuous; lay low; keep your head down)

Journalists were clustering around the drink table like flies around a cow yard

You're a man with the minties (person with good tips on horses / horseraces)

Urger (derogatory term for someone who gives tips)

Pass muster (be acceptable)

Scrub up well (dressed nicely)

Chuck a spaz (get mad, upset, or way too uptight about something)

Dag (a real nerd)

Brekkie (short for breakfast)

Lunatic soup (alcohol)

Grog (beer)

Tinny (can of beer)

Tube (can of beer)

Plonk (cheap wine)

Fourpenny dark (cheap, red, fortified wine)

Snake's piss (bad alcohol)

Dead marine (empty beer bottle)

Stubby (a small Australian beer bottle)

That deal would choke a brown dog (horrible deal)

A mouth like Cocky's cage (hangover)

Have a yarn (have a conversation)

Ear basher (pub bore)

Talk you blind (what an ear basher or pub bore does)

Cheesy Sneaky (McDonald's cheeseburger or any fast-food place cheeseburger)

Tickle the Peter (minor stealing)

Poor box John (a minor thief)

A case of beer and a bag of prawns (taking it easy)

A glass of rum in a quiet, warm place (taking it easy)

Good as (something is really good by itself)

You're in a bad way (not doing too well)

As rough as guts (nasty act; horrible taste; piece of bad sportsmanship)

Beyond the black stump (crazy; just on the other side of normal; going to the bad side)

Down the hatch (a toast with a friend)

Here's looking at you sideways (a toast with a friend)

Two-pot screamer (a cheap drunk; someone who can get intoxicated very quickly)

On the turps (in the process of getting drunk)

Top night (getting drunk amongst friends)

Rort (an enjoyable party with dancing and violence)

Arseholed (drunk; intoxicated)

Blotto (drunk; intoxicated)

Floating on ice (drunk)

Pissed as a parrot (drunk)

Full as a state school (drunk)

Metho (a derelict)

Brumby (a wild horse; a wild card)

Cranky (bad-tempered or crazy)

Don't get sarky with me (sarcastic)

Mad as a cut snake (bad-tempered or crazy)

Hatter (crazy person; as in "mad hatter")

Two bricks short of a load (stupid; crazy)

Not the full bottle (crazy)

Off his face (crazy)

Dingbat (crazy but not dangerous)

In the mullock (in the sh**)

Show willing (ready to help or work hard)

Crack hardy (ready to help or work hard)

Crawler (ass-kisser)

Piss in the same pot (to suck up to someone)

Handy little nipper (helpful person or ass-kisser)

Crooked as a dog's hind leg (someone not to be trusted)

Bucket him (criticize and adversary)

Dead set unlucky

It's had the bloody claw (no longer works)

Dead cert (guaranteed to do well; a winner)

He's on compo (on worker's compensation)

Bugger (bastard)

A pantywaist (a sissy)

Dag (a wimp or dull person; a piece of crap)

Go to buggery (tell someone to piss off)

Take a powder (tell someone to piss off)

Spit chips (someone who is fired up and pissed off)

Pull your head in (shut up)

Piss poor (bad performance)

You have bugger all (you have nothing)

A bodgie job (messed up)

Tell 'em where to get off (tell him off; set him straight)

Off like a bride's nightie (leave or exit quickly)

Boofhead (dull or stupid person)

Let's have a bit of shoosh, ladies and gents (everyone shut up; be quiet)

You've got two chances, mate, yours and Buckley's (which means you really have only one chance)

Ridgy-didge (original, genuine)

Yiddish / Hebrew Phrases — Stuff You Need To Know and What "M.O.T's" May Say

The Prompt

FOR THOSE M.O.T.'s (Members of the Tribe) who do know Hebrew/Yiddish, please forgive my attempt at trying to spell it how I believe it sounds. I am trying to help the goyim say it right.

She knows how to put people together… she is a real "Yenta"

The guy went to bat for me, he's a true "Mensch"

You are a "Meshugana" if you think I am going to pay that price

We are getting together Friday night with the whole "Mishpucha" (pronounced "mish-pooka")

Mensch (a man's man, good person, good boy)

Haymisha mensch (warm and friendly good person)

Gonif (thief)

Goy (non-Jewish person)

Goyim (non-Jewish people)

Shiksa (non-Jewish girl)

Chutzpah (nerves; balls)—You have real "chutzpah" to ask me that question

Oy vey (oh my goodness, how terrible)

Oy gevalt (oh, my goodness)

Mazel Tov (a common wish of good luck or congratulations—for marriage, baby, etc.)

Mischagoss (nonsense)—Instead of working, he is involved with his "mischagoss"

Yenta (a matchmaker)

Gelt (money)

Hanukkah gelt (money you get as a gift for the Jewish holiday Hanuukah)

Machatunnum (the in-laws)—pronounced (maccha-toon-um")

Mishpucha (family)—pronounced "mishpooka")

Meshugana (crazy person)

Kvetch (complain)—Stop "kvetching" about business

The whole magilla (everything; a really good deal)

Magilla (a big deal; a good deal)

Macher (a big shot)—pronounced "ma-ccher")

Maven (expert)—He thinks he is a "maven" with the stock market

Momser (a bastard)

Gornisht (nothing)—We bargained but it's still worth "gornisht"

Pisher (inexperienced young person)—You cannot quote a price, you are a "pisher"

Putz (jerk, creep, fool, dickhead, dick)

Schmuck (jerk, creep, fool, dickhead, dick)

Schnorer (cheapskate; beggar; a person who tries to get a good deal for little dollars)

Schnores (begs; tries to get something for nothing)—He "schnores" all the time

M.O.T.'s (members of the tribe)

Kibosh (put a stop to something)

Fershstay (understand)—I will not pay that, "fershstay"?

Shmata (rags, clothes that are not good quality)—I will not buy those "shmatas"

Chuchum (a smart-ass, smart-alec, would-be-know-it-all)—pronounced "cchu-cchum")

Mischigots (crazy)

Tzooris (trouble)

Schvitzing (sweating)

Mountains schmountains

Deal schmeal

Date schmate

Turtle schmurtle

What's with the hurry? Is there a fire?

What am I... a clock?

So the sun is out... what else is new?

I should be so lucky

Saturday we rest

Light the candles

Spin the dreidel

Smegma (yucky stuff)

Schmegma (yucky stuff)

Bubkus (nothing; of no value)

Ficockta (Fu**in', fake, phony)

Zoftig (soft; not toned)

Saykel (common sense)—You don't have any "saykel"

Tchotchkes (stuff, trinkets)—pronounced "chach-keys")

Kibbitz (gossip; talk shop, tease or joke around)—He likes to "kibbitz"

Hazarei (junk)—I don't want to be bothered with this "hazarei"

Dreck (no good junk)—This is "dreck"

Hebonics (slang expression for Jewish English)

Vay iz meer (an expression which closely resembles: "woe is me")

Koorveh (a call girl or prostitute; or a derogatory reference to a flashy shiksa)

Nafteh (same as a "koorveh")

Tattalah (an endearing term of love which means "little man")

Chaleria (a derogatory term which best refers to a female business associate or mother-in-law; aka bitch)

Kugel (a yummy blend of overcooked noodles, raisins, and curds of ripe cheese)

Borscht (a reddish, purple soup made from beets)

Schmendrick (a man who messes things up, always loses, and feels miserable)

Schlemiel (a jerk who cannot do anything right)

Schlemazel (the poor dumb putz a "schlemiel" is always spilling on or messing up)

Let's Get Down To Business

$$$

Q & A session with Dennis Gilbert
Chicago White Sox Executive and President of
Gilbert-Krupin (Los Angeles, CA)

Brief History Lesson

DENNIS GILBERT REVOLUTIONIZED the sport of baseball through the free agent system. As baseball's leading agent, Dennis had founded the Beverly Hills Sports Council in 1980 and represented such mega-stars as Barry Bonds, Jose Canseco, Ricky Henderson, Bobby Bonilla, Mike Piazza, Curt Schilling, and Trevor Hoffman, to name a few. In November 2000, the Chicago White Sox recruited Dennis Gilbert to serve as Special Assistant to Chairman Jerry Reinsdorf to go well

beyond the handling and negotiating of contracts into an expanded role of providing key input on personnel and scouting-related matters associated with the team. Dennis Gilbert knows and loves baseball. Continually demonstrating outstanding commitment to his community and his love and passion for the game, Dennis Gilbert has served on two committees for Major League Baseball (he currently serves on the Salary Arbitration Committee, and he served on the Player Development Committee), and he also sits as Chairman of the Professional Baseball Scouts Foundation (started in 2003). Moreover, he funded and built an inner-city baseball diamond at Southwest Community College in Los Angeles (now home to baseball's RBI Youth Program—Reviving Baseball in Innercities).

Dennis has returned to his initial occupation of life insurance to better assist his clients. His company, Gilbert-Krupin, deals with estate planning and insurance for some of our nation's highest net-worth sports figures, celebrities, and accomplished individuals. Randy Gordon was introduced to Dennis Gilbert in 2003 during Randy's time working for the Regal Entertainment Group. Randy had asked Dennis about his point-of-view on lingo, buzzwords, and terminology used in day-to day business dealings or prolonged negotiations, in the sports and entertainment worlds, as well as in the life insurance business.

QUESTION: Is there a certain language or protocol in which you, as an agent, would engage General Managers or your negotiating counterparts when you were working on your clients' contract deals?

ANSWER: I would not say that there is a certain "code" that is used when dealing with sophisticated and influential baseball men. I can tell you that it's not like the movies or shows like HBO's former hit series *Arliss*, because we simply did not slide numbers across a table when we were negotiating on behalf of our clients. I like to use the "Doctor Analogy" because I believe it best fits our unique approach to each negotiation. When you go to a doctor for the first time, he or she does not just give you a penicillin shot. The doctor may take your temperature, test your blood pressure, maybe do an X-Ray or an EKG test, but he or she also talks to you about what is ailing you, asks you to fill out forms on your past history, and looks to what can be done to make you feel better. It was and is the same way that we approach how we represent our clients. Hard work, comparative research, and historical data… we approached each negotiation as its own separate medical visit or surgery… pouring many hours into our own research and devil's-advocate scenarios to prepare for the discussions. This all went (and still does go) into complex negotiations, and usually winds up in a "well-pieced-together binder" or packet of pages with recommendations and alternatives before we ever come near the negotiation table.

QUESTION: Do you have your favorite expressions and phrases that you would gravitate towards in order to persuade your client to sign a deal or to leverage your position against a team (e.g., he has filthy stuff and throws split-finger and cut fastballs; he hits bombs; or, by doing this deal, you could be a hero for the organization)?

ANSWER: I may not be the best person or subject for your book. But I do want to help you. What happened in each negotiation or representation was spontaneous, and it was not a canned

speech. In fact, I do not really have lines that I say in situations. Every single negotiation has its own merit, its own life, and I did not script out what happened next nor did I pull strings or tricks to make things happen. Preparation was always the key. No two situations are exactly alike, so I would amass all of the information that I could in order to prepare. I would try to look at the negative issues that could be brought up about my client from the General Manager's or team's point-of-view, as well as from the coach's point-of-view. The other important thing was, and is, to be fair.

QUESTION: Now that you work for your clients in a slightly different capacity, that of doing deals in estate planning, life insurance, and other types of insurance, do some of the same philosophies that you used at the negotiating table still apply?

ANSWER: For 35 years, I have been selling intangibles that you cannot necessarily smell, feel, or hear. Maybe now the day-to-day is a bit simpler and with less drama. But, like I said, we were not using lines to begin with. My deals have been and still are about doing what is right for our clients. These deals will impact a client's life and their family.

QUESTION: Other than the obvious thinking on your feet, keeping your wits about you while showing a calm demeanor, and effectively communicating with your clients, what do you like about what goes into closing a deal?

ANSWER: You have to take the approach that the person you are dealing with has done the same amount of homework that you have. Whether a deal netted my client $3 million, $4 million, $5 million, $20 million, $35 million, or $40 million, it was still about empathizing with a General

Manager or coach about what their team needs to win, and then it would be, how my player may best fit that situation… where will they have a fit in the lineup… and how can we help improve the franchise's win-loss record, win some extra games, or take pressure off other veteran or returning players (e.g., what is it worth to you to win five more games or to have you use your other relievers less? Your team may be lacking XYZ, and that's where my guy fits). To be effective with my style of contract negotiations, you would want to be as thorough as you could, find out as many comparables as you could, find out the rationale on which a number was based, and, in dealing with the coach or General Manager, try to empathize their situation in order to understand their needs. Hopefully, everybody then gets what they want.

QUESTION: Could you always get people to see things your way?

ANSWER: They didn't always agree with me, and nothing was ever really easy or a slam dunk (no such thing in this business). This was not Monopoly money. This was real money, and these were real clients. I stayed in baseball and focused on it because I believed that I had quite a bit of knowledge about the game. We simply did the best we could for our clients, and we did not lie down in doing our deals.

In sum, though the book's section professes "Let's get down to business," it is not the flashy language that will necessarily get a deal done any better or any sooner. Sometimes, it is just about building relationships and treating people like they want to be treated… with empathy and respect for their individual and team needs and what it will take to win. At that point, once you know what they want, then hopefully you can help.

Negotiation /
Negotiation Terms / Deals /
Compromise

The Prompt

As the old saying goes: You do not get what you deserve—you get what you negotiate

Hammer out the final dealpoints… sign, seal, and deliver, or throw it back in their court

Hold their feet to the fire

Wiggle room

This is serious business

The upper hand

Who has the leverage?

Pistols at dawn? or swords?

Public posturing

Split the difference

Negotiate through the media

Negotiate through the press

Put the thumbscrews to him

The ball is in your court

All your eggs in one basket

The whole kit and caboodle

The whole enchilada

Ask for the kitchen sink

Punt

The deal fell through
The deal went through
Tender an offer
Sit tight and wait 'em out
Keep your powder dry
Who blinks first?
Done deal
Seal the deal
Close the deal
Fait accompli (a done deal)
Lock it up
Sew it up
Tag it and bag it
Pull out the sutures and close it
Scalpel, sutures, scissors, done
I will hold you to every letter of the contract
It's all there, black-and-white, in the contract
The rock and the hard place just became one and
    the same
Don't think for a nanosecond that we won't pull
    this off the table
Boilerplate
Legal-ese
Read the fine print
On the cheap
For a song
Bidding wars
Up the ante
Up the bid
Push a little harder
Sit tight
Bluffing game
Intensify the rhetoric
The art of the staged sell-in
Other fish to fry
Cash is king
Political maneuverings

Score some political points
Nest egg or goose egg
Concessions
Compromise
I'll meet you half-way
Let's meet in the middle
Let's split the difference
Look for the win-win
Pull the rip cord
The healthy solution
The healthy alternative
A dealbreaker
The kill switch
Put the brakes on the deal
Hammer out the deal points
We'll split the baby to get it done
Find the panacea that will cure everyone
What concessions are you willing to make?
If you don't make this deal, you'd be penalizing
    the entire organization
By making this deal, you have a chance to be a
    hero
That's a dealbreaker
Bail out
Dump it
Only sell rights to those who can exploit
Consider artistic integrity
Hide-and-seek
Nuclear response
Bounce it off them
Lob one over and see what they do with it
Let's deep dive on several issues
Hammer out the issues
We are miles apart
We are miles away
Open gash
Lowball 'em

Don't blink
Don't leave anything on the table
Can we agree to disagree?
Hold their backs to the wall
Etched in stone
Cast in concrete
Lip service
Throw him a bone
Pigeonholed
Stymied
The squeaky wheel gets the grease
Put a stake in the ground
Draw a line in the sand
Nickel-and-dime you
Cross that bridge when you come to it
Burn that bridge when you get to it
A verbal agreement is not worth the paper it's
    written on
The music industry is comprised of a monolithic
    handful of companies
The signed contract ideally is a reflection of a true
    balance of power
If there is an error, let's make it in our favor
Everything is for sale except the wife and kids…
    and they are for rent
Double-edged sword
Two sides to every coin
We've had preliminary discussions
It is too premature to speculate
Botch the negotiation
Industry-standard split
Standard 15% (media-related + sales commis-
    sions)
Standard 4% (athlete contracts)
Sharpen your pencils
Attach specifications
Printed and bound

Form and content
Split the difference
50-50
Fifty-fifty
Very few deal off the gross
Peanuts
Couple of bucks
Stake your claim
Posture for negotiation
That's a non-starter
Missed the boat
Jump on board the train
Thanks a million
Deal fluff
Signaling through other numbers
Lay your cards out
Let's put our cards on the table
Alright everybody, cards on the table
Don't show 'em your hand
Tip 'em off
Don't scare 'em away
Didn't find the bottom
A real cat and mouse game
Play both sides against the middle
From your lips to God's ears
Royalties are the time value of money
I cannot disclose any of the subject matter from
    those dealings
There's the pressure you feel and the pressure
    you apply
Worldbeater
Do we have some wiggle room on this one?
Deny the existence of any agreement
Never negotiate with an oxygen thief
It moved the needle
That number didn't scare the horses
Drive a hard bargain

Drive a tough deal
A lot of different kinds of silence
Use silence to your advantage
Silence can always be a response
Threat conditions
Evaluate the threats
War plan
Attack plan
Swing for the fences
The $64 dollar question

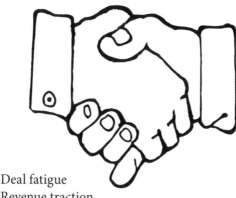

Deal fatigue
Revenue traction
Anti-punitive leverage
Sound asleep on that deal
Asleep at the wheel
Get your house in order
Cut it in half
Knock down the number a tad
That's a number with everything all in
Playing hardball
Let me confer with my clients
When you get a pitch like that, you gotta swing
      for a home run
Cash out
Take the money and run
Go straight for the jugular
Go for broke

In the works
Unconfirmed sources indicate
A deal is in the works
Sources close to management say
Make the lights and make the meeting
Touching base
Be careful for what you wish for
The notion that an agreement may happen
What's the ceiling?
What's the floor?
Less upfront but incentive-laden for the back
 end
Is there a back end?
Don't pull any punches
Close the book
Finagle (re-work the numbers; get them to fit the
 solution)
Deal flow
This one's a tweener
It's not in the cards
We have 'em by the short hairs
We have them over a barrel
Life is not a bowl of cherries and Von Dutch hats
We're holding court
Takes the cake (winner)
Takes the cheese (consolation prize or source of
 disappointment)

Getting Started / Starting Over / What To Do First / Doing What Is Necessary

The Prompt

IT'S A CLEAN sheet of paper
Let's get rolling
Let's kick things off
Get on the same page

Let's get off on the right foot
Our first line of defense
Bury the hatchet and move on
Cast differences aside and move forward
Start your economic engines
Go after the low-hanging fruit for starters
Do some reconnaissance
Do some due diligence
Do your homework
Run the numbers
Touch base
Your initial foray into…
It's freshly minted

Let's pull our plans in line
Let's define a method to the madness
Shake off the morning dew, my friend
There's dew on the melon
It's a go
Give 'em a fruit cup
Give 'em a fruit basket
Top of the windup
Throw out a litany of ideas
Put your best foot forward
Prepare the head by feeding the soul
Run it up the flagpole
First line of defense
Kickoff meeting
A whole new ballgame
It's a "go" job
Can we go to green?
Get to green
Greenlight
It seems like the cart before the horse
The price tag never leads the idea, but here
    goes...
We will need to pore through a wealth of infor-
    mation
Run it up the flagpole and see if anyone salutes
Red-line it
Red flag it
Put a stake in the ground
Draw a line in the sand
The first order of business is...
Top of the order
Top of the lineup
Leading off
Dawn of a new day
Kick things off
Blue sky all the way
Clean and green

The biggest fish to fry
A fish fry
Put together a "To Do" list
What is on the tick list?
Irons in the fire
Laundry list
Touch base
Peck check
Deep six it
86 it
Flares in the air
First line of defense
Backup plan
Plan A
Plan B

Sparking up the barbeque
Block and tackle
Heavy lifting
Wakey wakey, eggs and bakey
Let's get off the dime
Let's get off our duffs
Let's outline a method to the madness
In spite of the clutter, I would still like to go for it
Parallel path with your first contingency plan
Put the contingency plan in motion
Time to stuff the goose (load the camera)
Stuff the goose

Ultimatums / Friendly Warnings / Threats / Major Risks

The Prompt

Sink or swim
Sack up
Sh** or get off the pot
Fish or cut bait

You better grow eyes in the back of your head
I'm gonna drop you like a bad habit
I'm gonna knock you on your wallet
I'll come down there and eat your lunch for ya
Show some sack
Pound sand
F-off
Up yours
You're small potatoes
You're excused
Recuse yourself from all this
You should remove yourself out of the situation
Don't say I didn't warn you
Stick it
Shove it
You need to bounce
You should splitsky
Watch your back
Be careful of a bloodbath
Do not poison my water hole
Do not rain on my parade
Do not bend over to pick up the soap
Off to the gallows
Steer the ship

Well, we'll just see about that
I would like to see them try
Go ahead, try and stake your claim
Don't think for a nanosecond that we won't pull
    this off the table
Don't pull the bowl away from the Doberman
    when he's eating
Just remember who is ramrodding the cattle drive
Just remember who is captaining the ship
You can run with the dogs or piss with the pups
You can soar with the eagles or sputter with the
    turkeys
We'll see what happens when we push a little
    harder
The cut to the chase is simply this
Let's cut to the chase from this long diatribe
Let me give you a cut-bait date
Put the thumb screws to him
When push comes to shove
Don't overdo it
Don't try to beard the lion in his den
Just remember, job security is job one
Let's not blow things out of proportion
You're yelling… I'm yelling… we will get it done
With friends like you, who needs enemies?
Do or die
We gotta let you go
Watch your back with that guy
Win or go home
Publish or perish
Either make the rain or clean up after the storm
Lose and go home
Up to the suite or down to the street
Just give me the stuff and take off
Make no mistake about it
We're taking over
We're buying you out

Sports and Business

$$$

by (the late) Craig Tartasky
Former Chairman and Executive Director–
International SPORT SUMMIT

HAVING BEEN IN the sports business for more than 20 years, I have seen the evolution in jargon… and the buzz of the biz, if you will.

Our world has gone vertical in its integration, horizontal in its thinking, global in its economy and local in its focus. We live life in the macro sense, focusing on the micro view only to be confronted by multifaceted issues.

While the rest of the world looks to sports for its analogies, sports looks to business for our own. While others look to hit a home run with their product, we are looking to cross-integrate. While others are trying to get into the game, we are trying to create new arenas for our products. Business looks to sports to score the winning goal and sports looks to business as the way to keep score.

Everyone wants to get into the game, step to the plate, swing for the fences, snatch victory from the jaws of defeat. When pressed for answers, we look to go for the bomb, the hail mary, the last second heroics to save the day. In sports, we want to drive the bottom line, capture market share, and extend our brand.

The world has gone upside down. Sports has become more of a business while business has become more of a sport. Business is constantly looking for the go-to-guy, the new quarterback to lead the team. The CEO who was also an athlete gets more attention than the guy who ran a division profitably. Glory comes to those who have tasted victory, dined with champions, and who know what it takes to be an athlete.

A friend and fellow industry expert and I were having a discussion about the quality of the executives in our industry. He said our problem is that we have too many people who think tactically and few who think strategically. I had to stop for a moment and try to understand what he meant. Then, I realized, he meant that we have too many people who can implement and not enough who can envision. Of course, if he said it to me that way, I would never have appreciated the Ph.D. that follows his name.

Our catchphrases come from all over. However, there is nothing funnier than watching one of our catchphrases get lost in the translation. In 1995, I was at a conference in Brussels. The speaker, an American with a great Southern accent, was talking about how his company had "wanted to see if that dog would hunt, so they gave out 5 million tchotchkes." I could hear the contingent

from Paris saying to themselves "Quel sont ces tchotchkes?"

We have learned to measure the value of media in terms of audience reach, pass-through readership, cost-per-thousand, return on investment and on degrees of stickiness. We surf the net, TiVo the game, and blackberry ourselves in our spare time. What we call multi-tasking used to be called walking and chewing gum at the same time. We have leveraged our brand, positioned it, polished it, reinvigorated it and sometimes even re-branded it. We have captured our audience, penetrated the market, identified our clients, co-oped our consumers, corralled eyeballs and saturated our markets. I am not sure if we have conducted business or committed a mortal sin.

Our words get bigger, but our mission is the same. We have to develop products that drive the bottom line. Things like revenue inversion, market dichotomies, changes in the landscape, unforeseen circumstances, software glitches, or system crashes are wonderful phrases for failure. But winning is simple. Our profit met or exceeded expectations.

We have become so good at what we do that we can say so much and mean so little. Our goals can be multi-platformed, strategically-tiered, and value engineered so that, at the end of the day, we can say that we managed the expectation consistent with the marketing or business plan which was written before we took over and which, of course, reflects a reality that has been changed by intangibles not yet foreseen.

We have obfuscated the language to the point where even Yogi Berra wouldn't get it. Sports is simple. The team wins, we succeed. Rarely does a bad team sell out.

Oh, and before I forget, let's not forgive ESPN their trespasses (though I do congratulate them on 25 years of broadcasting magic). We set our clocks by SportsCenter. So, don't forget to hit your sales quotas with a big "Boo-Ya" or "We got all of that one." And remember, while "the Boss" to some still plays in the E Street Band, "the Boss" also owns the Yankees, and please don't confuse the two.

HOME RUN!

Thanks to the leagues, we have lottery picks, salary caps, luxury taxes, revenue sharing, Larry Bird exemptions, franchise players, and wild card playoffs. There used to be a time when the franchise player was the guy who carried your team, not just your payroll, and the wild card was the thing or person that could upset the apple cart.

If you don't speak the language, talk the talk, walk the walk, then you are not in the game. And no one wants to admit they aren't in the game. So egos get boosted at the expense of the language. And, after reading this, doesn't it make you wonder if I couldn't have dialed it down, flown beneath the radar, or simply taken one for the team?

Class dismissed.

Sports Terminology Applicable To Business Talk

Macrosports Talk

The Prompt

SPORTS MARKETING IS the art of using the assets or a sports property / event to move the sales of a product or brand from the point of conception to the point of consumption

The U.S.A. is a sporting island
Points of differentiation
Strive to win
The only two global events are Olympics and
   World Cup
Stars drive the globalization of sports
Olympianism
Sponsor fees escalating
Sole goal is maximization of revenue
Put a good product on the field
In five years… a 1,500-channel universe
In the future digital world, sports has value
Mega-events will continue to have value
Digital compression… many feeds in one pipe
Team revenues are up 12% but costs are up 35%
Dispersed fan base… 17% of America moves
   every year
Position the league as a fan's league
Fan-friendly policies
Lure the fan base
Constructing national marketing programs
Pay out of need and not out of greed
Acquisition of sports programming

Focused demographics

Broadcast parity

Internet power and offline media glory

No medium has grown faster than the Internet

Intense pleasure to be here

Strength of the audience base tested once the novelty wears off

Sports and properties need to step back and ask what brands mean to people

Fragmentation of the media market makes sports more powerful

More media means more ways for consumers to access sports

Mass consumption on a grand scale

Closing the loop

Multi-media tasking

A shift in tech land

Internet/TV convergence

Cohesive combination of online and offline media

Measurable interactivity

Rumor, innuendo, and unsupported allegations

Debrief candidate series

Size and scope increases risk and rewards

Recommend definitive measures

Put your house in order

Financially secure and politically stable

Desperate and far flung

Issue of financing is a double-edged sword

Culmination in a strategic marketing plan

Build and enhance the Olympic brand

The Olympic brand will transcend

Olympic rings are more recognizable than the Christian cross

Protect the ideals

Extraordinary patience

Episodes

Political machinations

Political infighting

Results can sometimes be measured media

Driver interview time

Real watershed chance

Niche boutique company capturing expertise with narrow focus

Be acquired by a predator

Cultured vision

Maintain autonomy and responsibility

Great mechanism

All of the eggs in one basket

Key to sponsorship is customization

The pay-per-view era will generate $25 million to $100 million

The rule of thumb is the sky is the limit

Rule of thumb

Adding brand value

As that person illuminated

Ideas that have been challenged

Cynicism about the role sports in our society

Dark cloud hiding

Courtship phase

Beyond emotional attachment

Sports can exemplify the core assets of a brand

Assets of the property

Attributes

Perceptions

Major economic downturn

Trend predictions

Tune-in programming to support integration

Competitive programming landscape

Category exclusivity goes without saying

Commercial rotation schedules

Premiere "A" pods

The A-team

The varsity

Preferred stockholders

Inner core

Core team

Starting lineup

Starting five

Starting eleven

Staring nine

Measured in column inches

Impact on sponsors versus stats

Transcend

The term Sponsor has become meaningless unless delivered in a meaningful context

Use brand to add value in a sponsorship role

Show consumers that we have matured --- start demanding more from properties

How to use association to increase awareness and purchase intent

Tired of the media's overwhelming whining of commercialization

Extend via properties that are sponsored

Explosive growth of sponsors

Manage sponsorship programs and develop marketing plans

Tap into lifestyles and passions

Unnecessary dilemma

Commerce names make the Olympics possible

They believe they are righteous in their principles

Explosion of sports in our culture

Stark differences

Wages, hours, and working

Profitable subsidiary

Exclusive right to negotiate under labor law

Know it intimately

Proliferation of player foundations

Have all the issues in front of you

Piggyback and passthrough rights

Fully integrated into marketing programs
If it's reasonably priced, let's do it
Passion play
Sports deliver the numbers
Advertising fits into all five strategic objectives
Positioning
Imagery
Integration
Volume
Volume-building
Relationship building
Superior acceptance platform
Media analysis
Assess from a CPM standpoint
R & F's
Build impressions
Purchase intent
Product favorability
Know something about 501C3's and a 300-page
   collective bargaining agreement
Sports provides the platform on which to build
   integrated communication messages
Setting the stage for a big event
Darling of the event
Crusaders
Pioneers
Visionaries
Gain acclaim
Aspirations
At a basic clip
Benchmarks
Feasibility study
Systematic and strategic shifts
Underlying initiatives
Overlying initiatives
Watershed events
Growth catalyst

Embrace patriotism
Embrace corporate America
Package the emotion
Corporate America stepped up
Assets successfully leveraged
In-store signage
In-store POP
POS materials
TV spots
Merchandising
Trade incentives
Grass-roots initiatives
Kids' initiatives
Online inititaives
Promotional campaigns
Sordid details
Maximize potential revenue streams
Signage inventory
Commitment to sport is shared by sponsors
Comprehensive multi-dimensional efforts
Nascar is the largest spectator sport in the U.S.
One of few sports to show annual growth for two
    straight decades
Support business efforts of best customers
Sum of the whole is greater than the value of the
    individual parts
Collective good
Maximize dollar value to shareholders
Split categories
New terminology
Consumers bombarded
Do not have the capacity to attain
National clutter
Local clutter
Sports marketing is 30 years old (since the
    1960's)
Contend that nothing is new

Marketing business using sports to meet sales objectives

Package the elements

Measurable results

Expansion of the digital world

Own compelling sports content

Does it matter geographically?

Predictable ratings

Desirable demographic

Fragile commodity

Don't kill the system

Don't point the finger

Best opportunity to show your best

Discernible added value to drive product sales and enhance brand imagery

Analyze the architecture of a sports brand with product brand to see if there is a fit

The role of sports in TV results in the highest male representation in viewership

Live programming is an important element in broadcasting

Benefits of renting include instant credibility, brand ID, predictable success rate

Negatives of renting are labor disputes and building another's brand

Benefits of owning are equity in brand, controlling costs, and content in perpetuity

Negatives of owning are brand development and startup costs

Professional Football League to combat free agency, high ticket prices, teams moving

Sports and Business—the Sponsorship Climate

The Prompt

THE ECONOMY IS not exactly roaring back—it's a moderate recovery in a down economy, but there is always someone willing to pay more for sports franchises, players, and sponsorships

Winning can cure a down economy in sports
You need Presidential sign-off
Streamline the business
Buck the trend
Run against the grain
Cut against the grain
Against the grain
It's not just buttons and banners
Post-flight surveys
Sports-endemic
War stories
Need to be a differentiator
Differentiator
The gold standard
Be iterative with the sponsor
Dollars to leverage
Dollar scrutiny
The ROI uptake
Set parameters and metrics
Quantifiable metrics
How do you aggregate it?
Measure against pre-set clicks
It's not measured against clicks
From selling signage to activation
Draw traffic
Traffic builder
Get your just due
It's my due

It's my time
Ink the deal
Canned paneling
What's your high-flier?
Office pools
Off-field behavior
On the arrest blotter
Steroid stallions
ROI as a function versus the previous year as the
      baseline
ROI against deliverables of what was promised
Hockey stick projections
Up and to the right
Crisis control department
Push it under the rug
Sweep it under the rug
Throw it under the bus
Throw him under the bus
Push him off the stage
Yes, have some
Taints the picture
Impairs the judgment
Spike in traffic
Desperate times call for desperate measures
Permeates
Assistance team
Two words for you: Media Training
Hit the bottle
Hit the sauce
Thug factor
Dancing on top of your S.U.V.
The American public is forgiving
Own the whole pie
Roadmap
On the roadmap
Cue it up
And he bailed

General Sports Gobbledygook We Hear On A Daily Basis

The Prompt

I WOULD LIKE to see a full court press on this
We're playing some heavy-stakes poker
Now, grab the ball and run with it if you want to
   be a Superstar

The quick six
In for a touch
All-star
An end run
The hook and ladder
Up the gut for six
A frozen rope
The whole nine yards
Hard-nosed baseball
Hostile territory
A toss-up
The way the ball bounces

HODGEPODGE & GOBBLEDYGOOK

Orange
Pill
Pumpkin
Rock
Orb
Kick it off
Tee it up
Take it all the way
Hoop all afternoon
Out of the gate
Cut and run
Tap the Titleist
Let's get busy
That's a two-putt green
Two-foot putt
Layup
Slam dunk

Ace

Red zone

Pinch hitter

Home run

The three keys to football are field position, ball security, and smashmouth

I need more than two minutes… I am not Roger Staubach, John Elway, or Joe Montana

I'm all in

Heavy-stakes poker

Milk the clock

Salt away some time

Salt away the game

The clock is running

The clock is ticking

Make big plays

No turnovers

Rapid response

Contingency plans

Schemes

Yoked up

On the juice

Closer

Firefighter

Two-minute warning

Field position football

Take it to the house

Six points

Two points

Game point

Match point

Ballgame

Defensive stopper

Franchise

Zonebuster

Gamer

Gamebreaker

Impact player
Big time
Money player
Paint the corners
Let the game come to you
Play your game
Evenstance affair
Play to a tie
Play to a draw
Run with it
Home field advantage
Team player
We need to eat our Wheaties
Behind the eightball
Keep the drive alive
Take a shot at the end zone
A shot in the arm (positive boost)
A real boost
Check out for the traps
Check the pin placement
As they say in golf, it's right in the Sahara
How many strokes?
How many blows?
Hit it, Alice
Lights out
Tough sledding
Tough going
Evaluate the season
Get in there for a touch
Paydirt
Jackpot
Get after 'em
Snuff it out
Put the kibosh on
Deadbolt locks
Closing speed
The goat

The hero of the ballgame
Big dance
Move the sticks
Top of my game
Bring your A-game
Bring your big boy hat
Eat clock
Stallball
Get yourself a big hunk of that
Big time
Catch air
Full court press
Alley oop
Snowbird
Hail mary
Win or go home
Hold serve
War of attrition
Ballhawks
The swagger
Two-minute drill
Advance the ball
We cannot be throwing 55-footers (coming up short)
Winners never quit and quitters never win
Third place is third place, no matter how you slice it
Attract the casual and the core
Begin in earnest
Good old-fashioned cost management
Renewal packages
Significant dividends
Association alliances
Acquisition and production
High-profile sports programming
Close to the action
In the mix
Structural changes

Focused demographics
Broadcast parity
Broadcast erosion
Money flow in advertising
Sell to who wants to buy
It's not yards tallied but points allowed
Defense wins championships
It's how you finish, not start
Increase familiarity with days and time blocks
Sports has become a commercial endorsement
    at every level
Maximize revenues through the corporate mar-
    keting program
At the end of the day, it's runs scored, not batting
    average or slugging percentage

Baseball–Specific Terms That Can Still Apply To Business Situations

Frozen rope
Homer zone
Walk-off homer
Belt high
Tater ball
Bleacher reachers
Leather and lumber
Flash the leather
Webgem
Base knock
Ducks on a pond
Hang the curve
Throw 'em the deuce
You were hit hard
You were shelled
Small ball
Just hit singles
Hit-and-run
Scores will be settled

Candy hop
Brush 'em back
Crowd the plate
Double dip
Chin music

Golf–Specific Terms That Can Still Apply To Business Situations

Right postage, wrong zipcode (it had the distance but was not on target)
Wormburner (safe but low and touching the ground or low and straight down the middle)
USA (you're still away)
FISO (fu** I'm still out—putting term)
SYT (still your turn—putting term)
NSF (not so fast—probably not a gimme)
Condom shot (safe but didn't feel good)
Nascar shot (always left or hooking left)
Lipped it
Lipped the cup
Lipper
Hit it, Alice
You could have used some more Wheaties
Get legs
I hit it fat
Blade it
Keep your head up
Good ball
Golf shot
That'll play
That dog will hunt all day long
That dog will hunt
Scratch golf
Drive for show and putt for dough
It's not how you drive, it's how you arrive
Just grip and rip it

Tools of the trade
Par for the course
Even the squirrel finds an occasional nut
Downhill lie
Bump and run
Uphill and into the wind
Stay dry
Waterball
It's wet
Drop zone
Nice shot, right on the beach
It's right in the Sahara
On the beach
Beach
Beachfront property shot
Beachcomber
Take sand
Pick it clean
Roll it in
Tap in
It's a gimmy
Inside the leather
Greenie
Whiff (swing and a miss)
Airball (swing and a miss)
Crushed it
Tagged it

"Trash Terms" For Pars Without Hitting Greens In Regulation:

Sandy (par after being in the sand)
Barky (par after going into the woods and/or hitting a tree)
Woody (par after going into the woods and/or hitting a tree)
Tar Baby (par after hitting the cart path)

Skippy (par after skipping in and over the water
    to safety)

Potty (par after hitting a Port-A-Potty or station-
    ary bathroom)

Fencey (par after hitting a boundary fence and
    staying in bounds)

Carpathia (par after hitting the cart path)

Missy (par after a whiff or swing and a miss)

Winfield (par after hitting a "live" bird)

RJ (par after hitting a "live" bird)

Parky (par after hitting a parked car)

Lucky (par after hitting a moving car and not
    hurting anybody)

Horse Racing–Specific Terms That Can Still Apply To Situations

Turn out to pasture
Out of the gate
And away they go
Let's get out of the gate fast
And, Down the stretch they come
Down the homestretch
Into the first turn
Frontrunner
Parlay
The drop
Neck and neck
Coming down to the wire
Workhorse

Thoroughbred
Wire to wire
Gate to wire
Here's the wire
Up to your knees in crap
Stall muckers
I've got a hot tip
Sticking close to the rail

Railbirds
Broke his maiden
By a nose
Daily double
Across the board
Dead heat
Photo finish
Fast track
Horse sense
Long shot
Handicapper
Blinders
Blinkers
Stallers
In the money

Boxing–Specific Terms That Can Still Apply To Business Situations

Haymaker
Sucker punch
Rabbit punch
Upper cut
Right cross
Jab
That's the fight game
The fight game
Stick and move
His shoes have eyeballs on 'em

Surfing–Specific Terms That Can Still Apply To Business Situations

In the green room (inside the pipe)
Get barreled, but don't snap it
The waves had fair shape
Freight train lefties
Shore break righties

Chargin' hard
Get out there and get after it
The sets were coming in nicely
A-frames
Tri-frames
Pull in
Shoulder highs
Rammin' and jammin'
Touch the face
Lip the face
In thar
Mushy peaks
Thrashed and shlarved
Shore break righties
The break
Gnarly rides
Mushy peaks
Grab your stick
Crunched and shlarved
Mushroom-headed cheez-its
Pumpin' from the West
Sardines give you a woody
Northwesterlies
4 foot on the face
Good shape
Hang ten

Basketball / Hoops Terms That Could Also Apply To Business

Orange
Pill
Pumpkin
Rock
The orb
The roundrock
The pill
Draw iron
Dish the rock
Head fake 'em
Take it to the bank
Snowbird
Full court press
Three quarters court
Sag zone
Loose zone
Box-in-one
Diamond-in-one
Two-three zone
Three-two-zone
Two-one-two zone
Zone press
Man-to-man
Man-on-man
Motion offense
Slow down game
Up-tempo game
Run-and-gun
Off the dribble
Take 'em off the dribble
Fingerroll
Reverse layup
Reverse jam
Tomahawk jam

Slam bam jam
Automatic from fifteen feet ("15")
Automatic from three ("3")
Release, rotation, splash
Pull up and hit
Pull up and knock it down
Drillin' reggies
From way downtown, bang!
Gat it
Area code J
Range J
Baller
Have some
Ya'll gotta give me that
Are you kiddin' me?
Somebody stop that guy
Spot up and shoot
Spot up
Pick and roll
Backdoor cut
Backdoor pass
D-up ("dee" up; play defense)
Pressure D
Draining treys
Draining 3's
Wraparound pass
Thread the needle
Zip it
Post up
Post up on the block
Pull up
Pull up J
Pull up and drain
Alley oop
Stay out of the lane
Open looks
Dribble drive

SLAM DUNK!

Dribble, drive, and dish
Stop, pop, and drop
Go to the hole
Go hole
Drive the lane
Take it to the rack
Take it to the house
Get the roll
Shooter's roll
Shooter's bounce
Too much French pastry
Too much hotdoggin'
Rain
Money
From way downtown
The shots weren't falling
Nothing but net
Mad game
Mad skills
Player
Player hater
The kid's got ups
Holler
Steal Game One
Fillin' it up
Cagers
Statement game
Career game
String music
Street cred

Head Honchos and Big Cheeses: The Leaders and Top Dogs

$$

by Scott M. Kaufman
CEO—Young & Successful Media Corp.
(Los Angeles, CA)
Author of: *Secrets Of The Young And Successful: How to Get Everything You Want Without Waiting a Lifetime*™

HOW DID THEY GET THERE? How did they ascend to the top of the food chain? People like Warren Buffett (Berkshire Hathaway), Michael Dell (Dell Computers), David Filo, Jerry Yang and Terry Simmel (Yahoo!), Larry Page and Sergey Brin (Google), Jeff Bezos (Amazon.com)— Just how did these people make it to the top? Are they the "Visionaries," "Field Generals" or "Hired Guns?" Are they "Dreamers with a deadline?" Are they people who "bootstrapped" their companies, or did they find "Angels" (or angel investors) or

"VC's" (venture capitalist firms) to fund their ideas? Were they "mavericks" or "charismatic leaders" who surrounded themselves with "rainmakers" that supported their dreams and vision?

Having started my first business at the age of 12, I quickly found myself thrust into an entrepreneurial world where I was constantly faced with having to learn the vernacular or *BusiBUZZ* of different industries. From technical and finance terms to common marketing jargon, I often wondered where the heck the dictionary was to look up this stuff!

As my "Grand Plan" took flight and I sought to build a company that could become the "category leader" in its industry, I have continually sought to learn the latest *BusiBUZZ* to stay "at the top of my game." Today, as our company works, supports, and interacts with young "movers and shakers" from over 100 countries, the global "macro-level" business landscape is rapidly changing. For anyone who seeks to become "Top Dog" in their field, it's more important than ever to take the time to understand the new vernacular and cultures of business. Solid first impressions count more than ever and if you're looking to become part of the "crème de le crème" in your field, this book can provide a "competitive advantage" as you assemble the tools and resources necessary for success in this "flattening world."

Randy has painstakingly done the hard work for you, by continuously documenting countless "*BusiBUZZ*" business terms for numerous years, and including them all here in one easily-accessible reference book. Written from a practical, straightforward, and humorous point-of-view, Randy provides examples of what others have said in the past and are just starting to say so that you can step up, "play the game" and become one of the "big shots" in your industry. This book will give you a window into the terms, words, phrases, and expressions that span from mundane water cooler talk to frequent technical and business speak.

From popularized acronyms dating back 50 or more years to the hot verbiage of today, *BusiBUZZ* is a must-read reference tool for anyone who is truly serious about "fast tracking" their business communications and success.

The Top Dog / Person In Charge / Boss Figures / The Leaders

The Prompt

Higher-ups
Mucky-mucks
The big cheese
The 800-pound gorilla
Chief baller

The top banana
Alpha dog
Head honcho
Cat's meow
Bigwig
Big cheese
Head cheese
The big guy
The big man
The big boys
Main man
The cheese that stands alone
General
Captain
Governor
Major
El Presidente
Chief
Boss

Partner
Principal
The guy
The sacred cow
Top brass
The brass
The brass ring
Kiss the ring
The HMFIC (head motherfu**er in charge)
Jefe (pronounced "heh-fay")
Hefe (pronounced "heh-fay")
He's a big swinging dick
BSD (big swinging dick)
Golden Boy
Golden Child
Golden Goose
Queen bee
The second coming
Big ticket
Hot ticket
Big Kahuna
Big Brother
Headliner
The belle of the ball
Reverse exclamation point
The pick of the litter
The CIO (Chief Idea Officer)
Kingpin
The lynchpin of the whole operation
The ringleader
A-number one
Ace
Muckety-mucks
Baller
Ruling class
Debutante
The rainmaker

Feature program
The star
The pinnacle
The summit
The peak
The apex
The optimum
The maximum
The zenith
The feature premiere
Golden parachute recipient
The point guard runs the show
The heavy artillery
Movers and shakers
The key players
Player
Power brokers
Big guns
Big boy stuff
Ring leaders
Ol' boy network
Old guard
Old school
Young guns
Hired gun
Big operators
Big-time
Top execs
Key execs
Blue chippers
Up-and-comers
Moguls
The cigars and pinky rings of the business
Ringknockers
Cha-ching
Player pimps
Hoi Polloi

Not small-time
Double comma club member (millionaire)
Oversees a triangular hierarchy
Oversees a flat hierarchy

Politics / Be Political / Org Chart / Play The Game / Territorial

The Prompt

PLAY THE POLITICAL game with search-and-destroy politics if you have to, but remember, it's lonely at the middle, and hidden agendas will get you every time

Up the ladder
Down the ladder
Play the political game
Play politics
Political animals
Political beasts
Political climbers
Political outcomes
Power brokers
Balance of power
Reflection of a true balance of power
Political influence
Don't step on any toes
Walking on eggshells
Wield political power
Political maneuverings
Score some political points
Cut the overheated political rhetoric
Expound and pontificate
Any time you get a one-on-one, it's a good thing
Movers and shakers
Leaders of men
Winning on your own terms

Influence peddlers
Trading illegal favors
Curry favor with the boss-man
Civic champions
Civic leaders
Policy makers
You need a favor... I need a favor
You need something... I need something
One hand washes the other
The ugly side of politics
Political work with the zebras
A little spice, a little sugar
You gotta know how to hit 'em and kiss 'em
Backscratchers
Asskissers
Brownnosers
Step on a few toes
Do it at your own political peril
The collective good
Collective cause

Common cause
How will it shake out?
Who do you back?
What do you back?
Hobnobbing with the big boys
Dealing with the mucky mucks
Dancing around the issue
Play the game
The Potomac two-step
Bullsh** artists
Bullsh**ters
Truthiness

Life In The Fast Lane

$$$

BusiBUZZ: "HOLLYWOOD MOVIETALK"
From "Bupkes" to Blackberry…
or
Who took the shtick out of show business?

$$$

by Tony Seiniger
The Critics' Collection
(Former President – Seiniger Advertising) –
    (Los Angeles, CA)

THE MOVIE BUSINESS was founded by Jews. Immigrant Jews, coming from Poland, Russia, Romania and Germany, coming to America with "bupkes" (nothing), and their dreams. They came to Hollywood for the same reason. They saw an opportunity—to make money and have fun in the sun at the same time. In the early days of the movie industry, Los Angeles had one-sixth the population it has now. Compared to the ghettoes of Eastern Europe (and even the Lower East Side of New York), Hollywood, Beverly Hills, and Bel-Air seemed like Heaven, if you believed in Heaven.

America learned Yiddish from show business.

The early moguls, Louis B. Mayer, Harry Cohn, and the Warner Brothers all used Yiddish, heavily mixed with English, as part of their everyday business language.

In 1974, Mel Brooks' *Blazing Saddles* brought Yiddish to Middle America. Dressed as a Native American tribal chief, Mel rode up to an African-American family traveling westwards by Conestoga wagon, and, upon seeing their complexion, looked at the audience and exclaimed "Schvartzes."

It wasn't long before other movies as well as network television series were full of people "shlepping," guys being "schmucks," other people being warned of "gonifs," and in the hot summer months, all across the country, we were "shvitzing." What was once the domain of Myron Cohen on the "Ed Sullivan Show" was now being used weekly by Krusty The Clown on "The Simpsons."

Perhaps the ultimate symbol of Yiddish becoming a permanent part of the American lexicon was the billboard for the Walt Disney / Pixar summer animated comedy *Finding Nemo*. "Fish Shtick"—the copy line for a Walt Disney movie? Who would have believed it?

With Yiddish becoming so mainstream, Hollywood had to create its own unique-speak once again. Besides, the immigrant influence had passed. The new breed of studio executive, agent, producer, writer, and director is highly educated. Many have degrees from the nation's best law schools. They're film school graduates, Ivy Leaguers, and MBAs. They may be of Jewish ancestry, and proud of it, but they don't necessarily want to sound it. So instead of Yiddish, today's movie folk speak in fake affection, or what we in the business like to call:

Lethal Warmth

They "love you." They love you so much, they bear-hug you to death, or slap your back so hard, they practically knock the wind out of you. When you invite them to see a cut of their movie in a private screening long before its actual release, and they think it's a real piece of dreck (crap), they hug you and say, "It's all up there on the screen." Or welled up with tears, they cling to you and whimper, "I don't know what to say."

Two screenwriters bumping into each other at The Palm will grab each other like professional wrestlers trying to squeeze each other's last breath out. "How's it going, man?" "It's going great, man. Just great," which means they're both spending every day the same way—staring at the telephone, waiting for their agent to call.

If a filmmaker gets a great deal to do a new project, his filmmaker buddies will hug the sh** out of him, wailing at the same time, "I'm so damn happy for you, man," which translated means, "If your next film out-grosses mine, I'll eat your heart out, personally, which is something my agent usually does for me."

Or if a friend makes a really artsy, but uncommercial film, you say "I see gold, man. This one's got Oscar written all over it." But, what you really mean is, "Your points in this turkey won't cover your next mortgage payment."

In a business with so much damn love in it, how come you can't get an appointment with a shrink? Once it was simple to end a conversation with, "So think about it, and give me a call," now, with pure Hollywood affection, you say, "Just let it marinate, and hit me on my Blackberry."

I have known Randy Gordon (or "RG," as I call him) since the early 90's, and he has done a quasi-decent job of capturing a smattering of the gobbledygook and phrasings that you still hear today in Hollywood marketing meetings. Oh, and by the way, make sure to look for the Yiddish pages of this book in the GOING GLOBAL section (he paid me for that endorsement). Good show, RG.

Theatrical Entertainment / Movie Industry Buzz

The Prompt

Though many of the terms are taken out of context, and, while some of these phrases or statements will not universally apply, this is what has been said and is still used in Hollywood

Theatrical success drives ancillary revenue streams
The script is boarded that way
Board the script
The money shot
Ambient sound
Windows of expectation

The sell-through video market

The majors have other profit centers

Recapture profit margins through distribution

It boards cheaper if you do it this way

PFD Deal (Production, Finance, Distribution)

The "P&A" (Prints (or movie) and Advertising costs)

Above-the-line costs (producer, director, principal actors)

An Equity Play (win-win with no downside guarantees)

Negative costs (what a film costs to make based on production)

A negative pickup (a picture financing term relating to acquisition)

The "dailies" (footage shot from that day)

The film has legs (a movie that will run for many weeks)

If the movie does not have legs, the exhibitors may lose big time

Time and a half (what people get paid after 12 hours of a workday)

Golden time (pay that is double the hourly wage)

Magic hour (time of the day when the sun is rising or setting)

Dirty dupe (black-and-white production)

Mute (print or negative that carries a picture without a soundtrack)

Loop the picture (re-record the dialogue)

Loopers (make sounds of crowd scenes)

Walla (background crowd sound)

Do you do highfalls? (stuntman term for falling)

Fast-food critics (the people / reviewers who provide immediate quotes)

It's a speculative business with many players and secrets

It's a capital-intensive business that blends art and commerce

It's the second largest export business in the U.S. behind aerospace

Movies are classic project management models with critical paths

2 out of 10 movies make money

There is a distinct need for deep pockets when there are risks at stake and profits to be made

Funding this picture would be a crapshoot with no real game plan

Recoup cash through windows of exploitation

Sometimes, singles are better than home runs because expectations are down

A day player

The feature exhibition

Standalone soundbytes

Blocked funds

Modest budgets

Stable of talent

As common as reshoots

As common as rewrites

We need a clear vision of project in sight

Clash of cultures

Juggle the elements to protect the film

Board it and hire for day's wage

SAG actors (Screen Actors' Guild—union)

I want final cut

Final cut

Let's get set up for ancillaries

Look for singles and doubles

If you cannot say yes, you have no power

The power to say yes

Playdate charts

You have a lot of faith to press the button

Kiss the ring

Once played it is value down

Firm terms create conflicts

Firm terms create conflicts and obstacles going in

Popcorn margins are tremendous

I saw him at the Dresden Room Friday night with a babe

Once played, the value goes down

It's a perception game

You have to roll the dice

We need visible actors for an economic price

It's playthroughs versus original bookings (holding a film over)

You can change the commerciality through the editing process

I am diametrically opposed to everything you do here

If the pot grows as a whole, the industry is better off

Politics and entertainment...it's the same business these days

The Producer and director should not impose on a writer when creating

Boom, it's like Patton hitting the beach

Slug line (exterior day, interior night)

A Production Manager and First AD are BTL but can still be big ticket numbers

Pay or Play deal (regardless if the movie goes or not, anybody and everybody could get paid)

The house nut (film exhibitor house / exhibition term for covering all monthly expenses)

Overextension and undercapitalization are pitfalls in domestic distribution

Film making is a collaborative effort

Visceral sense

Write what you know

Do not quell creativiity

All the people have to be fed and gaffed

Don't print everything in 35mm… just the good takes

Protect the downside of the picture

Motion picture biz is a typescripted business

Find a set director with an ego who wants up

Who wants up?

Spot the talent

Pay the commensurate wages

Grips set up and tear down for the crew

Wear emotion on your sleeve

Picture value

Go for the money shot

Gyroscopically controlled

Give picture a big look

You don't see the gradation... it's muddy

We need a genie (generator)

Explosion (stock footage)

Bag of shells

Bag of beans

Flash frame (editorial trick of white, then explosion)

Flashbang

Intermediation and interrelation

Find money with words and hide money in numbers

What's good for the picture? vs. What's good for
the wallet?

The producer's dilemma: re-board or raise more
money?

Need compromise and cooperation

It offends all reason

Interface with them to find out

In case of emergency, administer chocolate

You have to be predisposed to want to go to a movie

What's the likability factor?

Like a prelude to an opera

Publicity... keep building... don't peak

The klieg lights and the glitz

The back end of the train

It's a planned scramble

Research is an added voice, not a dictatorial process

You can't get into words what you can put up on a screen

Frame it this way

I'm reading the script, and I don't see it

Dial in bits of info to push the meter a little more

Business feeds off of negativity, not positive vibes

Interview them in an intercept situation

It may bode poorly with competitive clutter

The publicity campaign should mirror the marketing campaign

Good reviews don't help bad movies

Nuancal ways of doing things (based on "nuance")

That's the equation… it's success or failure… the majority is failure

The Golden Globe is a popularity poll

The release of the movie is the start of the revenue flow

MTV is just part of the landscape

A still image can sell a movie

Credits are a galactica all to themselves

Don't trust the audience to read anything

Music is a great engine for selling

Music fuels

Someone has to stake it

Seducing is a craft and an art form

Keep taking it through strainers until you get sauce

Give 'em a smell of what you think it will be

It's all a big chess board

Movies expand young

How 'bout in Lincoln, Nebraska?

Will it play in Peoria?

An "If Come" deal (TV business—paid only if it's made)

A "Hold" deal

It's greenlit… it's a go

Greenlight it

The script was greenlighted

It's a "go" job

Can we go to green?

Get to green

Assault them with your findings

Let your work create your reputation

Sell yourself, sell your work, sell both

Without a problem, there are no errors

Nuggets

Character + Reputation = Career

A plan is a stand-in while life happens around you

Range management and damage control

Tools, fools, and mules

The tilt factor

The sharing of scarcity and awareness creates
hype

Media enlarges a film's success

Give it spin

Attack the soft underbelly of the project

Technical workability

A combative fight scene doesn't necessarily buy
anything

Credibility in moviedom

It's all up there on the screen

This one's got Oscar written all over it

The release date is the single most important decision we make

The white-bread-with-mayonnaise audience

Let's give it a high-profile platform

You're always warmed by the eyes

Vegas… my favorite place aesthetically

The pinky rings and the cigars of the business

Let's see if the idea sprouts legs and takes off running

Corny and schmaltzy

We just touched off a firestorm

If you localize a campaign, people embrace it readily

He's a real firebrand… pisses off as many as he impresses

A hyena-like crowd

Pan and scan

Visible industry

There was indeed life before the steady cam

Board is translated to one-liners for schedules

Rehearsal on that is mammoth

Kill off day players and keep the weeklies

I've been in this business too long to lie to you. It's the "fu**ing" greatest movie I've ever seen.

Many roads to mecca (find your own)

The Martini shot (the last shot of the day)

The Abbey Singer shot (the second to last shot of the day; before the Martini shot)

Spend… then let it coast

There's nothing like execution

Create a buzz

Hot and sexy action

Newspaper is retail

CYA (cover your ass)

Always operate by CYA

A pacing and attitude piece

Do the scripts behave?

Ridder (wind machine)

Dissolves, fades, and wipes (transitions)

Do a burn-in (optical effect using television image)

Industry-standard tape recorder

Blue-screen process
Like a chroma-key blue
Fine cut
Finish cut
Some travel first class, some no class
Dress the set
Strike the set (take it down)
Need a cover set—alternate call
Sound dailies and dubbing
Longer to mix in stereo
Royalty fees
Comes to fold
A lot of featherbedding
Cross our "t's" and spot our cues
Backhand courtesy payments
Honorariums
Stipends
Drowning a kitten would be more of a challenge
Hittin' the sauce
Lie in a gutter and drink
Crop the photo
It's a perception game
You have to roll the dice
Quarter-inch mag tape that goes on the "nagra"
    (a sound device mixer)
DAT—Digital Audio Tape
Lock the picture (picture lock is image lock, then
    you start doing sound)
Spotting cues (for music)
Shoot it clicktrack (no sound) then ADR it later
    (ADR = dialogue replacement)
Set dressers
Location costs are enormous
Communicate dialogue
Construct change
Waaaay behind
Keep ahead of the sheriff

Optimistic media budget
Big horses to the table
Collective intellectual reservoir
Energize sluggish business
Down to brass tacks
Details and paper clips of it all
Bid 'em up… buy 'em up
The numbers don't jibe
Let's do a numbers run
Run the numbers
Turnaround transition team
Take copious notes
Master plan for calmer waters
Boundcrossing
Set memory presets
Less-literate brethren
Landlubber

Improve the bottom line of the P&L
Back to the drawing board, sharpen up the pencils
Go to the rack early and often
Intrapreneurship (within a company)
Pound salt (forget it)
It costs you more until you use it
The quicker you fall behind, the more time you
    have to make it up
Awards to warp the mantlepiece
Three types of business people: pleebs, paper push-
    ers, and presidents
The final product is never as good as the dailies…
    never as bad as first cut
If it's not on the page, it won't be on the screen
Exit polling
Edit bay
Chiron
A severe case of schizoid actions
Lamentably, I suspect something is amiss
Let's get off the dime

Let's get off our duffs
Time to stuff the goose (load the camera)
Stuff the goose
See you in a short
Yuppie idyll of domesticity
Serves a grisly purpose
A sanguine shower (upbeat)
Dangerous scum
We're in the mix
Range me
My life for freedom
Walker at a foley house
The sounds will be in the mix
Need palm print, retina scan, and urine sample
The only easy day was yesterday
Log the evolutions (part of class; breakdown and
    rebirth)
Depth of field may have to change from focus
    to focus
The logic behind the end result
Television is a close-up medium... not many long-
    shots
Split day (day and night)
Do not be greedy, know how to trade off and
    compromise
I suspect an orthographical lapse
Score and source music
Adaptability is the single most important element
    in production
Word gets around the set like lightning
Strike the set
Wrap the gurneys
Lenny arm (lunar crane, 25 ft high, 35 mm Fuji)
Send in the cleaners not agents (remove everyone
    rather than negotiate)
Rack focus (shifting focus from foreground to
    background or vice-versa)

What to look for in director of photography: quality, speed, flexibility, communication

Used to be goons, arcs, and HMI's (blue lights—night), now it's yellow lights to create artificial DP

Intensely valid

Getting scarce

There is always one word to summarize a decision

Social responsibility

That's an essay question

Limited gray matter

Flyover country

Artistic integrity

Substantive issues

TV is an insidious poison

Violence and sex are safety valves in film

Your argument has resonant chords

Butts in seats

Has it got legs?

Boobs bring in the rubes

Hot piece of tail

Double D's… double these

Tracking shot

It's a go

Gels (filters for lights)

Gaffer noise

Swish pan (camera move)

Smash cut (an abrupt edit)

New smash hit

New hit show

The make or break

The moment of truth

Actress to starlet

Hits-driven business

Moonshot titles

Two minutes of kill time

Twisted devil

Things Elvis Mitchell would say (NY Times)

There is a predisposition to want to be heard by your peers

The notion that an agreement may happen

Money is a vehicle of our guessing who we are

I never invited Madonna into my consciousness… but she's there

The opening weekend is the make or break of a film's revenue streams

It's results, not intentions, that allow it to happen… the gamble is the process

Sistine Chapel is the result of the ego of one man… decisions force the shrine into being

It does not stipulate that the 1st amendment guarantees you a development deal at WB

Technology will assault you, placing you in a sea of uncertainty

Mouseschwitz (derogatory name for the hours spent working at Disney)

Lighting

Mole

2K ("two-kay"—2,000-watt light)

4K ("four-kay"—4,000-watt light)

Inkee (small light)

Gels

Filters

Cookie (a Cuculoris; a lighting instrument)

Shoot it against Blue screen

Shoot it against Green screen

HMI's (blue lights for night shots)

Digital FX

Freezeframes

Flashframe

Fade to black
Slo-mo
Slow motions
Strobe
Mosaics
Superimpositions
Splitscreens
Dissolves
Grainy stock
Green screen
Blue screen
Flashbang (quick white screen frame that precedes
    an explosion)
Blow it out (overlight or over-expose the scene)
Swish pan (a camera move)
Smash cut (an abrupt edit)
Handheld (using the camera off the tripod)
Sticks (tripod for the camera)
Steadi-cam shot
Tracking shot
Dolly shot

TV Industry-specific

Test deal (pre-negotiated deal to agree to shoot a
    show while still screening multiple actors)
Backdoor pilot (self-contained 2-hour movie to
    see if certain characters resonate with the
    audience)
Two-hander (a show with two primary leads)
Pilot test
Holding deal
Hold deal
Green lights
Green light meeting
An "If Come" deal (if it is produced, then every-
    one gets paid)

"If Come" money

Piece of casting (mid-level stars whose names are not marquis enough to get something greenlighted)

Showrunner (TV writer who is big enough to get a show going)

Runner (a smaller storyline within a TV show that plays into the bigger picture of what is happening)

Above-the-line

Below-the-line

Script supervisor

Story editor

Music Industry-specific

Buzz (great word-of-mouth)

Stuffing the channel (overshipping an artist's new release)

Loading (same as stuffing the channel; overshipping an artist's new release)

Street date (day the CD hits the shelves)

Stiff (a record that is not selling)

Spins (how many times a day a radio station plays a certain record)

It's over (any record/CD that is not connecting with consumers even after heavy push)

An independent (promotion person or label)

Indy

Payola

Plugola

Plug

Concert economics

Load in

Load out

The crew

Roadies

The main lighting guy
Riggers
Gaffers
Green room (artists' lounge)
Talent (artists / musicians)
Mix position (mixing board at concerts)
Roving camera
Camera positions
Stage left
Stage right

Los Angeles Nicknames

The Prompt

WHILE NEW YORK is affectionally known as The Big Apple, The City, Gotham, New Jack City, and New Yawk… and with Chicago alternatively known to be Chi-town, The Windy City, and the City with the Big Shoulders… with San Francisco (also self-proclaimed to be) The City, The city by the Bay, Fog City and Fogtown, Oakland as Oaktown, Seattle as The Emerald City, Portland as Rip City, and both Orlando, FL and Birmingham, AL as The Magic City, how can it be that Los Angeles, California is known to so many by so many nicknames?

My personal favorites include the following:
Tinseltown
Lipstick City
The City of Angels
La-la-land

But try these on for size…
Glitterville
Smogtown
Smog City

Glass City
Plastic City
Silicone City
West Beach
Left Coast La-La
The Left Coast
Boomtown
Dolltown
Bigtown

Land of limos
Hollywood
Home to Hollywood
Horrywood
Los Angaleeze
Sin City (also Las Vegas)
Granola City (land of fruits, nuts, and flakes)
The largest city for cancer permits and jaywalking tickets
The town where lady luck courts a kid named greed
The city of klieg lights

Gaming / Videogaming Business / Console And Computer Gaming Terminology

The Prompt
SHIP-AND-DUCK
Beta testing
The disc went gold
MDF's (market development funds)

Frontline titles
Triple-A titles
AAA titles
Value games
Unsecured revs

Burning money
The burn rate
You're only as good as your team
Layered-in content
Constant idea flow
Pre-pro
Pre-prod
Post-pro
Post-prod
Proof of concept
POC (proof of concept)
Game design doc
Tech design doc
Push the boundaries
Deliver on the design
Game engine
Mathematical boundaries
Non-convex terrain
Digital terrain maps
Land usage data
Persistent worlds
End-player experience
Color
Lighting
Scale
Sound
Time constraints dictate
Cut feature list
Feature set
Frontline titles
Sense of progression
Level design
Recognize-reward
Long-play goals
Visually stunning
Tight
Asset tracking

The industry that started with a Bing and a Trip
Articulate the main idea of the game
In a more casual vein
On the fence
Watch what trends
Bazillion dollar industry
Jettison what you don't like
Directionally get a sense
Quantitative is projectible
Useful but contentious
Fielded the study
Reps the consumer in the marketplace
The game is rock tony solid
Climatically desirable
It's how you finish, not start
Cost, time, and efficiency
Platform sharing, like dimsum
Hardware drives the software in the early stages
Obsessive
Exploration
Extend the fantasy
Extended fantasy
Texture mapping
Animated moves
Polygons
Polygonal speed
Reflection lighting
Bones per character
Tight moves
Button masher
Beat-'em-up game
Reward mechanisms
Macro design
Customizable interface
Recognizable keys
No tutorial mode
Scripting language

Buck the trend

Front-end traction vs. back-end fulfillment

Affinity programs

Bouncebacks to retailers

Mutual admiration society

Buggy games

Co-op monies (same as MDF's)

Flashbang (million-candle strength)

Nailed the gameplay elements

Legacy of the franchise

Problems with closing the code

Footprint too big

Ports are a lot harder

Vanilla racing title—not a lot of sparkle

Let the license do the heavy lifting

Heavy lifting

You guys work together and "be simpatico"

Ping me back

Ping me

Expel it as a social reality

Character-savvy

Imagine yourself in a world with characters

Mastery

Recess currency

IP (intellectual property; not Internet rotocol)

IP is P1 (intellectual property is priority #1)

Creatively bankrupt

Entertainment parity

Distribution parity

Scale to meet the demands

Casual creep

Project creep

Question of continuation of flow of product—not exact same distribution channel

Between corporate and entrepreneurship exists a middle ground of Utopia called professionally managed

Cut down space, adjust down the AI, and cut down the number of missions

Renting not owning is a long-term problem because margins are smaller

Licensing fees are so high that there is nothing left for development

Heavy licensing fees are cutting right into the margins

Rights fees are astronomical in U.S., Japan, and Europe

The zigger… while others zagged

Mask the inefficiencies

Move the needle forward

Move the needle

Inspire and reward developer creativity

Strike a balance

Add value across global markets

Leverage product placement in a relevant way

Drive development costs down

We are being pigeonholed

New set of API's

API's

Social dynamic of gaming

Not worrying about network protocols

Fuel passion and spirit of promotional partners

Shared experience

Sequelize but do not cannibalize

Sequelization of entertainment

Living in a world of me-toos

It stank

It's a hits business

Products rushed to market

Buggy

Time to get it done or lose their rights

Drink the kool-aid

Story arc

Get it back in spades

Termination rights if breach
Termination right
Reps and warranties
Indemnification
Mutual indemnification
Inextricably part of our culture
Entertainment becomes collateral
Easier to get approval if not taking risks
Easier to take the cowardly way out and avoid not getting approvals
Controlled decontrolling of emotions to become civilized
Extract the essence of the underlying product
Control-Alt-Delete
Staring down the barrel of a gun
Checking the boxes
Console simplicity is built-in
Lightning-fast downloads
Be "always on"
Be epic, like films
Patterns emerge
Content is king
Cash is king
Competitive unity
Standards and conventions
Competitive chaos
How low is the churn?
The churn-rate?
The product cycle
Pay in real currency
Earn reputation points
Skyrocketing dev costs
Code of creative efforts
Push the boundaries
Shock value
Codes the moment in our memory
Zeitgeist (collective culture at any given time)

Mad skillz

Mad game

Owned

Jacked

PK-er (player killer)

Play CS or UO? (CounterStrike or Ultima Online)

Gaming clan

Clan

Dino

Luddite

We make 20-hour experiences

We want to kill TV

In the music business, back catalogs can carry you for years

The industry does not have cross-media business skills

Product placement is seen as crass

Broadband penetration plus content offering

Compatibility issues

The walled garden approach of the wireless world

Music marks the moment and emotion at any given time

The other shoe will drop (what is really coming?)

Intrapreneurial (key team owns and is proud of what they build within host corporation)

Bet on broadband (competing with Cable TV but easier to flip channel to next thing)

Who's helping whom?

Use content to target a different subset

1 million used to be an impressive number

Reverse trend of ongoing sales rather than just a first weekend gross

Our business was solitary, then machines took us away

Striving for the convergence device—more of a hub

Hire server engineers who think games are respectable

The guys who design game levels

Game design

The retailers do not own anything

Sequels counter the trend

The EA stock has had a big bet

No longer just competing on market windows

Free-roaming non-linear experiences

Base sale-ability conditions

Movie-quality resolution

Competent tech companies versus just acquisition companies

Design coding

Alpha

The beta

Beta test

Gold disc

3G roll-out

Wireless Wi-Fi

No Hollywood celebrity factors

How can videogaming add sex appeal?

You don't need big names and characters to make the X-Games cool

Ignore the market research and make the bets that pay off

Japan—phone to thumb versus San Francisco—phone to ears

200 yen to download wallpaper, ring tones, and videogame character screensavers

When you play with infrared technology, sophistication levels increase

Admin

Header

Newbie
Dweeb
Rook
Frosh
Bootychump
GL (good luck)
GG (good game)
Visually dynamic
Boss battle
Cel shading
Animation cel
Pixel shaders (for pixel lighting effects)
Vertex shaders
Shaders
Self-shadowing
Convergence of design and functionality
Be good ancestors
Mind-expanding journeys
Labyrinth of ideas
Creatively bankrupt?
Chic not geek
Story arc
Look for original ways to express the essence
Console driver
Platform driver
What if it slips?
Cut the feature list
Compound interactions
Home continuum (castle, pitstop, showplace, couch potato, theme park, cribs)
Controlled decontrolling of emotions to become civilized
Rent outward not inward
The difference between Woodstock and the moon versus Mars and Immortality
I.P. (intellectual property)—the key to interactive entertainment

Priority number one

How much do I own, versus how much do I rent
   out or short-term lease?

Max speed

Rich graphic intensity

Teens lead secret lives

Mediavores

Show me the numbers

The daunting challenge

Pitfalls

Rosiest future

Macro-view

That which is familiar is less threatening

Level playing field

Chaotic first stage of development

Feature creep

Feature drop

Spend money now and save money later

Dense organic look

Cost-inefficient in pre-production

Traditional documentation completely discarded

Five prototypes before fully funding

KISS method—Keep It Simple, Stupid

How to get the okay

Subliminal suggestion

Deserves to be seen by all of us

Get drawn in

Find something else to get distracted by

Legal defense fund

Stack up the chips

Monumental achievement

Sense of progression

Constant idea flow

Layered in content

Medium is a key risk

Why game? (fantasy, challenge, curiosity)—(sustained attention, reward)

Candy is psychological delivery; Gaming is mind delivery (flow)

The game can only be as good as the team

Make deals with less upfront and more sharing on the back end

Despise lack of originality

Exploit the strengths of your own medium

Terribly unsuccessful in getting this point across

Advanced AI

Character animation

Real-time physics

Hi-res (pronounced "high-rez"; high resolution)

Pressured rescue

The little moments

Trigger the event

Smoke clouds within game

Energy blasts

Particle stuff

Ender

Post-ending

The yin of the character

Passive viewer moment

Lone hero

Self-aware

Delve into it

Hook 'em in the moment

The hook-in territory

Detailed animations

All about the entertainment value

Pre-rendered loaded characters

Sliding and weight distribution

Little guy, extraordinary circumstances

Sound design supporting what is happening in a game

Done real well in real time

Not game camera work but cinematography

Engrossed in the moment

Connect with the character

This is where it is going in the future

Saw your name on the roster

That's a level pull

Real-life scenarios

Fight mode

Blows the illusion of life

How much attention is dedicated to code

Missed opportunities

Head-down developer types

All the bells and whistles

Actual in-game screen

In-dash engine not pre-rendered

Launch title (for a new platform or system)

New platform is a great time to launch a franchise

Characters paying attention to each other

Defining moments supported by animations and sound effects

Cinematography—pulling the camera back

Enchanted ghostly figure

Traditional documentation completely discarded

Core issues that were missing

Why games are like sex… not enough dials

Where's his axe, dude… where's the bazooka?

Process of building games and designing characters

Wish fulfillment

Evergreen

Next gen (next generation)

It has an engine

RTM (release to manufacture)

The game went gold

Blogging (web logs; web postings)

End user experience

Training mode (not tutorial mode)
Peer-to-peer versus server-based
Online multiplayer
MMO (massively multiplayer online)
MMOG (massively multiplayer online game)
MMORPG (MMO role-playing game)
The game genres
Action Sports
Sports
Racing
Action adventure
Fighting
Flight Combat
Flight sim
RTS (real time strategy)
RPG (role-playing game)
Sim (simulation)
Puzzle games
Turn-based games
Education-based games
Productivity software
Head-down developer types
Crunching code
Character depth
Game engine
Art and assets
Game mechanics
Game structure
Game storyline or narrative
Cell shading
Cheat codes
Atmospheric graphce

Las Vegas Terminology / On A Roll / Hot

The Prompt

IT'S VEGAS, BABY ! Vegas ! The city of Lost Wages
where you can do anything
Run the table, Double down, Be a big shooter, and
Let it all ride—Sin City awaits.

The vig (10% of the action)
The juice (10% of the action)
The cut (10% of the action)
House action
House take
Big hitter
Big player
This guy's the sun
Dare I say en fuego
En fuego
Hot as fire
Bet the farm
Bet it all
Split eights
Split aces
Hit me
Give me a hit
Take a card
I'll inherit another
I'll stand
I'll stand pat
Hold tight
A crap shoot
Everybody loves a shooter
Throw the dice
Roll them bones
Throw them bones
Late scratch

Chasing sunsets
Even money
Breaking even
Getting back to even
Broke even
Flatline
Hits and stingers (winners and losers in gambling)
I do not own a farm, but if I did, I would bet it
What's the spread?
What's the price?
Grab the ball and run with it
It's a sure thing
Sure-fire winners
Can't-miss picks
Winners
Beauties
Specials
Tapped out
Let the chips fall where they may
Ace or face
Face cards
Face time
Lucky seven
Split snowmen
Snowman (eight)
Bullets (aces)
Fish hooks (jacks)
Ladies (queens)
Bitches (queens)
Women (queens)
Big Guys (kings)
King pins (kings)
Cowboys (kings)
Perfects (tens)
All in
Nice pull
Modest winnings

Bet the house
Let it ride
Press your luck
Press it
All or nothing
Goose egg
Bupkus (nothing)
Cleaned out
An incredible run
On a roll
Ride the wave
Stay on board the train
We need to catch a break
End the losing streak
Losing skid
Having a bad run of luck
Bad run
Can't catch any cards
Wise up
Dial it back
Keep your powder dry
Texas Hold 'em
The flop
The turn
The river
Gentlemen, you can't lose what you don't put in
    the middle
This is a monster hand
You're going to fold with that monster hand?
Table stakes here
Shall we double the blinds?
You've got that alligator blood
Didn't know what hit 'em
And I thought you were holding some bullets
And I thought you had a pair of fish hooks
And I thought you had a pair of cowboys
And I thought you had some snowmen
Either fold or hang tough

That's the way, grind it out

Grind it out

What a frozen wave of cards

You can't seem to catch any cards tonight

Call or raise the bet

Let's go, while we're young

Are we playing cards or just watching the paint dry?

Are we playing cards or yammerin' about our problems

Are we playin' cards here or what?

This'll all blow over

Stake me

Seeya when I seeya

Get outta Dodge

Get outta town

I wouldn't be pokin' around here if I was you

The size of the stack is better than the quality of the cards

You had it the whole way

Lean on 'em until he falls over

There are some hungry wolves around here

Some sharks circling the table

Some rabid dogs around this table

It's like some rabid dogs salivating over a piece of meat

You don't know what you just walked into

Even the squirrel can find an occasional acorn

You can spot a man's tell

Keep it to yourself

What were the down cards? I don't quite remember

Don't draw against a made hand

That's Mister Son-Of-A-Bitch to you

Splash the pot

Don't splash the pot

Go into hock for more

You're thinking you're Mister Vegas

Do you have the stones to play
All you really need is one big hand an hour
All your outs are gone
There's one last card in the deck that can help
    you
Turn it around
Try to turn it around
A bunch of mopes at the table
No mopes at my table
You're short-stacked with long odds against
How did you get in such bad shape?
It smells kind of musty in here
Play heads up
Blinds 25 and 50?
That's very aggressive
You're being a little agro, don't ya think?
Re-raise
Check and raise
Aces against cowboys?

Poker Terminology

And what does Big Daddy bet?
Big Daddy bets...
I'm all in
I'll pay to see what you got
I'll bite
I'll pay to see 'em
Taking care of the tourists
You're looking around like building buyers
Dragging the occasional pot
That's good pot
The final table
Your Ali-like return to the ring?
Pulled a card out of my ass
Take each other's rolls
The telltales
Facial ticks

A hand over the mouth
A hand on the back of the neck
Nervous fingers
The way a cigar is smoked
The way a cigarette is smoked
Throw in your cards the moment you know you
  can't win
Don't try to make a hand out of it
It's noble work you're doing
So who wants to play some cards?
The rake
The drag
If a fish acts brave or strong, he's bluffing
If he acts meek, he has a hand
You think you got the hand to win?
Fold as soon as you know it's a loser
Play back at me
Tight but aggressive
Cut cards
River cards
Flops the nut straight
It dis-spirits you?
Three high cards to a flush
Nines or better wired
Play premium hands only
Play premium hands
Play it blind
Get the money in when you have the best of it
Quit yammering
Winners smile, losers say deal
Know when to release a shitty hand
Know when to release a crappy hand
Don't give anything away
Chew you up
Take your whole bankroll
Take your whole nest egg
Roll up your stake and go to Vegas
Full house

Full boat
Big blind
Small blind
One hundred dollars all day ($100 in total)
Aces rollin' over kings
Rolled up aces over kings
You made your boat
Did you make your boat?
I got the boat
Rich flounders
Rich sharks
It's immoral to let the tourists keep their money
Play all night
Check-raising tourists
Discard calls
Overhand run-ups
The double dupe
A real blood game
Blood game
Gettin' cold cards
Position raise
Can you handle the swings?
Life is on the wire, the rest is just waiting
If luck weren't involved, you might win every
     hand
No risk in this room
Chip placing
Trapping
Up to our old tricks
Back to our favorite stomping ground
Back to our favorite watering hole
Get paid off
Flush draw
Burn and turn
Always leave yourself outs
A lotta action
This is a lot of action
Are you carrying stacks of high society

High society
High society = $10,000 of chips
It was an easy clean
It was an easy take
A late night comeback like you read about
A late night comeback
Late night rally
Like you read about
He beat you straight up
Beat ya straight up
Check
Check check
Check-o-slo-vakia
Checkmate
Check it all the way
Check it—ba-va-ka-sha
Took a shot and missed… it happens
Bustin' you up all night
Flip 'em
He's betting into us
What's he got under there?
What's he holding down?
Lay with those names
Play with those names
Busted straight
Calculate odds on the spot
Fourth street (fourth card up in Texas Hold'em)
The river
Fifth street (River card; Last card up in Hold 'em)
Towers of checks
Chip count
The outstanding tough beat
Just lost to a slightly better hand, that's all
Cowboys bow to bullets
If it's good enough to call, you gotta be raising
It ain't almost poker
I was sure he was folding

Comes away with the whole pot

Burn cards

Suited pair

Off suit

Play to see the flop

Get to the turn or the river

Jump on board the train

We can handle that (calling a bet)

Trips win it (3-of-a-kind wins the hand)

Trip snowmen (3 eights)

River men

River winners

River players (people who usually win on the last card)

You're my hero for staying in with that hand

You have to pay a royalty for that patented play

Run the rabbit (see the cards anyway to see what would have happened)

Hell, pull the trigger (call the bet and stay in the game; or dare someone to make a bet)

Wireless / Web / Internet Terminology / On The Web / The Net

The Prompt

UNIQUE USERS, USER session lengths, Page views, Metrics—what's lies in store for us?

Wimax

Wide-Area Wireless

2.5G

3G

Bluetooth phones

Skype name

Skype me

AIM name (AOL Instant Messenger Name)

Packets

Acronym Soup

HTTP (Hyper Text Transer Protocol)

LAN (Local Area Network)

WLAN (Wireless LAN)

PAN (Personal Area Network)

WAP (Wireless Application Protocol)

SMS (Small Messaging Service)

RFID (Radio Frequency ID)

QOS issue (Quality Of Service Issue)

DSSS (Direct Sequence Spread Spectrum)

RSS (Really Simple Syndication)

CDMA protocol (Code Divided Multiple Access)

GSM (Global System for Mobile)

GPRS (General Packet Radio System)

WPA (Wi-fi Protected Access)

VOIP (Voice Over Internet Protocol)

VPN (Virtual Private Network)

Open Source

J2ME (Java 2 Mobile Edition)

BREW (Binary Runtime Environment for Wireless—from Qualcomm)

Non-Open Source

SSID

Crossfire

IEEE ("I-triple E"; Institute of Electrical and Electronics Engineers)

802.11A (IEEE protocol)

802.11B (IEEE protocol)

802.11G (IEEE protocol)

Walled gardens (location-based, high-speed ports for broadband delivery in airports)

Last Mile problem

Back-of-the-envelope calculation

Flash banners not compatible with tech specs

Firewalls

Surface area of attack

Cryptic

Encrypted
Wireless bridges
Wireless broadband
Real-time
Contextual
Situational
Service-centric
Service deployment
Solution archicture
Digital identity layer
Heads-up display
Higher uptake in mobility
Intermittent connectivity
Software technology stack solution
That's right on point
Ringtones
Polyphonic ringtones
Wallpaper
Untethered world
Horizontal and vertical apps (applications)
Always on
Exceedingly important
Protocol-talking methodology
Speed and encryption
Foundational groundwork
Mouse potato
Teenile
Trade prominence for revenue split
This may be the right sh**y deal right now
Give us a flavor or a taste of what it is
Dotted quad (same as an IP number; example: 125.167.231.4)
Ruggedized (rubberized hardware to protect against drops and dings)
Chips and salsa (hardware and software)
Multi-modal issues
Social functionality
Better information at the point where it matters

Business benefits

Cohesive context

Mobile development tools

Live message swap (old school, early 1990s)

Swap code (old school, early 1990s)

Reference the click-through URL externally via HTML

Uniques (unique or first-time visitors to the site)

Proxy (security feature allowing you to use different resources)

Techies (prononunced "tekkies")

Enterprise resource management

Hits (site hits)

Field force applications

Integrate seamlessly

Legacy infrastructure

Ad hoc network

Outside the visible spectrum

Filtering and redundance algorithms

You can trade cycles for reliability

Streaming content (the sound or video that is played when accessible from a host site)

Broadband (Internet access with a higer bandwidth than dial-up)

The Internet (network of computers and networks talking to each other via fiber optic cables)

Internet access (the provision of connectivity to the Internet)

Intranet (private networks usually maintained by corporations for internal communications)

IP number (a unique number consisting of four parts separated by dots; every Internet machine has one)

2.4 GHz speed versus 5 GHz speed (the higher the frequency, the greater the data transfer speed)

Impression (the viewing of a creative element by a visitor to a web site)

Java (programming language that enables web pages to contain miniature grams)

Keyword (a word or phrase often used to focus an online chat)

Kilobyte (One thousand bytes; usually 1,024 bytes)

Last mile (broadband—cable, DSL, ISDN, etc.)

Link (an electronic connection between two web sites

Lightning-fast speeds

Logging on (entering onto the Internet)

Login (the account name used to gain access to a computer system)

Lurk (hanging out in a chat room without adding to the conversation)

Mbps (Megabit per second; one million bits per second)

Megabyte (One million bytes; one thousand kilobytes)

Navigating (traveling across the Internet)

Netiquette (the etiquette on the Internet)

Netizen (citizen of the Internet; someone who uses network resources)

Newbie (a new user to the Internet)

Offline (not currently connected to the Internet)

Online (connected to the Internet)

Pageview (a metric for measuring traffic including all content, images, and frames on a page)

Posting (putting messages on public electronic bulletin boards or on a newsgroup)

Query (a request for information, usually to a search engine)

Real time (events that happen virtually at that particular moment)

Router (a device that connects LANs)

Search engine (a tool for accessing information on the web that searches key words and topics)

Serial port (a plug on a computer for connecting an external device, such as a modem)

Spam (an inappropriate attempt to use a mailing list by sending unwanted messages to many people)

Sundowner (someone who stays up all night surfing the net)

Surf (hopping from page to page on the web)

T1 (a T-1 is a leased phone line that is a type of data circuit that allows for high bandwidth)

T3 (a T-3 is a leased-line connection capable of carrying full-screen or full-motion video)

Tags (used to format text in HTML)

The Net (slang term for the Internet)

Thread (a series of messages that make up a discussion on a particular subject)

Uncle Joe (a web site that consistently loads slowly)

Virtual (the environment on the Internet)

Web (slang for World Wide Web)

Web address (URL)

Hotlink (a favorite link of an Internet user)

Hotlist (a list of favorite links on a website)

Hyperlink (Clickable link in text or graphics on a web page that takes you to another place off the site)

More Acronym Soup

AFAIK (As far as I know)

AFK (Away from keyboard)

BRB (Be right back)

BTW (By the way)

CPC (Cost-Per-Click)

CPA (Cost-Per-Acquisition)

DART (popular ad server)

PDF (file for graphic use)

FTP (File Transfer Protocol)

TIFF file

GIF (Graphic Interchange Format; can be displayed on web browsers; pronounced "giff")

JPEG (Joint Photographic Experts Group; pronounced "jay-peg"; graphic format newer than GIF)

HTTP (HyperText Transfer Protocol; the format of te World Wide Web)

ISDN (Integrated Digital Services Network; high-speed dial-up connections to the Internet)

DSL (Digital Subscriber Line; copper loop transmission technology through a dedicated phone line)

IDSL (ISDN DSL)

IMHO (In my humble opinion)

IP (Internet Protocol)

ISP (Internet Service Provider)

IRC (Internet Relay Chat)

IM (Instant Messenger)

IM (Instant Messaging)

OSP (Online Service Provider)

MIB (Management Information Base)

MODEM (MOdulator DEModulator; device to connect your computer to a phone line for net talk)

MORF (Male OR Female)

MSO (Multiple System Operator; cable industry term; a company operating more than one system)

NAP (Network Access Provider; typically DSL-related)

NOC (Network Operations Center; centralized point of network management within large-scale network)

PPP (Point-to-Point Protocol)

RTF (Rich Text Format)

SDSL (Symmetric Digital Subscriber Line)

SOHO (Small Office / Home Office)

TCP/IP (Transmission Control Protocol / Internet Protocol; suite pf protocols that defines the Internet)

TTFN (Ta Ta For Now)

UI (User Interface)

URL (Uniform Resource Locator; used with the web as an address, e.g. http://www.*BusiBUZZ*.com)

VDSL (Very-high-bit-rate DSL; 25 to 50+ Mbps transmission over very short distances)

WAN (Wide Area Network; a computer or communication network that covers a geographical area)

LAN (Local Area Network)

HTML (HyperText Markup Language; coding language to create documents on the WWW)

WWW (World Wide Web)

UFI (User Friendly Interface)

GUI (pronounced: "gooey"; Graphical User Interface)

FAQs (Frequently Asked Questions)

VLAN (Virtual LAN; a network of computers that act like they are connected to the same wire)

ADSL (Advanced Digital Subscriber Line—high-speed transmission technology)

Boards (message boards)

Bugs (Errors)

Blogs (web logs; posted editorial or opinions)

Dirt road (slow connection to a web site)

Low upstream rate Avatat (a graphic that represents an individual in a virtual environment)

Backbone (high-volume primary data carriers that make up long-haul capabilities of the network)

Binary file (contains non-textual data that can contain graphics, sounds, or programs)

Binaries (what programs used to be referred to as)

Bit (either a 1 or a 0; the smallest unit of computerized data; Bandwidth measures bit per second)

Byte (A set of bits that represent a single character; 8 Bits in a Byte)

Body (the section where you enter text in an HTML document)

Attachment (file linked to an e-mail message)

Bps (Bits-per-second; measurement of how fast data is moved; 56K)

Bookmark (shortcut to a website that is saved on the desktop)

Broadband (the "always-on" Internet)

Browser (application used to view information via the Internet)

Chat (conversation on the Internet)

Chip (The place to store information on a computer)

Client (A web browser; software program that contacts and obtains data from another server)

Server (A computer or software package that allows a user to connect to it to use and share information)

Cookie (Small piece of information sent by a web server to be stored on a web browser and read back)

Cyberspace (the whole range of information resources available through computer networks)

Debug (to find and remove errors (bugs) from a program or design)

Digerati (a group of people that seem to be knowledgeable or "in the know"about the digital revolution)

Domain name (unique name that serves as an address to identify and define an Internet site on the net)

Download (process by which a file can be retrieved by a distant computer and transferred to another)

E-mail (electronic message sent to anyone with an e-mail account)

Feeds (live lines from a data source such as a news service)

Firewall (A security barrier placed between an internal computer network and the Internet)

Flames (Derogatory comments made online)

Flame war (Heated exchanges; when an online discussion degenerates into a series of personal attacks)

Flooded (what happens to an online mailbox when there is too much e-mail)

Gateway (a hardware or software set-up that translates between two dissimilar protocols)

Hackers (a computer programmer who breaks into other computers illegally)

Hit (a request from a computer to display a web page)

Home page (the Web page that your browser is set to when it starts up; main Web page of a business)

Netheads

Net rangers

Web rangers

User sessions

Sticky site

Sticky

Ping me back

Pingable

Pop-ups

Click-throughs

Skyscrapers

Banners

468x60 banner
234x60 banner
120x120banner
Buttons
Interstitials
Clocks
Domain name
Browser
Surfing
Cookies
Web counts
Web geeks
Burning money
The burn rate
Customer acquisition
Sponsorships
Branding
Co-branding
Portal
Online presence
Tracking
Server
Fast-acting and volatile medium
Path to profitability
Media Metrix
Comscore
IRI
E-mauling
How many web counts?
How many hits?
Impressions
Proxy
Contemporaries
Technofiles
Flash banners
Rich media expert
Tracking clicks

Flash tech specs
Sniffer code
Sample sniffer code
Rich media tech specs
B-Box
Flash file
Embedded into the flash file
It's not just buttons and banners
DART-enabled site
Thwart the spammers
Anti-spamming software
Computer glitches
Gremlins
Buggy system
Crunch code
Rich media
Fat pipe
High-speed access
:-) (happy sign)
Animated GIF
Archive
High downstream rate
Bandwidth

Exit / I Need To Leave / I Will Be Out Of Touch / Away

The Prompt

IF WE ARE going to make the meeting across town, we have to jet right now

If we don't want to finish ass out, and be the last ones to arrive, we need to bounce

The wheels have left the tarmac, and we are en route to arrive shortly

I have a hard stop at 3pm, so we need to wrap this up

I Have To (fill-in-the-blank) By (a certain time):

Bail
Bag
Bounce
Boat
Book
Jet
Skate
Step
Bolt
Hop
Jump
Break
Split
Scram
Amscray
Vamoose
Skedaddle
Head out
Hit the trails
Be wheels up
Make like a baby and head out
Blow this joint
Blow this popsicle stand
Make like a tree and leaf
Time to get out of the kiddie pool

What To Say When Leaving:

Peace. Out.
Here's to the journey
Here's to the struggle
Adios
Adios amigo
Hasta la vista
Hasta luego

Hasta manana (pronounced "man-yana")
Later days
Later
Late
Lates
Catch ya later
Catch ya
Make trails
Make tracks
Seeya
Seeya when I seeya
Seeya, wouldn't wanna be ya
Later gator
Seeya later alligator
After a while, crocodile
See you on the other side
Catch you on the flip side
I am Outtie (Audi)
I am Outtie 5000
I am Outtie Five Thowdy
Time to get out of Dodge
Happy trails
Time to depart en route
I am en route
Let's rock and roll
Let's rock
Let's roll
Let's blow this joint
Let's blow this dump
Wheels up
I'm off like a prom dress
I'm 10-7 (operations / security radio lingo)
I'm 7
I'm O-O-T-O (out of the office)
I'll be out of pocket for a while
I'm incommunicado
Signing off
Sign off

In transit
Exit stage left
Take a walk
Take a sojourn
Leave of absence
Peace be the journey
Journey
Godspeed the journey
Godspeed
Let me dump this call
I'm on final approach
Vanish
Bye-Bye
Bye
Out of the gate
Cut and run
Shalom
Au revoir
Sayonara
Sayonara, sucker
See ya in the next life
Don't let the door hit you on the ass on the way
    out
Golden parachute
Talk to you in the PM
Cool runnings
Have a good roll
Have a nice flight
Go offline
Log off
Please prepare for arrival and cross-check
Hit the hay
Hit the road
Let's get the show on the road
Hold down the fort
Pull up stakes
I'm solid gone, man
This is an A and B conversation, so C you later

Drugs (Cocaine)

WHY IS THIS in here, you ask? Because some people in business do drugs, people sometimes act like they are on drugs, or hypothesize that someone else is on drugs; they talk about people who do drugs, and that is why something got messed up; When they throw out these terms or accusations, or act like they are on them (and some are), here are the terms you will hear:

Blow

Bouncing powder

Yeyo

Magic bus

White lines

Nose Candy

Blow candy

Blowcane

Blow smoke

Blow blue

Booster

Bubble gum

Bunk (fake cocaine)

Gaffel (fake cocaine)

Nose powder

Candy cane

Marching powder

Bolivian marching
    powder

Powder

Yay-Yo

Puleeski

Dust

Glass

Go

Amp

Base

Baseball

Ball

Barbs

Beam me up Scottie

Banano

Bazooka

Belushi

Bernice
Bernie
Bernie flakes
Big C
Big bloke
Big flake
Big rush
Billie hoke
Blizzard
Rock cocaine
Rock coke
Coke
Cola
Dama blanca
Double bubble
Dreamdust
Devil
Dust devil
Diablo
Diablito
Drug of choice
Foo foo stuff
Foo foo dust
Foolish powder
Frisco
Frisco special
Frisco speedball
Friskie powder
G-rock
Ghost busting
Girl
Girlfriend
Glad stuff
Goofball
Gold dust
Happy dust
Happy powder

Happy trails
Heaven dust
Haven dust
Henry the Eighth
Hitch up the reindeers
Ice
Icing
Inca message
Jam
Jelly
Joy powder
Junk
Lace
Lady
Lady cane
Lady snow
Go on a sleigh ride
Mama coca
Mayo
The man
Mojo
Movie star blow
Paradise
Paradise white
Pearl
Peruvian flake
Peruvian lady
Powder diamonds
Press
Pimp
Pop
Racehorse Charlie
Ready rock
Rock
Roxanne
Rhino rinse
Schoolboy

Scorpion
Scotty
She
Snow
Snowball
Snowbird
Snowcone
Snowcaps
Snow white
Sniff
Snort
Street cred
Sleigh ride
Society high
Stardust
Star-spangled powder
T
Tardust
Toot
Turkey
White girl
White horse
White house
White lady
White powder
Whiz bang
Wildcat
Wings
Witch
Zip
Crank
Crack
Crackers
Charlie
C
Coke bugs
C-dust

C-game
Cane
Candy
Candy C
California cornflakes
Carrie Nation
Chalk
Chippy
Chipper
Coconut
Coolie
Fluff
Flakes
Flaky
Florida snow
Miami snow
Tweekers
Tewts-a-rewsky
Tootsaroosky
Peaking
Champagne
Chasing the dragon
Get your own
Giddyup
Glitter
Gutter glitter
Heavy stuff
Incentive
Merk
Sugar
Snort
Space blasting
Speed
Speedball
Wacky dust
Weasel dust
Angie

Aunt Nora
Snow lights
Saltwater taffy

Connecticoke
Yellow sub

Drugs (Crystal Meth— "Methamphetamine")

Ice
L.A. Ice
Glass
Critty
Speed
Speed freak
Hot ice
Super ice
L.A. Glass
Quill
Tweek
Crystal
Christy
Christina
Chris
Crypto

Crank
Crink
Chalk
Croak
Bombita
Meth
Meth head
Meth monster
White cross
Yellow bam
Poor man's speedball
  (with heroin)
Teen-i-nsee
Teenage (one-sixteenth
  of a gram)

Drugs (Marijuana)

WHY IS THIS in here, you ask? Because some people in business do drugs, people sometimes act like they are on drugs, or hypothesize that someone else is on drugs; they talk about people who do drugs, and that is why something got messed up; When they throw out these terms or accusations, or act like they are on them (and some are), here are the terms you will hear:

Mary Jane
Spleef
Grass

Weed
Mary-ja-wanna
Joint

MJ	Jive stick
J	Jolly green
Pot	Joy smoke
Leaf	Joy stick
Buds	Juan Valdez
Bud	Kaya
Wacky weed	Kentucky Blue
Wake and bake	Killer Green Bud
Fire up	KGB
Light up	Kick stick
Ganja	Killer weed
Ganj	Kumba
Gunga	NoCal Sensimilla
Grass	Sensemilla
Man-ja	Senz
Funny stuff	Sen
Giggle weed	Sezz
Sparky	Skunk
Sugar weed	Siddi
Stems	Spark it up
Herb	Laughing grass
Reefer	Laughing weed
Root	Light stuff
Burn	Loaf
Bammy	Lobo
Buddha	Love boat
Cess	Love weed
Chillums	Panama red
Collieweed	Pack
Hash	Pack of rocks
Hash brownies	Pakistani black
Hash-ish	Panama cut
Indo	Panama gold
Jane	Panatella
Jay smoke	Rainy day woman
Jay	Rasta weed
Jive	Rockets

Rose marie
Seeds
Sweet Lucy
Tex mex
Tea party
Thai sticks
Torch up
Twistum
Twist
Wheat
Wooly blunts
Woolies
Wetdaddy
Yellow submarine
Yen pop
Yerba
Zambi
Crazy Eddie
4-20
Four twenty
Fry sweet
Candy blunt
Muggles
Peace weed
Sticky green buds
Phillies Blunt
Blunts
Parsley
Pocket rocket
Potten bush
Pretendo
Primo
Puff, puff, pass
Zombie weed
Acapulco gold
African black
African bush

Airplane
AK-47
Ash
Aunt Mary
Bale
Bash
Black Bart
Black ganja
Blanket
Blue sky blonde
Blonde
Blueberry
Blunt
Bomber
Bone
Boo
Bubbleberry
Burn one
Burnie
Cam trip
Cambodian red
Canadian black
Cannabis
Cannabis tea
Catnip
Cheeba
Chiba Chiba
Cheeo
Citrol
Cocoa puff
Colorado cocktail
Colombian
Crying weed
Ragweed
Goofball
Kind bud
Green bud

Puff the magic dragon
Captain Jack
Macon
Magic smoke
Manhattan silver
Mary and Johnny
Mexican brown
Mexican red
Mighty mezz
Monty
Moota
Mother
Mow the grass
Ding
Dinkie dow
Donna wanna
Donna Juanita
Dope
Roll a joint
Roll the bone
Dry high
Endo
Smoke some endo
Flower
Flower tops
Fly Aeromexico
Fry daddy
Gasper stick
Gasper
Happy cigarette
Hawaiian
Maui wowie
Maui wauie
Contact buzz
Contact high
Ditchweed
Gunney
Hit

Hemp
Hydroponic pot
Hay
Herb
Herb and Al (marijuana
   and alcohol)
Hay
Hit the hay
Hocus
Hot stick
Giggle smoke
Gimmie
Gold
Gold star
Golden leaf
Good butt
Grass brownies
Moocah
Shotgun smoke
Sticks
Super grass
Canadian super grass
Super weed
Tiajuana
TJ
Toak
Wacky terbacky
Throat bomb
Nico weed
Lung rocket
Coffin nail
Tonsil fire
Fire
Fry
Get a gage up
Get the wind
Griff

Drugs (Heroin)

Horse
Sweet Jesus
Smack
Mister Brownstone

H is for horse
Brother
Harry Jones
Heavy stuff
Schmack
Score
Sh**
Sleepwalkin'
Speedball
Super flu
Chick
China white
Chinese heroin
Cotton shooter
Judas
King Kong
Chasing the dragon
Chasing the tiger
Dancing with Mister Brownstone
Mister Brownstone
China cat
Chinese red
Daytime
Dip and dab
Do up
Floating
Goods
Ack ack (Asian slang)
Angel food
Red chicken (Chinese heroin)

Nixon
Belly habit
Black tar heroin
Blue velvet
Party from the people
Pineapple
Tease and pies
Tease and blues
Teddies and betties
Bad bundle
Bad seed
Belushi
Birdie powder
Big H
Big Harry
Black stuff
Black tar
Bomb
Bonita
Boy
Bozo
Brick gum
Brown crystal
Brown sugar
Bundle
Capital H
Courage pills
Crown crap
Dirt
Dogfood
Dope
Dooley
Dust
Dyno
Eightball
Eighth
Ferry dust

Flea powder
Golden girl
Good H
Good and plenty
Goofball
Gravy
Galloping horse
Kentucky Derby
Hairy
Hero
Hard candy
Hell dust
Him
Hombre
Honey white
Hot dope
Antifreeze
Atom bomb
A-bomb
Aunt Hazel
HRN
H-caps
Jolly pop
Jones
Joy flakes
Karachi
Lemonade
Load
Mexican horse

Mexican mud
Mojo
Moonrock
Mud
Muzzle
Oil
Old Steve
P-dope
P-funk
Poppy
Powder
Rambo
Reindeer dust
Red eagle
Salt
Skid
Sleeper
Slime
Spider blue
Stuff
Whack
White boy
White junk
White nurse
White horse
Witch hazel
Chiva
Cheva

Drugs (Places / Equipment / Paraphernalia)

Places
Crack house
Crack den
C-joint
Coke bar

Base house
Coke den
Miami highrise
Highrise
Low lounge

Equipment / Paraphernalia

Bong
Peace pipe
Load (25 bags)
Hookah pipe
B (amount to fill a
    matchbox)
Base pipe
Crack pipe
Hookah
Hubbly bubbly
Bag
Dimebag
Nickelbag
Deucebag
Spoon (¹⁄₁₆ ounce)
Matchbox (¼ ounce or
    6 mj cigarettes)
Horn
Tin (container for mari-
    juana)

Toke
Roach clip
Roach
Taste
Line
Rail (single dose)
Scale
Shaker Baker Water
Torch cooking
Blowtorch
Butane
Kitchen flame
Body packer
Tap the bags
Cook down
Cook
Bindle (small packet of
    drug powder)

Drugs (People)

Supplier
Pusher
Connection
Hook-up
Player
Distibutor
Intermediary
Cartel twice removed

Balloon
Pimp
Snowbird
Paperboy
Beeper
Handler
Parker (does not
    share)

Fight Time / Bring It On / Somebody Wins, Somebody Loses

Fighting / There Will Be A Fight / An Explosive Situation

The Prompt

Y OU WANNA THROW hands? There's nothing like a good ol' fashioned street fight
You better bring your big boy suit, pull out your rules for brawling… and come out swinging

The cannons are rolling around on the deck
I heard shots fired
It's the Hatfields and the McCoys all over again
The townies and the gownies
The snotty bluebloods against the country bump-
     kins
The sharks and the jets
Us versus them
Let's get it on
It's go time
Get ready to rope-a-dope
Dog fight

You wanna drop the peaches?
Drop the peaches
You wanna go?
It's brawl time
Prepare to bloody the knuckles
Crack the knuckles
Batten down the hatches
Better watch out for that blindside hit
Watch out for the haymaker
Sucker punch
Get your goat
Bazookas are honed in on me
The devil finds work for idle fists
What's the deal?
Is there a problem, officer?
We gotta problem?
Anyone, anyplace, anytime
I'll lick any man in the house
Hot under the collar
Hot and bothered
Roll up the sleeves
Get out the iodine
Rumble city
Can we take a punch?
A sock in the kisser
Blood will spill
The drinks will flow, and the blood will spill
Come out swinging
Sharpen the cutlery
You better grow eyes in the back of your head...
    because you won't know when it's coming
Rally the troops
Throw hands
Let us fling
We take all comers
Bucklin' down
The full-on beat down
Prep the trenches

Tighten up the chin strap
Tighten up the helmet
A real grinder
Fisticuffs
Someone's trying to pull rank
Someone's trying to big-time you
Lower the boom
A knock-down, drag-out
Called on the carpet
This is a pretext for war
Those are fightin' words
Those are feudin' words
A material breach
Punch your lights out
Punch your ticket
You'll get yours
Knuckle sandwich
Deploy the system
Egging him on
His ass is grass
Sock it to 'em
Punch 'em right in the kisser
Hit 'em high
Take 'em out
Sweep the knee
Blood in the water
Hold on to your lunch pail
Add fuel to the fire
Fire the flare gun
We have a situation
Get your coconut cracked
Get your cranium cracked
Hullabaloo
Commotion
Grind through
Fan the flames
Get into a scrape
It's raining cats and dogs

It's coming down in sheets

There is a deterrent effect, but only to certain limitations... after that, just beat his ass

With any bully, you have to walk up and punch 'em in the mouth

Like dropping a match in a barrel full of gunpowder

We've been through the wars

You mess with the bull, and you get the horns

Second-stage power alert

It was a rabbit punch... it came out of nowhere

Throw the haymaker

Silence is the ultimate escalation

Just BAQ (beat ass quick)

Beat you upside the head

Get into a real pissing contest

Muddy the waters

Jamming the bubba

Belt buckle to belt buckle

Puffed-out chest to puffed-out chest

Catfight

A carpetbombing

Take the hill

Homicidal violence expected

Pick and choose your battles... or just battle

It is not between you and me, we are just soldiers

Nip it in the bud before there's a big ol'problem

Pull in the leash on that one... she's not party-trained

Just ask yourself if that's the hill you want to die on? (is that the battle to fight?)

Get ready for the firefight

Open up a real can of worms

Pissing off the fireants is never a good idea

Be ready to fall on the sword

Soldiers of the war

When push comes to shove

Wanna take it outside?
Take it outside
Put the gloves on
Take the gloves off
Kick your butt
Kick your ass
Whoop your ass
That's life in the big city
Let 'em duke it out
Let 'em phone call it out
Give him a beatin'
Beat 'em down
Kick 'em to the curb
Bitchslap 'em
Make 'em your bitch
Shoot on sight
Smack talk
Smack chatter
The trash talkin' is potent
Verbal jabs
Verbal sparring
What's your answer, if anything?
Don't let him get under your skin
Don't let him get inside your head
I'm gonna drop you like a bad habit
I'm gonna drop you on your wallet
Get into a punch-up
Get kinged (punched)
King hit (sucker punched)
A shot to the snot locker
Fire a shot across their bow, and let them know
	we mean business
Mean business
Taken without a fight
Taken without them firing a shot
Here comes the shock and awe approach
Ruffle your feathers
Texas stand-off

Get into a tussle
Staredown
Extract some attitude
Let's see a rebuttal
No holds barred
It's anything goes
Cage match
Sweep the knee
Brass balls
Can we take a punch
It's on
Gotta fight for it
No hard feelings
It bothers me big-league
Ask for maximum restraint
Take them to task
C'mon guy (pronounced "come on, guy")
Bust out the whoopin' stick
Fighting tooth and nail
Well, there you go
Don't pull any punches
Getting into a scrape (British; UK—getting into a fight)
Good old fashioned street fight
Knock-down, drag-out fight
Slugfest
Rubber match (a fight or match to settle the score)
Settle the score
Never pick a fight with someone who buys ink by the barrel
A dogfight will ensue
Resigoo from the fight
Patience is wearing thin
Trouble spots
Flare ups
Hot spots
Batten down the hatches

Take 'em down hard
He must go down, and he must go down hard
Ride it out
Clip 'em
Bang heads
Knock heads
Bear down
Ass over tea kettle
Rough patch
Paint the target
Mount an attack
Pin 'em down
Bust some heads

Cutdowns / Insults / Putdowns / Comebacks / Insinuations

The Prompt

ALL OF THESE would be good for ruffling someone's feathers and getting their dander up:

There is a party in your mouth and everybody is
    coming
You are so small potatoes
Did you just fall off the turnip truck?
Well, it just proves that no one gets too old to learn
    a new way of being stupid

You've been relegated to right field (a demotion
    or a stepdown)
You are just a pawn of the game
You are a little slow on the uptake
You are not too quick on the uptake
Stand on your toes, it's going over your head
Did you go to school on the big bus or the little
    bus?
You are thinking and walking in loose granular
We'll egg you on
How 'bout a round of verbal jabs?

A little slow on the uptake
Ready to spar?
Wanna take it outside?
Time for a little trash-talkin' potency?
Some people smack talk, you smack chatter
You are merely rank and file
Errand boy
Order taker
Crash and burn
Behind the times
Bamboozled
Like ugly on an ape
You are a walking disorder
Dementia
You are a PBS mind in an MTV world
Cut me some slack
Fumble
And your point is?
Whatever
The light at the end of the tunnel might be a freight
    train coming your way
Your remarks are slightly obnoxious but some-
    what amusing
We will keep you around for the entertainment
    value you unknowingly provide
Try to pick us a winner (when someone is pick-
    ing their nose)
Try to pick us a Ford (when someone is picking
    their nose)
A lateral move is still down a half-notch
If you park here tonight, your car will be recycled
You are higher than domed-roof scaffolding
You're the kind of guy who likes to piss into the
    wind, don't you?
Stop doing things so ass-backwards
Doing the right thing in reverse
What you need is a sock in the kisser
He is no rocket scientist

His elevator does not make it all the way to the observation deck

The angle of the dangle equals the heat of the meat

Who is steering the ship?...it's not you

Don't get caught sitting on your hands

I like you... you remind me of when I was young and still stupid

You are validating my inherent mistrust of strangers

I see you've set aside this special time to humiliate yourself in public

I'll try being nicer if you'll try being smarter

I'm already visualizing the duct tape over your mouth

The fact that no one understands you does not mean that you're an artist

This is pure bush league

Bush league

Any connection between your reality and mine is purely coincidental

What am I... flypaper for freaks?

I'm gonna drop you like a bad habit

I'm gonna drop you on your wallet

I'm not being rude... you're just insignificant

You sound reasonable... therefore, it's time for me to up my medication

Who, me? I just wander from room to room like all the other lemmings around here

And your crybaby, whiny-butt opinion would be...?

Want some more crybaby soup?

You... off my planet !

Does your train of thought have a caboose?

Are you out of it?

Is your head even in the game?

Get your head out of your ass

Leave it out, will ya?

Whatever kind of look you were going for… you missed

I'm trying to imagine you with a personality

Too many freaks… not enough circuses

Nice perfume / cologne… must you marinate in it?

You are depriving some village of an idiot

Frosty

You are out of the box… and off this planet

A total glamour don't

A fashion no-no

Plain Jane

Very plain Jane

Vanilla

The tail is wagging the dog

That's just putting the cart before the horse

That's simply ass-en-nine

They do not know sh** from Cheyenne

They do not know sh** from Shinola

Only a Sicilian can tell you your face is dirty

How does that grab ya?

Stick that in your pipe and smoke it

Try that on for size

You're full of piss and vinegar

You're like a bull in a china shop

Looks like someone woke up on the wrong side of the bed

You have a case of the morbids

I wouldn't piss in your ear if your brain was on fire

I don't give two hoops in Hades

You unmitigated ass

I'll wreck your day in a helluva hurry

I'll mess up your day

Sarcasm is just one more service we offer

Everyone has a photographic memory, some don't have film

He who laughs last thinks the slowest

A fashion faux pas (pronounced "fo-paah")… what were you thinking?

Electroencephalographically challenged

You always seem to be running late… did your ancestors arrive on the Juneflower?

In these enlightened times when hubby is at work and you are sitting on your butt

Don't think for a nanosecond that we won't pull this off the table

You are colder than the boobs of a witch doing pushups in the snow

We'll see what happens when we push a little harder

Don't get yellular with me

Like I care

Whatever

Pull on this leg, it plays Jingle Bells

Look, it's Mister Laughs (sarcastic tone)

Quit wasting your time in the kiddie pool

I'll take your roll

A little blue humor?

Are you working blue?

A little black humor?

You'd chase a dog off a gut wagon

You'd lag behind on a coffee break

He ain't a factor

Sheep

Simpletons

Pleebs

Grognardians

Knuckledraggers

Worker bees

Ants

The people in flyover country

Lemmings

Hey, titular head, knock it off

Limited gray matter

Get out of my grill

Face time

Nice mug

Nice face… did your neck just vomit

He swapped legs with a jaybird and got cheated
out of his ass

Piss-ant

Slimeball

Sleazeball

Sleazebag

Panzy

Peckerhead

Doutsche bag

Bitch boy

Pleeb

Lemming

Blame / Blame It On Someone / Disgust / Stupidity

Silver Bullets

Blame is bouncing around like spit on a
griddle

Time to play the blame game

He is no rocket scientist

There's a whole lotta finger-pointing going on

They suck

It blows

He's a finger-pointer

A lot of finger-pointing

A lot of "woe is me" going on

I can spit anywhere and hit an idiot

Get a handle on it

Pass the buck

Accept full responsibility

Sidestep it all, why don't you?

Shift the responsibility

Sh** rolls downhill

Water off a duck's back… but I can't worry about it

It bounces off me and lands on you

Just get it done next time

Check for a paper trail

Fool me once, your fault, fool me twice, my fault

It's always the other guy's fault

Mea culpa

Mea maxima culpa

Errors have been made… others will be blamed

The devil finds work for idle hands

There's a built-in fudge factor

Fudge factor

That is just plain stupid

Stee-yupid

Rounding errors

Blame your fall on the carpet snakes

What's the deal?

Where's the scent? I don't get where we lost it.

Vapor lock… where did we go wrong?

Third place is third place no matter how you slice it

Second place is still the first loser

Show me a good loser and I'll show you a loser

His elevator does not make it all the way to the observation deck

I guess when things go wrong, you just pass the
   buck

The Goldilocks factor… it's either too hot or too
   cold but never just right

If we win, we win as a team, but lose… and YOU
   guys didn't do enough to get it done

You don't go teach your grandmother how to
   suck eggs

Contemporary Wartalk

The Prompt

DECAPITATION STRIKE, TROOP buildup, Human
shields, Flush out the insurgents. Looking
back, which terms and phrases will we remember
from the waged war on terror?

Regime forces
Coalition forces
Decapitation strike
Mowing down innocent victims
Troop concentrations
Stop the insurgents
Bunker shots
Threat condition
War plan
Attack plan
Fight tooth and nail
Suicide vests
Orange alert (severe)
Yellow alert (alerted)
Condition Orange
Condition Yellow
Bring in the artillery
Bring in the Bradleys
Send in some RPG's
RPGs (rocket-propelled grenades)
Let the play develop

Let it play out
The Brass rings
The top brass
Battallion
Assistance team
Border control
Self-rule
Decisive force
Free and independent Iraq
External aggression
Internal subversion
Roadside bombs
Powergrab
Suspected foreign fighter
Enemy gunfire
This is serious business
Find the common ground
Firm resolve and clear purpose
Enemy action
Attacks, kidnappings, and beheadings
Stability creep
Stabilizing
Get the birds in the air
Green zone
Red zone
Hot spots
The heart of Baghdad
Baghdad
Fallujah
Tikrit
North Korea
The Gaza Strip
Gaza
Win the spin
War rooms
If you gotta big pitch, you had better throw it
    now

Pocket veto
It died in committee
Tag it and bag it
Mobilize forces
Wiretaps
Ground sensors
Cell phone intercepts
Elaborate communication intercept systems
Slow to anger
The crucible of war
The black eye of war
The price of victory is high, but the price of defeat
    is higher
Declassify the information
Intense 30-day period of scrutiny
Phased withdrawal
Airspace configurations
Iraqi sovereignty
Field test requirements
Our interests in the region
A flawed policy wrapped in illusion
Post-Combat Stress Disorder
Stress test techniques

Winning / Losing / Ballgame / Game Over

Silver Bullets
You ONLY LOSE when you stop trying to win
I got all the hits and stingers (winners and
    losers in gambling)
Pile it on and win big
The little guy can be a megaloser

A "W" is a "W" is a "W"
Winning ugly is still winning
Winning breeds more winning

Winning is a habit
The big winner
It sure beats the hell out of losing
Him or me
Western justice
Won by a landslide
Landslide victory
One-sided victory
Killed 'em
Slayed 'em
Cakewalk
We won, fair and square
We won, lock, stock, and barrel
Winners smile, losers say deal
Decisions are made by those who show up
Check the win-loss record
Second place is the first loser
Sucking wind in a bad way
Megaloser
You got the Lucy
A major drubbing
Drubbing
Run up the score
Overmatched
Smoked
Smacked

Beat down
Creamed
Battered
Lambasted
Thrashed
Blasted
Boatraced
In the crosshairs
Show me a good loser, and I'll show you a loser
Defeat is a badly disguised opportunity
In the end, it's not the years in your life that count,
    but the life in your years
Bags 'em
Party foul
Reverse commute
That win was flagship
Two on a trot (UK—British); for two wins in a
    row

Nutballs, "Do-overs," Yawners, Blowhards, and Axe-men

Crazy

The Prompt

THE GUY HAS lost his marbles
He's not playing with a full deck... the lights are on, but no one's home
His elevator does not make it all the way to the observation deck
He is full-on loco

Take your meds
You need your medication
You should never have stopped your medication
Loco, Esse
Loco
Dementia
Out of it
Crazy people
Crazy old bird
Crazy bird
Whack job
Certified whack-o
Loony bin
Loon
Loony birds
Loonies
Nut house
Nut case
Nut ball
Nut factory

Flaky

Space cadet

He's a Cuckoo clock (pronounced "koo-koo clock")

Cuckoo for Cocoa Puffs (pronounced "koo-koo")

Cuckoo (pronounced "koo-koo")

Out to lunch

In his own world

Go postal

He's a real screwball

Screwball idea

Screwball

Cock-a-mamie idea

The wilding-type

Monkey business

You're a few sandwiches short of a picnic

What colors are the skies in your world?

What are you smoking?

I see fiery balls of gas

Bust out the straitjacket

Call Bellevue

Have you been in solitary?

All over the map

Opened up Pandora's box

Very hit and miss

A severe case of schizoid actions

Bats in the belfry

Driving in the fast lane with the blinker on

No one gets too old to learn a new way of being stupid

Out there where the buses don't run

You're a walking disorder and off the beaten path to boot

You are higher than domed-roof scaffolding

Do we need to fit you for a straitjacket?

Throw It Away / Dismissive / Discharge / Do Over / Done

The Prompt

CHUCK IT AND start over
Lock it up
Cut it loose
Water under the bridge

Fait accompli (a done deal)
Lost cause
War of attrition
Wave the white flag
Say uncle
Dead to rights
Ka-put
Stick a fork in it, it's done
Game over
Dump it
Hey, … what are you gonna do?
A whole new ballgame
Call it a day
Water over the dam
Smile, nod, and regroup
Sew it up
Tag it and bag it
Pull out the sutures and close it
Scalpel, sutures, scissors, done
A turkey shoot
Up in smoke
Give 'em a fruit basket and call it a day
Put the period at the end of the sentence
Make them crumble and crinkle it over the phone
Redline it
Flatline
Pull the plug

Deep-six it
86-it (cancel it)
Spilt milk
We have other fish to fry
We have other more pressing items
Let's nip it in the bud
Punt
Done deal
Seal the deal
Close the deal
Late scratch
Put a stake in the ground
Draw a line in the sand
Beating a dead horse
Vestigial (get rid of it)
The finality of it
It's toast
It's so last year
It's history

Boring / Long / Drawn Out / Ordinary / Vanilla / Plain Jane

Silver Bullets

I AM BORED out of my mind
The meeting was a total snore
I should have brought my pajamas
Somebody must have slipped me a mickey

Cookie-cutter
Boilerplate
A total yawn
A yawner
An eye-roller
Bor-rrring
It rocked me to sleep
It induces quick sleep
That was fine for a nap
Vanilla statements
Vanilla documents
Vanilla extract
Vanilla
Plain Jane
Thanks for the warm milk
Just give me some warm milk
Thanks for the nap
Pleasant dreams
Sweet dreams
Dead brain mode
Generic
Throw some coffee in my eyes… it'll work faster
Let's just say that I need to wake up
It was a nice rest

Blunt-edge, not cutting-edge
Blunt edge
An elongated process
Longer lead than usual
It's template
Same ol' same ol'
And I thought a red-eye was flying coast-to-coast
    overnight… this meeting gave me red-eye
Pink eye, in this case could just be conjunctivitis…
    but probably it was the speech
I am experiencing some patchy coastal fog
I was in "REM" stage during the meeting (rapid
    eye movement stage within sleep)
Glance at it when you get bored with someone
    else's presentation
It's like trying to read an organic chemistry text-
    book with baited breath

Bragging / Perceived Power / Brag And Boast

Silver Bullets

ALL HAT AND no cowboy
He is all brag and boast
He's a kiss the ring kind of guy
He thinks he's all that and a bag of chips

A little too full of himself
All brag and boast
All hat and no cattle
All cowboy and no giddyup
All foam and no beer
A lot of hot air
A lot of talk and a badge
You're all talk
All that
A real windbag
Ear bore
That championship swagger
Swagger

Narcissistic in his approach
He thinks he's the don
He thinks he's hot sh**
He thinks he hung the moon
He thinks he's God's gift
He thinks his sh** doesn't stink
There is no method to the madness
He is quite the worldbeater, isn't he?
He's got pull
Blowing smoke
Lip service
That's prison strong
Best in the West
Beast from the East
Swagger?, that's what we call that bein' from Texas
It's all happy camper syndrome… or at least that is what you tell everybody
He opens up his mouth and takes credit for everything

Busy / Not Enough Time To Get It All Done / Multi-functional / Multi-tasking / Stressed

Silver Bullets

I DO NOT have enough bandwidth to deal
You cannot do the minute waltz in thirty seconds
I am busier than the only island whore on Marine payday
Busy as all get out

Busy bees
Busy beavers
Up to my ears in alligators
Zero bandwidth
Out of bandwidth

Too many things on my plate
My plate is full
The deck is full
The flightpad is full
I've had it up to here
Omni-directional
Multi-faceted
Utility player
Wigged
Edgy
Strapped
Tapped
Bent

Bent out of shape
Maxxed out
Maxxed
Amped up
Incredabusy
Crushing workload
Buried
Armed with information overload
You can juggle too, can't you?
Need to come up for air
I can't see my way clear
Burning the candle at both ends
When I have some free time… to quote a joke
Workin' away… emphasis on "away"
Busier than a one-legged man in an ass-kicking
    contest
Busier than a one-armed paper hanger with the
    hives
I need more than two minutes… I am not Roger
    Staubach, John Elway, or Joe Montana

Make Cuts / Cutbacks / Reduction In Force / Right-sizing

Silver Bullets
The axe has fallen
Lower the boom
Marching orders
Walking papers

Drop the hammer
We're gonna have to let you go
Make deep cuts
Outsourced
Downsized
Eliminated
Unfunded
Career changed
Layoff time
Off to the gallows
Internal cuts
Overlap
Head count reduction
Decommission
De-install
Compromised
Early retirement
Excessed

De-hired
Involuntary release
You just slit your own wrist
You just slit your own throat
You just fired yourself
You just eliminated yourself from competition
Demoted
Not part of next year's business plan
Sent down a league
Lop off some heads
Run the numbers and lose some people
What's the kill code?
It's vestigial (can get rid of it)
On final approach for employee X
Rendered useless to the company
Right-size the company
We've been through the wars
Relegated to right field (stepdown)
The tribe has spoken
You've been voted off the island
A lateral move is still down a half-notch
Find the pick of the litter... toss the rest
Pink slip

Head Count / Staffing / H.R. / Depthchart / People Plan For The Backfill

The thankless daily HR grind of rearranging the files and the sock drawer

The department of redundancy department

People plan for the backfill

HR sleaze

Just waiting around for the next PC conference (Political Correctness)

Run some numbers and find out who is the weakest link?

The 52-hour work week (average work week)

Standard HR questions

The qualifier interview

They get snowed all the time

Do the due diligence

Check the references

Reference calls
Lodge a complaint
File a complaint
Write someone up
Write 'em up
Write the reviews
Have a sitdown
Have a clarification session
The benefits people
HR slime
Attend to the benefits
Plan the holiday parties
Severance packages
Cutbacks
Downsizing
Rightsizing
We need to talk
Time for a sit down
Pink slip
Weakest link

Workplace Items To Be Directed Elsewhere

Questions
Comments
Concerns
Complaints
Frustrations
Irritations
Aggravations
Insinuations
Allegations
Accusations
Contemplations
Consternations
Input

Do It Fast, And Get It Done, … But Be Careful And Watch Your Back

Fast Decision-Making / Decision-Making / Force A Decision / Reach A Decision / Urgent Attention

Silver Bullets

YOU NEED TO make a decision PDQ (pretty damn quick)

It's time to sh** or get off the pot

You have to decide relatively immediately… either fish or cut bait

Make the call

Drive-by management
PDQ (Pretty Damn Quick)
A "PDQ" decision
Actionable advice
It's a "go" job
Can we go to green?
Get to green
Greenlight
Take the wheel
Right the ship
Steer the ship
Ramrod the cattle drive
ASAP or sooner
Post-haste
Urgent or sooner
Go with the hot hand
Go with whoever has the hot hand

Stick with what brung ya
Stick with what got you here
Do-able recos (recommendations)
Off to the gallows
Chug-a-lug
Chug it
Power chug
Power down
Spring into action
Turn the corner
Strike while the iron is hot
Just give me a yes or no
Let's go, chop-chop
Chop-chop
Lickety-split
Make the call
Decision-time
Faster than a cheetah with a hot foot
Let's move into the left lane
What does your gut tell you?
Green light the incursion
Split-second decision
Executive decision
The power to say yes
Fish or cut bait
You have broad latitude in the decision process
Power to greenlight an idea
Toss the coin
Make the decision to course-correct
Hot off the press
White hot
In the here and now
En fuego
Political hot potato
Call-to-action
7-10 split
Pull the trigger
Make it so

Follow Through / Complete / Keep Things Moving

Silver Bullets
We just got it in under the wire
Who has the hammer to get it done?
Stick a fork in it… it's done… done deal
Case closed

If you want it done right, there is only one man
for the job
In spite of the clutter, I would still like to go for
it
You mess with the bull and you get the horns
En route
In transit
Follow up
Follow through
Follow through or die trying
Put some topspin on it
Come full circle
Under the wire
Just in the nick of time
In the nick of time
Run with it
Close it up
Finish it up
Wind down
Over and done with
Moved too far down the path at this point
Past the point of no return
No turning back
CYA (cover your ass)

Work It Out / Settle Down / Get Under Control / Cool Down

Silver Bullets

Flesh it out
Extend an olive branch
Cast your differences aside… and move on with your lives
Bury the hatchet

Get it over with
Like clockwork
Chill out
Be chill
Chill like big daddies
Deep breath
Ferret it out
Figure it out
Smoke the peace pipe

Expedite the process
Let's dial it down a notch
I'm going to speak soft, so listen hard
Let's turn down the volume just a tad
Pull in the reins on this one
Just close ranks and bond
Slow and steady wins the race
Show some composure
Forge ahead with educated guesses
Throw out a litany of ideas
Consider it all a do-over
More than one way to skin a cat
60 days to fix deficiencies
Temper the full effect
Don't botch the negotiation
After all, how much justice can you afford?
Clean up your house
Clean house
Swing for the fences
Ready for the storm surge
Level-five hurricane warning
Chill the fu** down
Chill the fu** out
Take a chill pill
Simmer down now
Drop a Valium
Take an Ambien

Be Careful With The Situation / Be Defensive / Conservative

Silver Bullets

YOU DON'T WAKE a snake to kill it
Exercise extreme caution
Don't get caught sitting on your hands
Don't paint yourself into a corner

Do not try to beard the lion in its den
Husbanding your money
Heads up
Show restraint
Sharpen your ears
Tighten up like your bank account
Stand sentry
Exhaust the possibilities
Tighten your belt, you starving artist
Throw caution to the wind
Don't paint yourself into a corner

Don't box yourself in by your own syntax
Exhaust administrative remedies
Hand holding
Touchy-feely
Watertight like a frog's ass
The devil finds work for idle hands
Make the budget work for you
Do not push the envelope
Check out for the traps
Check the pin placement
Measure twice, cut once
Safety net
Need palm print, retina scan, and urine sample
Proceed with caution
Exercise caution
We do not want any value-added that will impact
     the promotional budget
Make your dupes, so if the trapeze breaks, you
     have a safety net
Politically correct

Other Nuggets and Good Stuff

$$

by Jeff Powers
Marketing Superpower /
*   Account Management—*
*   Viacom Outdoor (formerly of G-Shock)*
*   (New York, New York)*

"Boobies, Sticks, and Stones"… the More Things Change, the More They Stay the Same.

IT ALL STARTS with boobies. It all ends with boobies. Yes, boobies. What a great word! Why? Because it has stopping power. I mean, it has real stopping power. And it also has a real, special meaning that people immediately understand. "Boobies" is part of *BusiBUZZ*. Throughout my

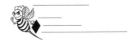

career, I have heard many words or phrases like boobies, and sometimes I have even coined a few myself. In either case, I am a believer in, and more importantly, a user of *BusiBUZZ*. In today's business climate, *BusiBUZZ* is a necessary tool for survival of the fittest. We have learned that we have to choose our moments wisely, and make our choice of words even more wisely.

When we were kids playing in a sandbox, we all used *BusiBUZZ*. "Sticks and stones may break my bones, but words will never hurt me." That's where *BusiBUZZ* started, as we chose our words and yelled them at the top of our lungs in the sandbox. Kids always stopped, listened, and took notice when they heard a word that had special meaning or a word they didn't really know. They would start to chant it, repeating it over and over again on their way home. "You're a booby! Yeah, you're a booby!! Jeff is a booby, Jeff is a booby!!! And then, the word spread. *BusiBUZZ* was born.

Have you noticed how the boardroom is not so different from the sandbox? The only difference is that instead of wearing our favorite Oshkosh overalls, we wear our power Brooks Brothers suits. Instead of building sand castles, we are creating houses of cards. *BusiBUZZ* is just another evolution of the English language; in short, extraordinary words used to describe ordinary things.

Too many times I have been in a brainstorming meeting with grown men and women, and a co-worker turns to a peer and says, "That idea sucks, you're a boob, a total boob." You've been there and you can't believe it. Did he just call him a boob? Are we back in the sandbox?

I was in a meeting once and the financial reports didn't look good. They actually were extremely disappointing; the sales forecast had crashed and burned because the national sales manager had inflated the numbers. (What else is new?) I heard someone in the room say, "Why do you have to be such a fake boob?" His numbers were inflated, yes, but unlike so many fake boobs, the sales manager wasn't really something you would look at with interest or desire.

Depending on your perspective the word "boobies" could be interpreted as "nuggets" or as "good stuff." I think Randy asked me to write this because I have been fortunate to learn, experience and excel at many different things throughout my career. And I have been more fortunate to have creative ideas and to see trends before they happened. My grandmother said, "You should learn something new every day." Well, I took that to heart, and I try to learn a new nugget or some other good stuff every day.

From candy land to toy land to the city that never sleeps (Lifesavers to Jakks Pacific to Citibank), *BusiBUZZ* is everywhere. I've worked on a myriad of big brands and product launches, and I've sat in on a lot of marathon meetings. Early in my agency career, when meetings began to drag on and on, I would request a "TV Timeout!" Yes, a TV Timeout. Back then, there were no TV Timeouts as there are in today's five-hour baseball games. Since we were in the business of making advertisements, I incorporated the phrase TV Timeout in lieu of a traditional commercial break. TV Timeouts can be powerful *BusiBUZZ* tools. Please use TV Timeouts appropriately, one for every 30-minute meeting, and two for every 60-minute meeting.

I met Randy years ago when I was the Marketing Director for G-Shock and Baby-G watches. We were negotiating what is now called "in-game branding." During our meeting, we were going back and forth, having a nice, gentle tug of war, when one of my Japanese co-workers asked, "What is the chance of success?" I replied simply, "it's like staying married." My Japanese friend smiled, while everyone else in the room gave a little chuckle. For him the odds of success were 100%, but we all knew what it meant, the chance for success was really 50/50. Yes, "staying married" is *BusiBUZZ*. As it turned out, when the meeting was over, my new friend and business associate Randy asked if I could give him a ride to the airport. "Sure, where are you going?" "I am getting married this weekend!" responded Randy. Funny, our business deals and our friendship have lasted longer than his marriage.

I am not a good writer, but I am an avid reader and admirer of great writers with an unbelievable command of the English language, to name a few—William Safire, George Vescey and Andy Rooney. In fact, one note in William Safire's rules for writers is, "Take the bull by the hand and avoid mixing metaphors." Well, when it comes to *BusiBUZZ*, Mr. Safire may be a little upset. As may, Andy Rooney, who is a practitioner of using proper English. He will probably do a bit on "*60 Minutes*" on how he heard about this horrific book called *BusiBUZZ*, and he will question why there are hundreds and thousands of great words in the English language and so why the heck do we need any more? Very simply, we really never leave the sandbox or stop saying boobies.

BusiBUZZ is not just limited to the words we speak. I am a big believer in txt msging. In fact, I spend most of my time, writing like this… thats a gr8 idea, very xcitin, i wood share it w/ sales, ill c u l8r, pls dont b late 4 our 8, n dont 4get 2 bring ur budgets. Many of these txt msgs will B the *BusiBUZZ* of 2moro.

Keep in mind, *BusiBUZZ* will always evolve… 2moro, the next day, in your next meeting, your co-worker will say something like "the flop," "the turn," or "the river" or some other poker term he picked up last night watching "Texas Hold'em." Or he might say, did you see So-And-So's boobies last night on celebrity poker. Like I said, it always comes back to one thing, boobies, other nuggets and good stuff.

Good People / Positive People / Preferred / Familiarity

Silver Bullets

GOOD EGG
SOS (someone special)
Short list
Pick of the litter

Top shelf
Good man
Smart cookie
One of us
Straight shooter
Stand-up guy
Man's man
He's the man
A-team
Salt of the earth
Mensch
He's the shed's sharp tool
He's an Irie man
You're a lock
He's Doctor Feelgood
Self-starter
He's a chum
Mister Fancy Pants
A sigh of relief
Player's coach
Coach's coach
Of that ilk
We are cut from the same global fabric
He's lived a little bit
Watchdog group

Bad People / Negative People / Not Preferred / Second String

Silver Bullets

B-TEAM
Second string
They do not know shit from Cheyenne
They do not know shit from Shinola

Has an air about him
He's a scrub
Scrubs
Scrappers
Bottom feeders
Hangers on
Sheep
Pleebs
Subs
Scabs
Newbies
Dweebs
Rooks
Frosh
Bootychumps
Dingleberries
Windbags
Losers
Scumbags
Sleazebags
Scum of the earth
Pondscum
Scummy
Greasy
Peckerheads
Snapperheads
Jerkies
Jerkwaters

He's a J'moke
The guy is "fugozzi"
Baddies
Trash
Dreck
Trailer trash
Slicksters
Hucksters
Snake oil salesman
Really bad element
Bad seeds
Demon seeds
Legbreakers
He's a real Joey Bagodonuts
Huey, Louie, and Dewey
Moose and Rocko
Adam Henry (a**hole)
He's from the firm of Dewey, Cheatem & Howe
He's from the firm of Dewey, Screwem & Howe

Salesmen / Barkers / Shills / Hucksters

Silver Bullets

Dynamiters (high-pressure stock salesmen)
Needlemen
Pitchmen
Dealmakers

Peddlers
Shoe peddlers
Hustlers
Moneymakers
Hip shooters
High-steppers
Gunslingers
Wolves

Carnival barkers
Product movers
Glib salespeople
Slick spinmasters
Faciltators
Deal cutters
Used car salesmen
Snake oil salesmen
Salesmen of sorts
Sellin' their snake oil
Ear bashers
Windbags
Yaks
Call boys
Account Reps
Reps
Account Execs
Shysters
Entertainers
Swag givers
Fronters (inexperienced stock sellers)
Coxeys (like "fronters"; front call men)
The Razz (high-pressure pitch)
Sell the wares
Peddle the wares

Retail Terminology / "Sales Speak"

Silver Bullets

WILL THEY TAKE any more product in… or do we need to wait until re-orders?
Where are we so far versus hitting our targets?
Fish where the fish are
He can sell a glass of water to a drowning man

Sell-through
Sell-in
Set up and catch-up

Pitch and follow-up
Pitch and catch
Purchase probability
Purchase intent
Nagging vendors
Buyer sleaze
Buyer scum
Cut the deal
Make a deal
Lock in a price
Lock in an order
Price protection
Well-oiled words
Handshake deal
Spike the sales
Show a spike
Move the needle
Write it up, fight it up
Ring the meter
Inflate the numbers
Quarter end deals
MDF's (Market Development Funds)
Co-op monies
Done deal
Write it up (done deal)
The goal is truly attainable
Fill rate (minimum inventory levels)
He can sell ice to the Eskimos
Open-To-Buy
I don't have any more Open-To-Buy (no budget left)
How's the sell-through?
The churn (cycle of sell-through)
How are the turns? (cycles selling a product through)
Sandbagging (purposely setting low expectations for goals that will be met)

We are like sailors pointing to the mark… and
    just trying our best to get there

Let's get on the same page and try to to work this
    out together

Our ideas are in concert with the corporate direc-
    tion

Hard Work / Try To Work Things Out / Tough It Out

Silver Bullets

THEY KNOW YOU'RE a hard worker when your
hands are brown and not your nose

Stick to it… keep your nose to the grindstone

Stay low, keep moving

Fles it out

Cut the mustard

Ferret it out

Ferret out the program

Fish or cut bait

Cut bait date

Sweat it out

Suck it up

Keep the focus

Stay competitive

Pencil-pushing

Bulldoze through it

Bite the bullet

Take it on the chin

Take it in the shorts

Heavy lifting

Block-and-tackle

The 52-hour work week (average work week)

The daily grind

Run some numbers

We don't need bodies, we need specialists

At least it's climatically desirable
Not planners but implementers
When the going gets tough, everybody leaves
When I have some free time… to quote a joke
There is a lot of heavy lifting involved
There is a lot of block-and-tackle that needs to
be done
People who are not afraid to roll up their sleeves
and get their hands dirty

Extra / Superfluous / No Effect / Unnecessary / Off-track

It has about as much impact as a postage stamp
Too many bells and whistles
Fluff and flab
Take it offline

Zero net effect
Offline
Off-track
Out of the ballpark
Outside the guidelines
Outside the lines
Inconsequential
Off the reservation
Flabby
Fluff
Fluff stuff
Fatty tissue
Too many extras
Not part of the meat

Postage stamp impact
Rollover stuff
Non-issue
Irrelevant
Away from what's
important
Tangential conversa-
tion
Tangential
Extraneous
Secondary
Tertiary
Icing but not the cake
Not critical path

Column 1-2-3 Game

T AKE ANY 3-DIGIT number and produce a phrase
that can be dropped into any report with a
sincere ring of decisive and/or knowledgeable
authority). No one will have a remote idea what
you said, but they are not going to admit it.

Example: #257 (systematized logistical projec-
tion)

#	Column 1	Column 2	Column 3
0	integrated	management	options
1	heuristic	organiza-tional	flexibility
2	systematized	monitored	capability
3	parallel	reciprocal	mobility
4	functional	digital	programming
5	responsive	logistical	scenarios
6	optional	transitional	time phase
7	synchronized	incremental	projection
8	compatible	third generation	hardware
9	futuristic	policy	contingency

Balls / Chutzpah "Hootz-pah" / Guts

Silver Bullets

You've gotta have sack for this business

Brass balls

Cuhones

Onions

The stones

The steel

Steel balls

Nads

The sand

The sand to do it

Jewels

Nuts

Game

Cujones

Huevos

Guayvos

Minerals

The sack

Sack up

Show some sack

Radja

Check yourself down there

Check inside your fly

Build Up Your Favors / Increase Your Chances / Chits / Favor Bank / Scoreboard Keepers

Silver Bullets

BUILD UP YOUR chits
Pile up the points
Build up the favor bank
Karma credits

I need a favor
Stockpile your nuts
Build up your chits
The Favor Bank
The Favor Scoreboard
Scoreboard keepers
Karma dividends
I owe you one
What goes around comes around
What comes around goes around
Let's barter favors
Radio Station WIIFM (What's In It For Me?)
I'm up one-nothing on the favor scoreboard
It's called the Potomac Two-step of political favor dancing
You scratch my back and I'll scratch yours

Even Money / Zero Sum Game / Stalemate / No Difference

Silver Bullets

NOTHING VENTURED, NOTHING gained
It's a wash
Even up
Even Steven

Even money
Break even
Broke even
Flatline
No blood, no foul
No blood
No foul
A good no call
No harm done
A tie
Game ended in a tie
A kiss your sister
We recovered our own fumble
All things considered, it's still zero-zero
Grind to a halt
At an impasse
Cat's game
Dead heat
Dead even
Peaks and valleys
Overmatched
Outmanned
Up and down
Didn't make a "hill of beans" difference
No difference
It did not upset the apple cart

Next Steps / What To Do Next / Road Map

Silver Bullets
Put together a 'To Do' list
What is on the tick list?
Irons in the fire
Laundry list

Touch base
Peck check
Flares in the air
First line of defense
Backup plan
Honey-do list
Plan A
Plan B
Close ranks and bond
From the get-go
From the opening bell
From the word go
Let's get off the dime
Let's get off our duffs
Play the scenario out... what would happen?
Play the scenario out
Keep it on board for now
Let 'er rip
Make a persuasive argument for us to do it
Helicopter up and see the big picture
Shoot first and ask questions later
Redouble your efforts
Take a stab at it
Ballpark it
Let's get the show on the road
Hazard a guess
Make a rough guess
Draw up a roadmap
Chart a course
Make a gameplan
Do a back-of-the-envelope calculation before you get started
Just worry about the shark that's closest to your body

Out of Control / Reckless / No Structure / Hard To Understand

Silver Bullets

A BLUE-SKY, UNBUTTONED format
Driving with the emergency brake on
Throw caution to the wind
All over the board

No real blueprint
No real gameplan
He's off his rails
What the fu**?
Why the hell not?
All over the map
Fu** it; some things you just gotta do
It's really out of bounds at this point
I do not have my PC hat on right now
Wide-open
It's quickly becoming a free-for-all
We're losing our grip on the situation
We cannot hold back the break in the dam
We cannot contain this for much longer
It's going to explode
We need to plan for damage control
Alert the media
Send out an APB (all points bulletin)
He's a wild man
Whack job
Breakneck speed
This thing is moving at light speed
We cannot stay on top of the situation
Get a handle on it
Blowing smoke
We were blindsided
We're behind the eightball
Out on a limb

Driving like a madman
TOOC (totally out of control)
Blown out of proportion
A severe case of schizoid actions
Dangerous scum
A danger to society
He presented a threat to our security
He presented a threat
Security threat
A walking timebomb
It's a volcano, spewing ash
They're escalating the situation
We're being provoked
Dirty pool
Unfair tactics
Desperate times call for desperate measures

Normal / Average / Static Situations

Silver Bullets

BUSINESS AS USUAL
Everything is hunky-dorey
Steady as she goes
Situation normal

It's soup of the day
All systems go
All systems five by five
Green lights all the way
The deck is clear
The pad is clear
Hum drum
Par for the course
Clean and green
All quiet on the Western front
Not much goin' on
Not much happening

Set your bearings and keep them there
Etched in stone
Cast in concrete
The rock of Gibraltar
Rock solid
Fixed
Stationary
Set
Bankable
You can set a clock by it
Very quiet out there
It's goin'
Stay dry
Hang sround and shoot the sh**
Same ol' same ol'
It is what it is
You know how it is
Back to what we know
Tried and true
Unflappable
Unwavering
Stay the course
On course
Predictable
Plugging along

P.R. / Communications

The Prompt

Float out a story
Start first by denying everything
VNR (Video News Release)
Talking points

Deskside briefings
Consistent messaging
Crisis communications program

Disaster plan
Celebrity tie-ins
Celebrity spokespeople
Development meetings
Get on the same page
Feature story packages
Pub circulation
Media tours
Dailies
Weeklies
Shoppers
Monthlies
Quarterlies
Lead times
Pitch letters
Angles
Press conferences
Press releases
Preview programs
Garner coverage
Assignment editor
Assets
Crisis communications program
Development meetings
Editorial calendars
Investor relations
Launch kits
Satellite feeds
Coverage
Win the spin
Spin it and win it
Spin control
Doctor Spingod
Damage control
Bust dust
Keep it contained
Keep it hush hush

I'll deny ever saying this
Take the big bullet
More of the same
It died in committee
Unsubstantiated reports
Instant scandals
Speakers bureau (consistent group of executives available to speak at conferences)
Publicity (getting visibility for product or people or company in print or broadcast media)
NAPS (North American Precis Syndicate)
Mats (reproduction proofs)
Media training (coaching senior executives and spokespeople in dealing with the media)
Investor Relations (communicating the company story to stock analysts)
Media alerts (short one-page notice that is a mix of a press release and an invitation to an event)
Assignment editor (person at TV or radio station who dispatches camera crews and reporters)
B-roll (quick video compilation designed to give to a TV producer "raw" footage of a story)

Market Research-related Terminology

Silver Bullets

One-on-ones
Focus groups
Online surveys
Ask the right questions

Do a deep dive
Do a deep dive and climb into the numbers
Take me on a numbers run

In a more casual vein

Look inside the numbers

On the fence

Watch what trends

What is trending?

Trending in a positive direction

Jettison what you don't like

Directionally get a sense of what is happening

Qualitative interviews

Exit surveys

Mall intercepts

Anecdotal evidence

Quantitative is projectable

Useful but contentious

Fielded the study

It represents the consumer in the marketplace

Analyze the data the right way

Normative data bases

Proprietary concept tool

Enablers versus Big Hooks

Do it on paper to avoid groupthink

Ideas, opinions, and insights

Qualitative test

HHI (HouseHold Income)

Median HHI

Milestones

Feature sets

Random digit dial that is projectable to the U.S. population

Random digit dial

Going in the wrong direction

Post-flight surveys

Back into the numbers

Run the numbers

Build models

Focus tests

Qualify the sample

Sample size

Variance

Anecdotal evidence

Empirical data

Degree of confidence

Quantify the data (likely measure the ROI, the return on investment)

Let's validate our findings (too afraid to make a decision)

Torture the data until it says what you want it to

Listen to the consumer (it is time to do focus groups or in-home interviews)

Develop some fresh insights (we likely need to start from scratch with new data)

Mother-In-Law research (I asked my Mother-In-Law about this, and she said...)

Actionable data

Cook the data (make the data show what you want it to show in order to tell a story a certain way)

Mine the data we already have (perhaps too cost-prohibitive (and maybe lazy) to conduct new research)

Data dump (having tons of information to sift through; "Let's start with a data dump")

Speaking from a focus group of one (same as saying what I see / hear from my own point-of-view)

Will It Last? / It May Fall Short / Take A Chance / Hopeless / Give In / Settle / Cave

The Prompt

DOES IT HAVE legs?
Can we make this lame turkey fly?
It does not quite feed the bulldog
Make sure to go on a tire-kicking expedition

Can it sustain?
Do you think it will fly?
Is there a there there?
Take a deep shot
Let's hope that sticks
Hold the break in the dam
Let's roll with what we got
Let's go with what we have right now
We may not get a better look at the basket
Better try and make the most of it
Let's throw one up in the direction of the end
    zone
Hail mary time
Throw one up there
Better tack on to the lead while we have it
Play stallball
The ducks are in a row as best they can be
Let's get out while the getting is good
It's our best chance at victory at this point
We had better run a check
Let's cut our losses and take what we can get
We're maxxed out
We topped out
Take what we can get
Breathe some life into it
Take it up another notch
It kind of takes the air out of the balloon

A deflation sensation
It all may come down to luck and timing
It may be a house of cards
It's like beating a dead horse
I would do it if it were realistic
It was deprioritized
Check the pulse
Kick the tires
It does not quite butter the bread
It does not scare the horses
It does not serve all the masters
That dog won't hunt
Surrender
Roll over
Bend but don't break
Just the way it goes sometimes
Just one of those things
It may just come down to, is the product available
   when they go to buy?

Acceptance / Accept The Situation / Approval / Validation / On Time

Silver Bullets

I AGREE WITH you 1,000%
Welcome to the fraternity
You passed the litmus test
The ceremonious pat on the back

Credentialed
Blanket clearance
He's one of us
Passed the litmus test
Passed the sniff test
Feather in your cap
He has all his ducks in a row

Welcome to the family

Roll out the welcome wagon

You get it

We speak the same language

We are cut from the same global fabric

Welcome to the team

Welcome to the club

Tapped into the club

You know how it works

There ya go

Happy camper syndrome

Yes, in a big way

Feather in your cap

Pat on the tush

Attaboy

Make the budget work for you

Do not push the envelope

Always on time

You could cook a turkey by it

Johnny-on-the-spot

Timetable

Thanks a million

Yes in a big way

Roll with the punches

Do-able

It comes with the territory

That's just part of the gig

It's my job to do it

On time and under budget; Eh, what are ya gonna do?

Did they pass the airplane test? (live through sitting next to someone on a long flight)

We must have the openness to accept good ideas and the strength to reject bad ones

Silence is not necessarily agreement, but then again, it might be

Coffee Chat / Coffee Talk

Silver Bullets

WAKE UP AND smell the coffee
Shoot the sh**
Chit-chat
Talk turkey

When can we coffee?
When can we cocktail?
Can we have a heart-to-heart?
Let's kibbitz
Let's shoot the sh**
Let's grab some lattes
Hobnobbing
Talk shop
Wise up
Throw it in my eyes, it'll work faster
Snap out of it
Smell the coffee
How about a cup of coffee?
Java
Cup o' Joe
Beans
Mug of moe
Crock of crud
Lug of lava
Brewski
Wake-up juice
Café
Big ol' cup of Jeremiah

Cigarettes / Smokebreak / Smoking

Cancer Sticks
Smokes
Gaspers
Throat bombs
Lung rockets

Nicoweed
Tonsil fire
Coffin nails
Cancer sticks
Death sticks
White sticks
Butts
Rollies
Whiteys
Timber
Sparky
Flame
Fire
Makings
Fags (British and Australian)
Bumpers (Australian)
Can I bum a smoke?
Can you slide me one?
Can you roll me one?
Do you roll your own?
Smoke 'em if you got 'em

Possession / Ownership

Silver Bullets
YOU CAN NEVER truly own golf, you can only borrow it for a little while
That actually belongs in our camp
We have first dibs on that

Compliments of our meat hooks
First dibs
In the barn
We own your ass
I have title on that
We own them
The IP we own (intellectual property)
Owning IP versus renting
Be your own boss
Check the bill of lading; it's ours
What's mine is mine, and what's yours is mine
My contacts are my contacts, and your contacts
    are my contacts
Possession is nine-tenths of the law

Call Back On Phone Or Via E-mail / Get Back In Touch

Silver Bullets

I'LL HIT YOU back later
Let me bounce you back
I will endeavor to get back to you
We are playing some telephone tag, but we will
connect

Let's hook and ladder
Ping me back
Ping me
Ping you back
Hit you back
Buzz you back
Ring you up
Telephone tennis
I'll get back to you
Catch you on an 'E' (on email)
Catch you on the flip side
Hit me back on my Blackberry
Blackberry me

Emotional/ Gutteral/ Visceral/ Safeguarding/ Sensitive

Silver Bullets

Too much bad theater
What does your gut tell you?
Touchy-feely
Fall on your sword

Theater of the mind
Carry the flag
Smells like victory
How's it smell?
How's it feel?
Like nails on a blackboard
Pick and choose your battles
A fight is brewing
There is a disturbance in the force
It doesn't feel right
Something is not right
The force is strong with the new kid
Pick your battles
Soldiers of the war
Hand-holding
Tissue issue
Gut reaction
Beltbuckle feel
They don't know sh** from Cheyenne
They don't know sh** from Shinola
It is not between you and me; we are just soldiers
Just ask yourself if that's the hill you want to die on (fight the battle)
More nervous than a long-tailed cat in a room full of rocking chairs

Add To It / Offer Suggestions / Build Upon Something / Think About It / Dress It Up / Embellish

Silver Bullets

THE DOCUMENT NEEDS more weight
Let's spice it up
Add some noise to it
Run it up the flagpole and see if anyone salutes

Let me build on that
Offer up any suggestions
Needs some light editing
It needs some more Tabasco
Throw out a litany of ideas
Any last-minute ideas?
Soup it up
Deal sweeteners
Add some sweeteners
Let me workshop that idea
Take it with a grain of salt
Give it some thought
Chew on this for a while
Noodle on this
Olive branch
Put on your thinking cap
Run it up the flagpole
Out-of-the-box
Be that as it may, let's…
Make the most of it
Wanna throw another idea into the mix?
Let's do a deep dive and see what else we can
come up with
Everyone wants to put their mark on your work

Thanks For The Introduction / Appreciation of Comments / Obliged

Silver Bullets

Much OBLIGED
Thanks for letting me write the cue cards
I will give you the ten bucks later
Thanks for the alley oop

The one and the same
That's me… in the flesh
Guilty as charged
Well, you look right perty, too
It's always nice to say flattering things about management
Getting paid to say nice things
Pleased to meet you as well
I must say, beautifully designed and well-written
Thanks for doing me the favor
I guess that makes me valuable intellectual property
I feel like I made it to Cooperstown
I feel like I made it to Canton
I feel like I made it to Springfield
Thanks for the ego feed
I just jumped up and touched the moon
I am as sure as the world
That is a very honoring thing to say as long as you do not believe it

Everything / Totality

Silver Bullets

The WHOLE SHOOTIN' match
The whole nine yards
The whole kit and caboodle
The whole enchilada

The whole lot
The full monty
Full-on
Fully loaded
Full boat
The whole shebang
Hodgepodge of everything
Mixed bag
It had all the trimmings
Frosting on the cake
Icing on the cake
And the cherry on top
All your eggs in one basket
Everything but the kitchen sink
The kitchen sink
All the marbles
Melting pot
Bet the farm
Might as well let it ride
All in
All on the line
Everything and a bag of chips
The total package
With an exclamation point
Go to the mat
Walk it through the garden (put everything on the sandwich)
Make it a Dagwood (put everything on the sandwich)
The Dagwood version
All the trimmings
All the fixins

No Explanation / No Reason

Silver Bullets

THERE ARE NO excuses for stupid actions which have no explanations

Do not look for scapegoats on this one... you won't find any

Brain freeze

Vapor lock

Some things just happen

It's just one of those things

Sometimes fate makes things work out that way

Fate weaves the web

It is just pre-determined destiny stuff

You were sitting on your hands

You had your hands in your pocket

You were just flat-footed

Fudge factor

Rounding errors

Carpet snakes

Invisible barriers

The glass ceiling

Bad voodoo

It just disappeared into thin air

Into thin air

Ain't happening

Saint happening

Expect a no storm

It just happens that way

Who can really explain it?

Ask a higher power

There may be no logical explanation that exists

Stand on your toes next time; it's going over your head

Deer in the headlights

The devil finds work for idle hands, that's all I know

Third place is third place no matter how you slice it

Sometimes it is not about reading tea leaves and crystal balls

We must have the openness to accept good ideas and the strength to reject bad ones

Everything happens for a reason... sometimes we never find out that reason

Who knows why his elevator does not make it all the way to his observation deck?

Comparisons / Controversies / Contrasts

Silver Bullets

Grade A versus Grade B
Apples versus oranges
Hatfields and the McCoys
Horses of a different color

Two peas in a pod
These two were made for each other
You deserve each other
Night and day
Black and white
Two big bullies on the block

Parameters / Constraints / Barriers

Silver Bullets

Take a look at the capabilities and constraints
Boundaries
What kind of latitude do you have on this?
Are your hands tied?

Get a handle on it
Where are the boundaries?

Is it rock-solid?

Latitude

The lines have been drawn

Territoriality

Territory

It's in their camp

That falls under our jurisdiction

Jurisdiction

Are you handcuffed?

Handcuffed?

Do you have any leeway?

Leeway?

Do you have free reign?

Retrofit the idea to the strategy

Back into the numbers

Back into it

You can find money with words and you can hide money in numbers

Pinch pennies and spend dollars

Background / Part of The Background / Background Info

Silver Bullets

THE BACKGROUND CHECK turned up nothing

Part of the landscape

Part of the backdrop

Is there a rap sheet?

Is there a paper trail?

What do we know about them?

Fill-in-the-blanks

Check his past history

Idea Generation / Brainstorm

Silver Bullets

Run it up the flagpole and see who salutes
Brain-misting session
Let's idea-ate
Bull session

Pow-wow session
Pow-wow
Brain dump
Brain drain
Let me bend your ear on something
Let me throw this out there
Let me bounce it off you
Throw out a litany of ideas
The pricetag never leads the idea
Pull our thoughts in line
Need for strong, core ideas
Add some noise to it
Add some weight to it
Light bulb went on
Shazaam!
Eureka!
Wowie-zowie!
Two heads are better than one
Sounding board
Let me give you a thumbnail sketch (review) on what I think it'll be

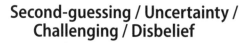

Second-guessing / Uncertainty / Challenging / Disbelief

Silver Bullets

PLAYING MONDAY MORNING quarterback with
hindsight is always easier
I would hazard a guess
It's a crapshoot… a big dice roll
Guesswsork

Guesswork
Bottle it up
Flip a coin
Bite your tongue
Looks like a little smoke and mirrors
You might as well run it up the flagpole
Last-ditch effort to make it work
You cannot polish crap
Six one-way, half-dozen the other
Seven-ten split
Shouldda, wouldda, couldda
Hindsight is twenty-twenty
If I had it to do all over again
If I knew then what I know now
Slow to anger
It begs the question, hmmmmm?
Do you think it will fly?
Can we make this lame turkey fly?
It came in like a lion, but will it leave like a lamb?
It may be in and out of style so fast it may make your head spin

What's Happening?

Silver Bullets

WHAT DO YOU hear on the down-low?
What's the 4-1-1?
'Sup?
What's the deal?

What up?
What's the scent?
What's the dilly-o?
What's the dilly?
What the deezy?
What the deal, chief?
What's the haps?
What's shakin'?
What do you got for us?
Any anything?
Any flash updates?
Flash updates
Priority score alerts?
What have you heard on the QT?
Anything under the radar?
Anything on the radar?
Let's hang out and shoot the sh**

Keeping Up-To-Date / In The Loop / In The Know / On Same Page

Silver Bullets

IN THE HOPPER
In the mix
In the loop
On the same page

Plug into global movements
Staying in tune
Up-to-date
Up-to-speed
Tapped-in
Dialed-in
Take a ride on my train
We're in the mix
Hop on board
Climb aboard

Looking Back / In Retrospect

Silver Bullets

WHEN I THINK back to the party at Max Yasker's farm
In hindsight
Back in the olden days
As I reflect back now as I am long in the tooth

In my day
Those were the days
The good old days
Over the years
We've been through the wars
Back in the day
Forward and backward thinking
Did you put on your hazard lights before backing into that one?
Behind the times
Memory like a steel dam trap
Memory like a steel trap—rusty

Commitment / Pride / Loyalty / Stick-to-it-ive-ness

Silver Bullets

Sustained and demonstrated commitment

Locked in and not going anywhere

Hogtied and happy

Signed in and on board

Pride of a lion

Through thick and thin

Tar on his heels

He'll stick

Will fall on the sword

Will take a bullet for you

He'll fight to the bitter end

No defeat, no surrender

On the same page

Stick to the fight

Fight the good fight

To the struggle

In concert

Like a pit bull

Gritty

He'll grind it out with you

Kick ass and take names

You want him in the foxhole with you

Intelligence / Street Smarts

Silver Bullets

A lot upstairs

Gray matter prevalent

The lights are definitely on

Engaged in mental gymnastics

Thought-intensive
Cagey
Seasoned
Heady
Smart cookie
Crafty
Scheming
A lot above the neck
Got the intell
Brain surgeon status
Borderline genius
He's the shed's sharp tool
Doesn't think like a box of rocks
Doesn't think like a pack of hammers
You subscribe to bastions of higher learning

Looking To The Future / What Future Can Bring / Contingency Plans

Silver Bullets

I't's interesting opening the mail each day
Be forward-thinking...and always have some
irons in the fire
To be forewarned is to be forearmed, and if I am
forewarned, I'll hit 'em with a forearm
Think a couple of moves ahead

Make a To Do list
Substance sustains
Touch base
Laundry list
Irons in the fire
Flares in the air
Backup plan
Plan A
Plan B

Looking down the road
Looking up the road
Peck check
Tick list
To do list
Crystal balling
Don't look at the present value, but at the value of future cash flows
Christmas is just around the corner; no wait, it's down the hall and 3rd door on your left

Denial / Delay / Not Taking Responsibility

Silver Bullets

DELAY IS THE worst form of denial
The quicker you fall behind… the more time you have to make it up
Not willing to shoulder the blame or the responsibility
Throw a cryogenic freeze over the situation

Cross that bridge when you come to it
Burn that bridge behind you
It's not us
You're not dealing with reality
Don't tarry
Shirking your responsibility
You're not stepping up
It's on you, get it?
Blamestorming
Living in denial
Play a slowdown game
Ain't happening
Flying by the seat of your pants
Expect a no storm
More on their plate than they san say grace for

Proof / Realization / Discovery

Silver Bullets

Take me on a numbers run
Prove to me beyond a reasonable doubt
Show me where I'm wrong
Suddenly, the lightbulb goes on

Crystal-clear
Crystal
Show me how the numbers jibe
Show me the numbers
The proof is in the pudding
The numbers don't lie
It's right
Eureka !
We got something
I get it
Affirmative

Opportunity Cost / What You Lose / Speculation

Silver Bullets

The piece you must give up in order to get
what you want
Be willing to compromise
Here's what you're giving up
What can we get for it?

The cost of guessing can hurt you big-time
One man's trash is another man's treasure
Dodged a bullet
There may be a consolation prize for losing sight
    of what you really wanted

Face / Mug / Grill / In Your Face

Silver Bullets

Get out of my grill
Face time
Nice mug
Your beak

Your dome
Your noggin
Your china
Up close and personal
Chin to chin
Beak to beak
Nice face… did your neck just vomit?

Uptight / Tight / Confidential / Guarded

Silver Bullets

Wound up real tight
Anal
Frosty
Chilly

Way too uptight
Too freakin' uptight
Wound up tighter than an alarm clock
Hold it down
Security on alert
A high security situation
Orange alert
Keep it on the QT
The down-low
Need a palm print, retina scan, and urine sample
Keep it on the down-low

Stay Up Late / Constantly Running

Silver Bullets

BURNING THE MIDNIGHT oil
Twenty-four-seven (24-7)
Pumpin' on all cylinders
Working the night shift

Full steam ahead
Full speed ahead
Spike up
The night owl
Night owl hours
Up all night
Whatever works
Mainline the caffeine
Mainline the Red Bull
Take some pinks
Plug in
Tune in
Push the envelope
Max it out
Top out
Power through
Push through
Gotta push it
Max speed

Be Ready / Preparation

Silver Bullets

Make sure your ducks are in a row
Prepare the head by feeding the soul
The early bird gets the worm… I'll see you at 0-dark-30
Dot all the i's and cross all the t's

Keep your head on a swivel
Sit up like Jackie
Look alive
Get set
Plan the work, work the plan
Block everything out
Heads up
Stay alert
Rehearse it in your mind
Take smelling salts… whatever it takes
Boot camp
Whatever it takes
Nothing prepares like preparation
Keep a good head on your shoulders
Jacked, ready, and double tough
Let's get off the dime
Let's get off our duffs
Ready, Freddie?
Work with me, people
Put out the feelers

Consolation Prize / Booby Prize

Silver Bullets

IT'S LIKE A tie… it's a "kiss-your-sister"
The second prize is a set of steak knives
A real lemon
B-team

Second string
Sloppy seconds
Scraps

Behind / Behind Schedule / Long Way To Go

Silver Bullets

THE QUICKER YOU fall behind, the more time you have to make it up
Behind the eightball
It's a major uphill battle from here
Missed a few milestones… time to play catch-up

A tough row to hoe (the right way to say it)
A tough road to hoe (the wrong way to say it)
You're missing milestones
A high burn rate
Too far back to catch up
Need to try make up the difference
Bring it back to even

Unrealistic / Not Feasible / Useless

Silver Bullets

NOT GONNA HAPPEN… no way, shape, or form
Like carrying coals to Newcastle
Like selling ice to the Eskimos
A bunch of pop fluff

Kaput
That's a real knee-slapper
Secondary stuff
Tertiary stuff

Put Pressure On / Thumbscrews / Feet To The Fire / Turn Up The Heat

Silver Bullets

Put the thumbscrews to 'em
Turn up the heat
Throw it back in their court
Full court press

Give them some end to end coverage
Turn the screws to 'em
Hold their feet to the fire
Hit it, Alice
Consolidate and dominate

Not In Touch / Not In Communication / Wishful / Wishlist

Silver Bullets

Out of pocket
NORDO (no radio contact)
Out there
Incommunicado

Pie in the sky
Blue sky wishes
Higher than a kite
Dreamin' on a star
Dreamscape
In a perfect world
Best case scenario
Higher than domed-roof scaffolding
We always want additional real estate at no cost…
    and we're kidding ourselves

Big Picture / In Sum / In The Grand Scheme of Things

Silver Bullets
Here's the skinny
When the dust settles
When the smoke clears
When the last ball has bounced

The grand scheme of things
I am working in a world that is unquantifiable
Broad strokes
Broad brush
House of cards
Thumbnail sketch
It serves all the masters
It doth not protest too much
The gist ("jist")
Uber
Mondo

Uncertainty / Dice Roll

Silver Bullets
THE LIGHT AT the end of the tunnel might be a freight train coming your way
It makes the question mark appear
Very gray area
It's a crap shoot

Pass the litmus test
It's a dice roll
It's a toss up
Russian roulette
Uncharted waters
Are our oars in the water?
It's a gray area

Too close to call

Like a puppy getting off a leash, I don't know where it's going

Like catching up to an avalanche to give it direction

Airplane test (living through sitting next to someone on a long flight)

Maximize / Working Late

Silver Bullets

Burning the midnight oil

Twenty-four-seven; (24-7)

It's all the way to bright

Top out

Top off

Maxxed out

Make the pie bigger

Bite off more than you can chew

Exhaust the possibilities

Exhaust administrative remedies

Blinding insight

Make hay while the sun shines

Make the most of it

Not all the way to bright yet (reaching a goal)

We always want additional real estate at no cost

Walk it through the garden (put everything on the sandwich)

They know you're a hard worker when your hands are brown and not your nose

Ahead Of The Game

Silver Bullets

YOU ARE WAY ahead of the curve
You're leading the pack
You're setting the benchmark
There is nothing like preparation

Setting the pace
Raising the bar
Upping the standards

Micro / Small / Details

Silver Bullets

DOWN TO THE details and paper clips of it all
Down to brass tacks
You're caught up in the minutia
Granular

Minutia
Teen-eye-ntzy details
Smallest spec
Pull out the microscope
Like dissecting atoms
Slicing up amoebas
Nit picky
Nit picking
Ticky tack
Tic tac
Minor details
Legal boilerplate
The fine print

Standard / Average

Silver Bullets
Boiler plate
Cookie cutter
Garden variety
Same ol' same ol'

Industry standard
Right on the mean
Top of the bell curve
Nothing special
AVG (average)
Vanilla
Vanilla statements
Vanilla documents

Too Much Input From Too Many People

Silver Bullets
LIKE HEARING FROM the department of redundancy department
Too many cooks spoil the broth
Too many cooks in the kitchen
I'm swamped

I am overwhelmed to say the least
Information overload
404—computer message indicating file not found
Spread thin
Spread pretty thin
I'm swarmed
It's causing me to have a wild sceddy (schedule)
It's way overdone
It's way overblown

Swarm of bees all over me
Get 'em all off my back
Too many chiefs and not enough Indians

Circumvent Process / Go Around / Go Over One's Head

Silver Bullets

AN END AROUND
An end run
Stay under the radar
Serpentine

Go around him
Go around their backs
Stay to the outside
Backroom deals
Slice out the middleman
Go direct to the source and around the guards

Pay For It / Get The Check / Pick Up The Tab

Silver Bullets

GIVE US YOUR credit card, and it will be like you are there
Don't pull a "short arms, long pockets" move on us
Get the check
Pick up the tab

Close out the tab
Tab out
Cash out
Run the card
Check please
Expense it

What's the damage?
What do I owe?
Check please
T & E it (travel & expense budget)
Don't have alligator hands on us, put up your share

Construction / Designing / Fabrication

Silver Bullets
Inventory tracking
Repurpose
Refurb
Recondition

The specs (specifications; size requirements)
4-color
2-color
Black-and-white
Footprints
Electronic Galleys
Check the galleys
Cover proofs
Mechanicals
DPI (dots per inch)
Inkwells
Safety
Trim
Trim size
Trim specs
The cutting / trimming tolerance
Spine thickness
Bleed
Additional bleed
Glossy
Matted

Perfect bound
Pre-fab
Substrate (surface)
Brush metal
Drill down
DIMs (dimensions)
TEMPs (templates)
GOBOs (gobo lights)
Never restorize your vector
Drayage
Bill of lading
FIP (foam-in-place)
Staging area
Mechanicals
Auto cads
Bluelines
Blues
Proofs

Tickets / Swag - Related

Swag (stuff we always get)
Duckets
Any Scooby snacks
Glom (give the loser our merchandise)

Superficial/ Signaling / On The Surface/ Subtle Communication

This is just scratching the surface
Public posturing
Subtle jargon
A precursory examination reveals

Fluid / Changes All The Time

Chameleon-like
Motion commotion
Can't get a grip on it
Slippery slope

Macro / Big / Perspective

Broad strokes
Broad brush
Uber
Mondo

Randy Gordon Nicknames

Gordo
The Red Dragon
G-Man
Jumpshot Randy G
Jumpshot
J
Code Red
LRC (Little Red Caboose)
Ran DMC
Big Red
Red Alert
Red Storm
Gorgon
Gordage
Gargoyle
The Bud Fox of Advertising
The Jew from Birmingham
Rags
Rando
Rondo
Randall
The candyman
Rangoon Ruby
G-Unit
G-Force
DF (Designated Freshman)
RG Intergalactic
Flash
Suitcase
Gorgonzola
Rand-"i"
Rand-"eye"

About the Author

JAY "RANDY" GORDON most recently worked for experiential marketing agency ignition, Inc. on Sony Pictures Digital business (FusionFlashConcerts.com), and he has consulted in the past for Adscape Media, GameLive Events, Telltale Games, and Red Bull's Ad Agency of Record Kastner & Partners. He has sold pre-movie trailer cinema advertising space to videogame companies and their ad agencies (for then Regal Entertainment Group's Regal CineMedia), and he served for over two years as Vice President of Marketing Services for Ubi Soft Entertainment, a French-based developer and global publisher of PC and videogames. In a working capacity, Randy brings proven process and a wealth of creativity and contacts (from both sports and entertainment). He operates under a unique style of sales-driving thoughts, big ideas with a promotional / PR slant, a keen sense of how to initiate and leverage relationships with other marketers, and a refreshing leadership role that fosters team play where he empowers those with whom he works to get things done. Randy authored "Gimme Five" for *Inside Sports* magazine October 1989 issue (a unique look at the beginning, meaning, and implication of "the high five" in sports and our culture), and Randy has been the subject of 2 business articles: ("Marketing Continues at InterAct" (*MCV Weekly* – Oct 29, 1999) and "This pixel brought to you by…" (*Shift Magazine* from Canada – May 1999) which discusses logo branding within games. Randy did just that for Sony PlayStation from 1997 to 1999.

In May of 2000, Randy Gordon joined the U.S Headquarters (San Francisco office) of Ubisoft Entertainment as Director of Brand Development and Promotions. His primary role was to "plus" marketing and promotional efforts and to fortify branding initiatives. Prior to his work at Ubisoft, Randy served as Director of Marketing for InterAct (at one time, the world's leading manufacturer and seller of videogame peripherals / accessories and the GameShark product line). Having also formulated "in-game branding" and cross-promotional programs at Sony Computer Entertainment America (as Manager of (In-Game Branding) and Consumer Promotions), Randy built a solid reputation of productivity within the videogaming space after only starting in April of 1997.

His work experience in marketing covers the gamut. He served as Manager of Sponsor Partner Development for the Coca-Cola Company (and the Coca-Cola Olympic City theme park) leading up to, during, and after the Summer Olympic Games in Atlanta, worked in Newport Beach for renowned sports agent Leigh Steinberg overseeing the daily account management of the U.S. World Cup team, worked as Marketing Manager for EA SportsLab / SportsLab, Inc. and spent 2 years in advertising (account management) for Universal McCann (New York, NY) where he serviced the ESPN account (Bristol, CT), as well as working for Bates USA (New York, NY) in media planning for M&M/Mars (Hackettstown, NJ).

Randy received his M.B.A. (1993) from The Anderson School (U.C.L.A.) and his B.S. in Business Administration from the University of North Carolina at Chapel Hill (1989). A Board Member (June 2001-2002) for the Academy of Interactive Arts and Sciences, Randy remains a member as he has since 1998, and he served as Executive

Committee Member of the Oakland Alameda County Sports Commission which was one of three finalists out of eleven cities vying to host Super Bowl 2005. He has also been a member of MENG (Marketing Executive Networking Group), LinkedIn, BAIPA (Bay Area Independent Publishers Association) and the National Sports Marketing Network.

Game credits to date include:

Sony PlayStation titles
Jet Moto 2, MLB '99, CoolBoarders 2, Cool Boarders 3, Contender
Sunny Garcia Surfing, Deathrow, Planet Of The Apes (Ubisoft Entertainment titles)
Telltale Texas Hold'Em (Telltale Games)

He lives in Marin County, CA (just North of San Francisco), and he is originally from Birmingham, AL.

Special Thanks To:

A

Richard Anderson, Brian Adams, Allen Adler, Dorothy Alires, Phil Alexander, Andre Abecassis, Lawrence Antoine, Donna Armentor, Freddie Avner, Dan Aston, Rick Arnstein, Zennie Abraham, Frank Alizaga, Ken Allen, , Chris Atkinson, Andrew Allen, David Abroms, Warren Allgyer, Kelly Allgyer, David Anthony, Jeff Agoos, Shell Ausman, Shelli Azoff, , Desmond Armstrong, Stephen Ackroyd, Stephanie Amiot, Danny Arnold, Vincent Aversano, Eamon Alvarez, Jonathan Arkin, Rick Alessandri, Adrien Agoado, Academy of Interactive Arts & Sciences;

B

David Burchianti, Rob Burchianti, Donald Beeson, Andrea Bobinski, George Biava, Nat Brookhouse, David Bernstein, Mindy Binderman, Ron Bruno, Paul Baldwin, Chip Blundell, Michael Betti, David Bamberger, Terry Bamberger, Linda Baldwin, Keith Boesky, Peter Bogart, Steffi Bogart, Dan Baker, Dhardra Blake, Sam Bayne, Katie Bayne, Mark Bernstein, Rob Bagot, Larry Block, Sheila Buckley, Dawn Bingham, Djuana Barnes, Dan Bornstein, Alicia Brit-Quintana, Lionel Bea, Thomas Bateman, Chris Berman, Mary Bihr, Kevin Bruner, Sean Brown, Gene Bartow, Chris Browning, Harry Bressler, Jeff Black, Bill Benjamin, John Billington, Julia Barfield, Kim Bardakian, Chuck Ball, Mary Alice Ball, Howard Berman, Cathy Byrd, Randy Bernstein, Mark E. Benson, Carole Bidnick, Ami Blaire, Dave Brown, Gary Bauer, David Brownstein, Edwin Byck, Celia Bechtel, Marcus Beer, Diana Benedikt, Thomas Bateman, Jeff Black, Charles Bellfield, Jen Burns, Mike "Baller" Brown, Mike Bonifer, Bob Biernacki, Matthew Berkson, Alexandra Brell, Will Blair, Michele Brouillard, Brad Barrish, Andy Brilliant, Laurence Buisson-Nollent, Paul Boschi, Kurtis Buckmaster, Keith Boesky, Dave Brown, Lauren Brignone, Marcelo Balboa, Bob Biernacki, Sarah Berridge, Steve Baker, Ross Borden, Leeman Bennett, Jonathan Blackman, Jeff Black, Bryan Brousseau, MaryFrances Bonvini, Silvio Bonvini, John Boas, K.B. Bose, David Borgenicht, Kim Bardakian, Gordon Bennett, Stacey Bender, Vickie Braden, Brianne Barack, Lauren Berzines, Andre Blanadet, Phil Battat, Norman Bellingham, Gary Barton, Patricia Broderick, Chuck Battey, Michael Becker, Thomas Bonk, Thomas Browne, J.P. Bommel, Jimmy Buffett, Dean Bender, Barry Bonds, Bear Bryant, Ed Bradley, Terry Bradshaw, Brenda Burcun, Mary Biondi, Nolan Bushnell, Mark Bernstein, John Boas, Robert Brown, Don Blue, Ralph Barbieri, Rick Burgess, Bubba Bussey;

C

Antonio Capretta, Ricardo Capretta, Patrick Carroll, Dan Cohen, Todd Cromer, Terry Cooper, John Cassimus, David Clark, Pete Christian, Lisa Carlson, Jay Cohen, Matt Campbell, Meg Campbell, Glenn Chin, Karen Conroe, Andrew Carra, Bob Crowe, Olga Crowe, Bill Criswell, Deb Criswell, Jeanne Courtney, Perry Cutshall, Tom Carr, Rebecca Coleman, Chuck Corcoran, Michael Cookson, Jennifer Croft, Sean Carey, David Choromanski, Donna Choromanski, Dan Connors, Paul Cappelli, John Cummings, Robin Carr, Tony Cacheria, Dan Courteomache, Neil Cohen, Mitch Charlens, Renee Chernus, Shannon Coy, Gus "Alex" Castillo, Renato Capobianco, Mike Cervanek, Dave Cox, Cory Clemetson, Ed Coleman, Anne Chen, Malcolm Campbell, Mike Cohen, Hal Carlson, Dan Connors, Tim Christian, Robin Carr, Joe Craciun, David Cornwell, Mark Caplan, Lisa Cleff, C.J. Connoy, Cecile Cornet, Paul Caligiuri, Chris Corman, John Clarke, Bruce Caldwell, Bob Costas, David Cook, David Casey, Renata Circeo, Tim Christian, Rob Carney, Frank Carrere, Carolyne Connor, Joe Cosentino, Chris Caris, Bonnie Carlson, Barbara Carey, Beth Cahn, Clark Crowdus, Howard Cosell, Benjamin Colteaux, Staysea Colteaux, Dave Cox, Adam Carolla, Debi Caprio;

D

Laurent Detoc, David Dunn, David Diamond, Matt Diamond, Brian Dammacco, Ali Dibb, Beth Doherty, John Diaz, Peter Dille, Dan Diamond, Hilary Dunne, Eric Daubert, Mark Driscoll, Susan Driscoll, Randy Dorilag, Dwight Debree, Steve Disson, Brad Durrusseau, Keith Dobkowski, Robin Davis, Rich DeAugustinis, Sean Downey, Daniel Dao, Amanda Daniels, Bobby "Bobby D" Danelski, Karen Schwartz Decker, Ray Decker, Paul Dalessio, Michael Driscoll, Danny Dann, Rob Dyer, Thomas Dooley, Lee Douglas, Marjorie DeGraca, Haven Dubrul, Don Dobbie, Brian Dimmick, Jeffrey Dickstein, Jenna Dawson, Annette Davis, Dennis Dunkelberger, Jarrod Dillon, Don DeSchmidt, Todd DeStefano, Jeff Daniel, Jackie Dupont-Walker, Aime Duell, Rick Dellacquila, John Diaz, Linda D'adamo;

E

Fred Erben, Joe Erben, Woody Eversz, Marvin Epstein, Jeffry Eaton, Robert Earle, John Emrich, Chris Emley, Doug Elvers, Susan Ely, Olivier Ernst, John Eckel, John Ellertson, Bill Edelman, Steve Espinoza, Chris Eames;

F

Stu Finkelstein, Doug Faust, Bob Fischer, Tom Finnegan, Matthew Feyling, Andrew Felder, Melissa Felder, Shannon Feldheim, Fred Fried, Robbie Friedman, Greg Fant, John Flippen, Brian Finnerty, Marc Fortier, Chaz Fitzhugh, Carolyn Feinstein, Eric Forman, Alan Furst, John Foster, Meredith Fierman, Mark Friedler, Scott Ferrall, Howard Flashenberg, Marc Franklin, Doug Freeman,

Janie Frank, Joe Forget, Tracy Foster, Miami Mike Fernandez, Joe Fuller, Alan Frankel, Marc Franklin, Mike Fischer, Gordon Freedman, Rob Fleisher, Wendy Fein, Ken Fong, Buffy Filippel, Mark Friedman, Michael Feldman, Michael Flaherty, Jack Fishman, Guy Farrow, Doug Faust, Kelly Flock;

G

Bruce Gordon, Beverlee Gordon, Beatty Gordon, Nikki Gordon-Still, Robert Gordon, Beatrice Gordon, George Gordon, Kingman Gordon, Marty Gilliland, Mary Lee Gilliland, David Giat, Sam Gradess, Ben Granados, Dan Gilsenan, T.J. Gilsenan, Miles Gilsenan, Craig Goldstein, Jeff Gregor, Mitch Green, John Thomas Griffith, Mary Gray, John Geoghegan, John Gerson, Lynn Gerson, Linda Jay Geldens, Ed Geldens, Jill Gregory, Bob Gayman, Dana Gard, Jen Groeling, Joanne Gaines, Dina Schon-Gioeli, Joe Gioeli, David Greenspan, Austin Gavin, Wendy Green, Donna Graves, Morton Goldfarb, (the late) Curt Gowdy, Bryant Gumbel, Greg Gumbel, George Geis, Ronnie Goldfinger, John Ganz, Dr. David Geisinger, Anthony George, Shelly Gaynor, Don Garber, Paul Gamberdella, David "House" Grant, Jay Gangi, Ted Gangi, Lia Gangi , Russell Gangi, Ktimene Gembol, Rob Goldberg, Dan Geiger, Yves Guillemot, Benedikt Grindel, Michel Guillemot, Ralph Greene, Tanya Greenblatt, Gabe Griego, Mark Gorski, Mark Goodrich, John Guppy, Brad Gerdeman, Anthony George, Greg Gallardo, Rob Gardner, Austin Gavin, Ronald Goodstein, Bill Gladstone, Jenny Green, Victoria Gangi, Morton Goldfarb, Chris Gilbert, Andrea Gordon, Ryan Gordon;

H

David Hartzell, Michael Helfant, Robert Holmes and his family, Michael Herman, Mark Herman, Oliver Heil, David Hughes, David Hanchrow, Kathy Hassett, Todd Hays, John Hays, Evan Hainey, P.J. Harari, Dr. Charles Harris, Andrea Harris, Jason Herskowitz, Jeff Harper, David House , Kevin Horn, Andrew House, Kaz Hirai, Dale Hopkins, Bo Heiner, Shelley Howell, Gary Himes, Leon Harmon, Munir Haddad, Hal Halpin, Phil Harrison, James Huntley, Lee Heffernan, Mona Hamilton, Trip Hawkins, Steve Hekker , John Hussey, Stephanie Hyland, Dr. Aaron Hass, Damian Hurtado, Thomas Hardy, Solomon Hutchinson, Tim Harris, Catherine Hurley, Frank Higgins, Scott Higgins, Pam Hertzel, Chick Hearn, Jed Hart, Dan Hirsch, Steve Hutcherson, Jay Heil, Kerry Hopkins, Mikey Hersom, Kristen Hecht, Marcel Hudson, Paul Hechmer, Rose Harkins, Peter Hughes, Pat Hedges, Jeff Hoff, Kurt Hall, Jennifer Hemmer, Dr. Richard Hunter, Todd Huffman, Tom Hanks;

I

Mindi Idell, Portia Igarashi, Joel Isenberg, Jason Isenberg, Yoshimi Iyadomi, Ann Ingold, Michelle Irwin;

J

Robert Jacobs, Eric Johnson, Ross Johnston, Sydney James, Pete Jacobs, Jim Johnson, Helene Juguet, Darlene Jordan, Rick Jones, Susan Jimenez, Jimmy Johnson, Wriston Jones, Paul Jimenez, Karim Jundi, Lisa Jackson, Mike Joyce, Monique Jones, Michael Jordan, Cobi Jones, Simon Jeffery, Fred Jackson, Julie Jodoin, Leo Jodoin, Georgette Jodoin, Billy Joel;

K

Mike Kaufman, Stu Klein, Gordon Kline, David Kupiec, Matt Knoles, Rich Kubiszewski, Caroline Kim, Tina Kowaleski, Edward Katz, Lisa Katz, Steve Koonin, Genie Kim, Doug Kennedy, Sandy Koplon, Vince Kurr, Bob Kramer, Erica Kohnke, Todd Kinney, Bill Ketchum, Pete Kutch, Alan Kass, Peter Karp, Angela Karp, Linda Kemper, Jennifer Karpf, Jan Katzoff, Chuck Kinyon, David Kinney, Stefani Kimche, Jennifer Kullman, Matthew King, Dick Kuegeman, Jeremy Kove, Jimmy Kinnel, Andrew Klein, Mari Kohn, Ynon Kreiz, Judy Kinyon, Derek "D-nice" Herbert Kroninger, Scott Kaufman, Carol Kruse, Chris Kimbell, James Krawczyk, Jamie Kerr, Jennifer Kushell, Ed Krent, Gerry Kelly, Carolyn Kremins, John Kape, Chris Kramer, Emma Kingman, Ferris Kawar, Gary Keith, Evan Katz, Michael Katz, Beverly Katz, Bradley Kesden, David Kim, Ray Knight, Will Kassoy, Kevin & Bean, Darlene Kindler;

L

Jon Lewis, Shari Leventhal, Bill Linn, Howard Liebeskind, Jeff Lang, Kyung Lee, Hyun Lee, Eric Lee, Criag Lee, Mike Lynch, Debbie Lynch, Nancy Lavender, Michael Lynch, Amy Landino, Nick Landino, Todd Lindenbaum, Dr. Larry Lemak, Marvin Lutz, Guy Lamothe, David Landsberg, Aaron Levin, Adam Lippard, Patricia Lamar, Paul Lapadat, Jeff Leonard, Eddie Leitman, Mike Lindsay, Mark Lane, Patrick Lugo, Bari Levin, Jim Lampley, Craig Lowenstern, David Lee, Dean Linke, Doug Lowenstein, Jodi Lipe-Tull, Christopher Levy, Aaron Levin, Adam Lippard, Theresa Lohrbach-Lin, Amy Landino, Jill Lublin, Jim Lampley, Nick Landino, Dr. Jeff Leonard, Doug Lowenstein, Elizabeth Lawson, Andre Leighton, Algon Leighton, Natalie Larrick, Mike Lustenberger, Dr. George Little, Jeff Leonard, Kristin Little, Laura Levitan, Laura Lashua, Elizabeth Lawson, Nancy Lombardino, Chip Lange, Jon Lefferts, John Lyons, David Letterman, LinkedIn, Mark Lafreniere, Alison Lewis;

M

Ann Meschery, Craig Middleton, David McKillips, John Miller, Gordon Munroe, Andre Marciano, Brian Melstner, Paul Meyer, Todd MacKenzie, Eric Mokover, Stefan Markey, Cliff Marks, Bill Meyer, Matthew Miller, Sean Morrison, Kim Moyer, Martin Masters, Jeffrey Moorad, John McEnroe, Johnny Most, Todd Moeller, Gary Moritz, D'sena Morehead, Joe Meyer, Leslie Meyer, Pete McDonnell, Shannon McDonnell, Jacinta Martin, John

Madden, Adam Mirabella, Jan Miller, Ann Morris, George Morris, Scott Marcus, Peter McAniff, Peter Michalsky, Brian Murphy, Alison Moy, Troy Molander, Laura Mehaffey, Kevin Mansfield, Tony Meola, Jim McGinness, Claudia Mendoza, Marco Mendoza, David Macachor, Richard Motzkin, Norm Mandell, Jamie Mearns, Richard Motzkin, Karen Maher, Lori Madsen, Peter Magelof, Irving Margol and his family, Tyrone Miller, Bob Mischler, Jim Myers, Larry Moak, Karen Moore, John Murdaugh, Jeff Moorad, Ron McGaughey, Dennis Miller, Craig McAnsh, Rudy Martzke, John Moshay, Deborah Michael, James "Jim" Miller, Jeff Martirano, Michal Mayouhas, Nicolas Metro, Rob Mills, Yannis Mallat, Vincent Minoue, Dan Moalli, Tom Martorelli, Susan Holland-Moniz, Jeff Moniz, Dana Mansfield, Atkims Martinez, Michelle Manapat, John Manapat, Phil McElroy, Lea Murga, Sven Muller, Sean Murphy, Lori McLeese, Enrique Mesones, Steve McPartland, Jennifer Minigutti, Matt McSparrin, Kevin Mansfield, Pete Menotti, MENG Online, John Miller, Jon Miller, Mary Alice McMorrow;

N

R.J. Nelson, Bill Nuttall, Arlene Navarro, Tim Norris, Bill Nollman, Rob Nelson, Juanita Nessinger, Marc Nover, David Neubecker, Ray Nutt, Mike Nichols, Sue Nopar, David Newman, Susan Nourai, Mark Noonan, Tommy Nast, Alyssa Nollman, Larry Needle, Andy Norton, Jeff Norton, The National Sports Marketing Network, Ken Nolan, Dan Nunenmacher;

O

Frank O'Malley, Dr. Lee and Samantha Oppenheimer, John Oxford, Glenn Oratz, Gabrielle Oratz, David Ominsky, Joseph Olin, Joe Owens, Sean O'Connor, Jeff Ohlbaum, Hughie O'Malley, Bruce (Doc Fu) O'Leary, Erin O'Malley, Robert Olshever, Brian Olshever, David Gene Oh, Craig Ostrander, Bob Olive, Elizabeth Olson;

P

Laura Porter, Thomas Porter, Melissa Procanik, Jerry Procanik, Mike Pade, Don Post, Bea Perez, Tenny Park, Paul Provenzano, Stu Pollard, John Peirano, Arnold Peter, Jeff Powers, Randy Pollack, Jeffrey Pollack, Ed Padin, Bob Pimm, D.J. Pufferd, David Pfaff, Dave Pindar, Mitch Prusin, Todd Parker, Cedric Penix, Rich Perelman, Wallace Poulter, Sandy Pfeffer, Scott Pitts, John Piester, Dayton Paiva, Joel Pambid, Jeff Price, Steve Pearson, Brenda Panagrossi, Jeff Pearce, Cybelle Perry, Mike Plante, Billy Packer, Marty Piombo, Randy Peyser, Matthew Pollack, Digger Phelps Arnold Peter, Stefano Paoletti, Alex Pigeon, Tracy Patch, Mark Packer, Mark Pickering, Pamela Prince, Brian Phelps, Dr. Drew Pinsky;

Q

Russell Quinan, Mike Quigley, John Quinn;

R

David Riberi, Gina Riberi, Michael Reese, Brent Russell, Ann Roth-Card, John Rubey, Bob Rivituso, Steve Ross, Leo Reherman, Greg Rowan , Julie Rowan, Mike Rose, Joe Rongavilla, Amy Randall, Rossana Ruey, Chris Rouse, Craig Rechenmecher, Tom Russo, Haven Riviere, Lynda Richardson, Doug Rebert, Chris Riley, Jennifer Riley-Rowland Dennis Roy, Riley Russell, Eric Rodli, James Regan, Tom Roseberry, Steve Rich, Sandra Rich, Wendy Robinson, Jeff Rynkiewicz, Dave Rosenberg, Alison Ross, Dennis Rancont, Mark Roesler, Jason Rubinstein, Drew Reifenberger, Walter Reynolds, Alan Rasooli, Candace Roper, Andy Roeser, Lynn Raviv, Ronnie Ruddell, Dan Rosenstein, David Rosenstein, John Rousseau, Peter Raskin, Jason Rosen, Jill Rabius, Dave Roth, Eileen Rodriguez, Jeff Reyna, Randi Reiten, Kent Rippey, Mathieu Rolland, Steve Rosner, Jeff Rynkiewicz, Bill Ridenour, Brad Rothenberg, Andy Rooney, Mathieu Rolland, Phil Rosenberg, Kent Russell, Brett Robinson, Anthony Rodio, Bonnie Recca, Sharon Richards, Steve Raab, Jim Rome, Gary Radnich, Johnathan Reddy, Angela Reeves;

S

Nikki Still, Chris Still, Lillian Still, Maddie Still, Carolyn Sapp, Michael Safris, Barbara Safris , Corrie Safris, Shawn Safris, Harold Safris, Tobey Safris, Justin Siegel, Barry Siegel, Beth Schnitzer, Ray Schnitzer, Stephen Schnitzer, Gaye Sussman, John Stallcup, David Sebbag, Paul Serwitz, Arthur Serwitz, Mike Stein , Jim Steeg, Dean Stoyer, Scot Safon, Andre Sherlock, Greg Stern, Mike Shine, Garret Seevers, Drue Schuler, Meryl Schreibman, Tom Sherak, Kevin Scher, Dan Setlak, Jeff Serota, Peir Serota, Thomasene Smith, Marshal Salomon, Stacey Salomon, Dean Smith, Gregg Smith, Michael Sondheimer, Isaac Scott, Dale Strang, Kali Simpson, Andrew Sherrard, Dave Smith, Seth Steinberg, Jill Steinberg, Chris Sturr, Helene Sheeler, Molly Smith, Wendy Spander, Drew Sheinman, Cory Shakarian, Nicola Shocket, Shyama Sachi, Pete Stapp, Eric Schulz, Mike Savod, Todd Sitrin, Claudia Sloane, Andrew Shevin, Stuart Scott, Mitch Stern, Murray Schwartz, Erik Stroman, Mark Stroman, Dominic Scaglione, Jimmy Schwartz, Jane Schwartz, Karen Shimp, Andy Swanson, Kathi Sharpe-Ross, Reid Schneider, Tammy Schlachter, Tony Sciolla, Richard Sankey, Tiffany Spencer, Neil Sharma, Vin Scully, Rod Stewart, Stuart Snyder, Rob Sullivan, Stephen A. Smith, Ronnie Stapp, Steve Stecher, Steve Stone, Steve Salyer, Sherry Santos, David Simon, Alan Stiles, Peter Surace, Ken Salottolo, Scott Sorensen, David Stallbaumer, Sigi Schmid, David Schriber, Rob Sullivan, Kristen Schwartz, Linda Sullivan, Steven Spector, Paula Savar, Mike Sorber, Stuart Sheldon, Dudley Shotwell, Joel Silverman, Bob Stohrer, Beth Scott, Pete Scott, Ben Smith, Arnold Schwarzenneger, Howard Stern, Pamela Snow-Prince, Nancy Smith, Alex Spence, Bernard Stolar, Ben Silverman, Wimp Sanderson, Sonny Smith;

T

Rollie Tillman, Terry Tumey, Vince Thompson, Ferris Thompson, Rob Trucks, Wayne Trucks, Larry Tolpin, Jack Tretton, Claude Torrey, Michelle Torrey, Earl Takasaki, Stan Taigen, Sutton Trout, Carrie Tice, Kristy Thomas, Tim Thomas, Andrew Thau, Kristy Thomas, Rob Tonkin, John Trevathan, Will Travis, Mike Trivisonno, Damien Taylor, Martin Tremblay, Stephen Tracy, Christine Trees, Ian Thompson, Terry Thomas, Amy Turner , Jack Ton, Richard Thalheimer, Forge Toro, (the late) Derrick Thomas, Gary Tautphaeus, Beth Townsend, Ilya Teplitsky, Mike Takacs, Elizabeth Tucker, Tom Tolbert, Mark Thompson, Ken Tayloe, Maria Tomas;

U

Lee Uniacke, Jennifer Usher, Michael Utley;

V

David Vinturella, Alex Vaickus, Dianna Von Kessel, Peter Vermes, Don Vercelli, Eric Van Gilder, Michelle Verselli, Frank Vuono, Ashley Vizzi, Anders Vestergaard, Beth VanStory, Steven Van Yoder, Cindy Vallar;

W

Matt Weiss, Gunnar Wilmot, Michael Weisman, Harris Wilson, Suzanne Weerts, Chris Weerts, Rich Winograd, Mike Walter, Kim Wermuth, Megan Wigert, George Wunder, Erik Whiteford, Scott Williamson, Doug Walker, Jag Wood, Steve Wilson, Gerry Wallfesh, Christa Wittenberg, Jeff Wyatt, Delvin Williams, Chris Wade-West, Rob Wells, Sam Wheeler, Dan West, Kevin Wall, Jeff Warren, Terri Warren, Simon Whitcombe, Willie Wareham, Jenn Wallrapp, Lisa Welch-Nehring, Kim Willus, Eva Wilensky, Shelton Wilensky, Dick Wnuk, Harry Wilker, Stan Wakefield, Ted Weinstein, Michael Wayne, Lisa Wilson, Keehln Wheeler, Mike Wharton, Bob Winneg, Kevin Winston, Richard Watts, Herb Winches, Marilyn Weyant, Mary Weir, Jeff Wildey, Jay Wilson, Rich Winograd, James Worthy, Meril Weinstein-Salzburg, Cathy Weiss, Brent Watson, Dan Willis, Daniel Wolfe, Andrew Whitman, Gerald White, Darin Woodard, Roy Williams, James Worthy;

X

Carol Xanthos;

Y

Steve Young, David Yehle, Marci Yamaguchi, Fathy Yassa, Jennice Yee-Chiu, Steve Yanofsky, Robynne Yoss-Elkin, Marc Yassinger, Ken Yamada, Larry Yannes, Rannie Yu, YOU;

Z

Alan Zack, John Zissimos, Andrew Zeiger, Brett Zane, Leigh Zaremba, Elizabeth Zwiller, Brent Zeller, Nima Zarraba.